DRAWN
FROM
LIFE

Mark Twain

DRAWN FROM LIFE

by

S. J. Woolf

WHITTLESEY HOUSE

NEW YORK AND LONDON

Published by

WHITTLESEY HOUSE

A Division of the

McGRAW-HILL BOOK COMPANY, INC.

Printed in the United States of America

Acknowledgments

GRATEFUL acknowledgment is made to the *New York Times* for the right to use such material as has appeared in its columns. Thanks are also due to the *New York Herald Tribune*, Mrs. Henry Moskowitz, George C. Smith, Jr., Esq., Samuel Finley Thomas, Esq., the Germantown Friends School and the Schwartz Galleries for permission to reproduce some of the drawings, and to Harlow MacDonald & Company who own the copyright of the lithograph of Mark Twain.

Contents

〖 x 〗

List of Drawings

〖 xiv 〗

DRAWN
FROM
LIFE

I

For some years I have been hunting the great. With portfolio and charcoal and with pad and pencil I have been making not only lineal impressions of them but also verbal ones. In New York as well as Washington, in Berlin, London, Rome, Paris, and Prague I have pursued those whom the world holds in esteem.

A long procession of shadowy figures passes before me and a host of memories attends them. Statesmen and authors, painters and poets, financiers and scientists are all in the ranks. As the procession has passed, from time to time I have halted it and out of the crowd have picked one here, one there, and from these I have made this book.

In writing about a man one has met, certain restrictions impose themselves. Confidences must be respected, while personal opinions must be subordinated if an impartial portrait is to be presented. Moreover, men long prominent become more or less fixed figures in the public mind. Often the impression that is firmly rooted, though very different from the man himself, has become so identified with the individual that it takes more than one article to dispel the false picture, if indeed it can be dispelled at all.

I have found the taciturn Coolidge talkative, the domineering Mussolini docile, the satiric Shaw sympathetic. Under Italian skies the cold, cruel former Crown Prince of Germany has been kindly and humorous, and Einstein, remote and absorbed in theories, has dunked his coffee in homely style before me. No man is said to be a hero to his valet, but while the valet lays out the clothes for his partially dressed master, the artist also has an opportunity of really seeing his subject despite the apparel which in most cases does not proclaim the man.

There is no surer way of getting to know a person than by drawing his picture. The silence that is broken only by the scratch of charcoal upon paper or brush on canvas seems to remove restraint. The artist has his sitter at an unfair advantage. One is working; the other sits quietly self-conscious. It rarely happens that the subject does not relax and as a usual thing in a short time he starts to talk. In this respect the man who also draws has an advantage over his less fortunate brother who only writes. His victim is disarmed. Nothing makes for taciturnity or at least care in what is said so much as a writer's pad and pencil; nothing is so likely to make even a shy person talk as the quietness of a room in which some one else is working.

And so, sitting in their offices, in their homes, or in their workshops, these men have talked to me while I have been drawing their portraits. The light and shade falling upon their heads brought out their features and I tried to reproduce what I saw, while at the same time I jotted down the high lights of their conversations on the margin of the paper.

In both cases I have endeavored to give the impression that the subjects made upon me. My drawings are not photographs nor are the articles phonograph reproductions. A broad sweeping line may better portray the contour of a face than a narrow halting one which delineates distracting details, and the same is true of quotations. A man's speech, in both manner and subject, has as many characteristics as his nose or eyes or mouth. In a drawing the artist seizes upon those forms which to him appear vital and perhaps exaggerates them in order to convey the impression that his sitter makes. I have done the same thing in words that I have done in line.

Yet it has been purely as an observer that I have met these men and drawn their pictures. There has been no attempt to delve into their innermost selves from a psychological point of view, nor to interpret what they said. That has been left for the reader. Yet despite the desire to draw what is seen and to write what is heard, it is impossible not to permit one's own feelings to enter into whatever one does. I have tried to keep mine in the background as much as possible so that they would not distort the pictures I have drawn, either by line or by word.

It goes without saying that some of the subjects appealed to me more than others. Some of the drawings almost made themselves; some of the articles required little work on my part; they took form in my mind before I had put a word on paper. Other subjects were more difficult, probably because I was not so much in sympathy with them. But the strange thing connected with this is the fact that the professions or occupations of these diverse personalities apparently played no part in the interest they evoked. I have found men presumably absorbed in business who were much more interesting than some of those who had devoted their lives to the pursuit of the muses; on the other hand I have seen business men to whom nothing but money meant anything.

By and large, men who have achieved success are about as interesting or as dull as the same number of individuals who have not. Some waiters are more diverting than some writers, some laborers more engrossing than some leaders of industry.

Men who are supposedly brilliant often were boring; others, presumably colorless, sometimes were entertaining. Some have gloated over their success and others have attributed it to anything but themselves. Some have liked to talk, others have been silent. They are as varied as their appearances, as different as their pursuits.

This is to be expected, and yet one unconsciously looks for some common element in all who achieve eminence, some characteristic which all possess. I hate to be trite. "Self Help" is a book which has done much harm. Picking up pins in a crowded London street is not a particular quality that goes to making successful bank presidents. The use of midnight oil is as likely to cause the conflagration of a city as to produce a burning success. And yet, looking back on all the men whom I have drawn, I am inclined to think that none of them reached the pinnacle with his eyes sometimes turned in another direction. No half-hearted attempts succeeded. Each one of them was absorbed in his particular calling.

This does not imply that they are of necessity narrow-minded, that nothing apart from their own particular activities holds any interest. There are scientists who love music, and musicians who dabble in science. Paderewski has been in politics, but he compares statesmanship to piano playing. His country has been a keyboard on which he performed the overture of a nation. Even this is no exception, for his service to his country was not given until years after his reputation as a musician had been made. Einstein's violin playing is but a diversion and plays no greater part in his life than does the bricklaying of Churchill.

And although no one comes to mind who has not apparently striven with all the energy of which he was capable to achieve his position, nevertheless, in addition to purposeful concentration, another element has entered. Another force over which the individual himself had no control has also been at work. Over and over again while drawing I have wondered if there were not something, call it luck or chance or opportunity, which has not also played an all important part. More and more have I come to believe that toil and toil alone is not enough, and that ability unattended by this other factor is not sufficient to reach the goal. Of course, opportunity probably knocks at all doors; the sense to open is requisite. Still, there is something that is more than just opportunity. When you hear of a man who through a mistake directed his letter to a wrong firm, and as a result obtained a position which he did not set out for, and which ultimately led to his becoming president of one of the largest companies in America, while you cannot deny his ability, you must still wonder what would have happened had he not misaddressed his letter. That, incidentally, is the story that Walter S. Gifford, president of the American Telephone and Telegraph Company, told me himself. It is uncertain what David Sarnoff of the Radio Corporation would be doing if by mistake he had not applied at a Postal Telegraph office for a job on a newspaper. Had there not happened to be a vacancy in the Physics Department of Oberlin College, Professor Millikan to-day might be teaching Greek instead of delving into the make-up of the universe. The examples are so countless that one wonders how many Michelangelos there have been who never chanced to meet those popes who were decorating Sistine Chapels.

I am not trying to tear halos from any one. I do not think the halos exist. I am not endeavoring to detract one whit from the genius of great men in any field. I do not for one minute attempt to imply that men achieve reputations without tremendous capacity. But I assuredly believe that more geniuses have been born and died unsung than have ever been heard of. Capability, by itself, is not sufficient. It must be accompanied by luck and it must secure recognition. Posthumous fame, though poetical to read about, is comparatively rare. The days of building mousetraps in the middle of a forest, if indeed they ever existed, are surely over now. With so many good roads men no longer have the time to beat paths through dense underbrush. To-day even great men must let the world know of their greatness.

But shrinking from publicity is something that is an uncertain and indefinite quality. I have heard much about it, but seldom encountered it. In most cases where I have, it has always seemed to me that perhaps it was but a more subtle way of securing publicity; for after all mystery is interesting. At heart the majority of people are much alike. It is a human failing to like to see one's name in print. If this were not so, such a large number of clipping agencies could not exist.

I remember trying to obtain a meeting with Sir Thomas Lipton. His personal secretary was not only abrupt but absolutely rude. I left the hotel at which they were stopping, having expressed my opinion. Within an hour I was called by another representative who, having arranged matters, laughingly remarked, "Some people are dreadful fools. We are paying a thousand dollars a week for less space than you are willing to give us free."

But merchant princes are not the only people who need publicity. Statesmen soon wither and die without it as quickly as actors; even poets and other writers require it, much as many profess to run from it. However, this is to be said: that many a man sincere in his desire to avoid notice has nevertheless consented to pose for his portrait. To see ourselves as others see us appears to be a most common human trait and to gratify it very often even a shy man will fall.

II

I**N LOOKING** back on the ways that many of these meetings were obtained, I think I can honestly say that the greatest obstacles that had to be overcome were private secretaries. Whether they are naturally stupid—they may be spoken about collectively, for with few exceptions they are alike—or whether they have some strange desire to shield their employers from unknown dangers, it is hard to say. They are kind, they are courteous and most encouraging in their conversation. There they stop and in the majority of cases, like Cerberus, bark at any further approach. Many a telegram sent to a man's home has secured a meeting which I had been informed by a secretary was out of the question.

As I write these words, the figure of one woman comes back to my memory. She was Mark Twain's secretary, and though it is years ago that I made a picture of him I can still remember her suave manner and the way she laughed at everything he said whether it was really humorous or not. She guarded him too well for my purposes. I had to go over her head and obtained an appointment through a friend.

Mark Twain was living then in an old red brick house at the corner of Ninth Street and Fifth Avenue in New York City. I was very young and he was the first celebrity who had ever posed for me. My heart was in my throat when I rang the bell and I can distinctly recall my embarrassment as I dropped some of my drawing materials on entering the long dreary parlor, with its tremendous melancholy organ. And then came the great man himself; and I was disappointed and disillusioned. He was so much smaller and more human than I had expected. The remaining spell was broken when he ran his hands through his bushy mane, which still retained a canary tinge, and asked whether I thought he had better go down to the Brevoort which was at the next corner and get a haircut. As I said, I was young at the time. It was not until years later that I saw a famous general in beleaguered Paris send his orderly upstairs for a mirror so that he might see if his hat were on at the proper angle for me to draw. When I drew Mark Twain I still thought that all eccentricity existed without premeditation.

It was shortly after his "Life of Joan of Arc" had been published. On the mantel in the front parlor prominently displayed was the bronze laurel leaf which a young girl dressed as the Maid of Orleans had placed on the humorist's brow but a few weeks before at his seventieth birthday dinner.

For the painting which I did of him he sat in the large bow window of one of his rooms. But my lithograph was made from a pencil sketch which I drew one day when he was not feeling well and had received me while he was still in his huge bed with its carved cherubim in the room on the second floor.

There was something sad about him at all times. Occasionally he would flash some witty remark, but for the most part he seemed to be living with his own thoughts. During most of the time he was posing his secretary played the organ—a mechanical affair—but I gathered that his interest in music was not an artistic one, for the pieces which apparently pleased him most were the sentimental ones connected with some event in his own life.

Despite the fame which he had attained, I carried away with me the feeling that he was a disappointed man. Perhaps it was his domestic griefs that had embittered him; perhaps it was his long struggle once more to regain his feet after he had been overwhelmed by financial disaster, but at all events it was hard to believe, as this old man with the beetled brows sat before me, that here was a writer who had made two continents laugh. It would have been easier to have imagined him as the author of "War and Peace" than of "Huckleberry Finn."

His thin, nervous hands constantly twisted a cigar. He was an inveterate smoker and the edge of his mustache about his mouth had that yellowish nicotine color, which in those days was so common but which to-day is as rare as the sulphur matches which were then used.

When I drew him with a book in his hand, he looked at the picture for a few minutes, and then quizzically remarked, "I suppose the book looks better, but a cigar would be more like me."

His voice was thinner than his leonine head would have led one to expect and about it was a suspicion of a southern drawl. He spoke slowly and almost weighed his words, and his conversation had none of the wit or sparkle that one would have imagined. He produced the impression that his humor was not spontaneous, that it was the outcome of logic and reason, rather than of sudden inspiration.

Of course, he was past seventy when I met him, and he had lived a full and sad life. The sun was already beginning to sink behind the clouds in the west when he posed for me, so perhaps the brilliance which I had looked for in vain had been dimmed. Memories appeared to overpower realities for him most of the time, though occasionally he would apparently tear himself away from the past.

Into that Fifth Avenue parlor with its Victorian respectability he brought a breath of the spirit of the pioneer Southwest. For notwithstanding a long residence in the land of the Yankee he seemingly bore a resentment against the effete affectations which to his mind surrounded the culture of the larger eastern cities. The artificiality of civilization palled upon him and he had more respect for the opinion of the man in the street than he had for book knowledge gathered in libraries.

"I remember," he said, "when the play which I wrote with Warner was first produced. How the critics damned it! But there was a human quality about Colonel Mulberry Sellers which the people recognized, and they came to see the show in spite of what the paid critics said.

"A critic," he drawled, "never made or killed a book or a play. It has always been the people who have been the final judges—it is their opinion which does the job—they are the last arbiters.

"After all, the final test is truth. But the trouble is that most writers realize that truth is their most valuable possession and they are extremely economical in its use."

A great part of the time I was working he sat smoking and said little. At one of the sittings Robert Reid, the artist, came in with his young nephew. Reid was well over six feet tall, and his nephew was as big. Mark Twain got up and took one by each arm and remarked, "One day the three of us will have to walk down the Avenue this way and people will say that Clemens is the cross bar of a capital H."

Much of his conversation was cursory. The most revealing episode that occurred in all my meetings with him was when one of the newspapers telephoned asking him for an interview. At first he refused. Then he relented and said that he would give it providing the paper would donate one hundred dollars to some charity. His offer was accepted and he immediately named an organization which looked after children. It was then that he seemed most like the Mark Twain whom I had pictured. It was then that his face lost its grim expression and the kindliness that was his came to the fore.

It was this meeting, now almost a quarter of a century behind me, which was one of the factors that turned my life into the channel in which it has run. But before it did this years passed—years in which I painted portraits and tried to make my sitters look like what they thought they were. I think it was Sargent who remarked that a portrait was a painting in which there was something wrong with the mouth. Only those who have made their living out of portrait painting fully realize the depth of the truth in that observation. Unless three-months-old babies clap their hands and say "Goo goo" before the canvas, unless pet dogs bark, and if every friend and acquaintance does not agree in saying the likeness is perfect, then the portrait must be altered.

Of all the people who sat for me in those early days only one stands out in isolated memory. That is Mr. Justice Holmes. I hesitate to put down more than a sketchy outline of the man, for it has been some years now since I made that drawing. I have had many sitters since, presidents and prime ministers, philosophers and mathematicians. And yet out of the whole number the tall, slightly bent figure looms. I can still see him greeting me in the second floor back room of his home in Washington, a courtliness and culture about him that are indissolubly associated with men who grew up in an earlier day.

Oliver Wendell Holmes

I have often felt that the men active in public life in Europe have a fuller outlook, a more rounded education, a scholarliness that is absent in our men of public affairs. One of the few exceptions has been this white-haired, pink-faced old gentleman. Surrounded by etchings which he loved and which he had collected, he spoke of art and life. Modernism to this octogenarian was a most absorbing subject. But though he was enthralled by the psychology of it, he still got his pleasure from the lines that Rembrandt and Van Dyke and Whistler had bitten on copper plates. Yet he did not close his eyes to the struggles that were going on among contemporary artists for a new mode of expression. While he respected their efforts, he acknowledged that he could not understand them. But he pointed out that it was only through movements such as this that the world progressed.

"The same thing," he said, "is true of every branch of human knowledge. The desire to get away from old ideas is a human trait. So is the clinging to them. Youth seeks to express itself in new ways. Age clings to what it knew in youth.

"This does not mean that youth is necessarily right or wrong. Nor does it mean that age is as a matter of course reactionary. It is the impulsiveness of the young, tempered by the experience of the old, that makes for progress."

He spoke of his father and he mentioned the "Autocrat of the Breakfast Table." He recalled how his father had written that when John and Mary were at the breakfast table there were six persons present—John as he really was, John as he thought he was and John as he appeared to Mary. The same was true of Mary.

"I suppose," he said, "in order to get a perfect likeness of me you would have to make me as I seem to myself, as I really am, and as I appear to you. I am afraid you have an impossible job ahead of you."

All the time I was drawing him his secretary was in the room.

"You know, Mr. Justice," he remarked, "when the portrait was started it looked like Justice ———— [mentioning the name of a particularly conservative member of the Supreme Court]. But now it looks like you."

"Well, don't you believe in evolution?" retorted the keen old jurist.

One of my regrets now is that I did not set down immediately many of the things that he said. However, at that time I was only drawing. It was not until some years later, and then almost accidentally, that I also began to write.

III

Just off the Strand, on Adelphi Terrace, stands a row of houses built long ago by the Adams brothers. It was in one of these that George Bernard Shaw lived when I first met him.

The ground floor of the corner house was taken up by offices but inside the first thing that struck the eye was a large sign—"Mr. and Mrs. G. Bernard Shaw"—while at the head of a flight of stairs a wooden gate reinforced by iron spikes prevented further progress and another sign gave notice that the floor above was private.

Here the visitor, if he managed to elude the wily janitor who told every stranger that Mr. Shaw was in the country, came to an impasse, and naturally it was here that I met my first obstacle. I managed to persuade the maid to permit me to speak to Miss Patch, Mr. Shaw's private secretary, who behaved in true private secretarial form. She did not find it necessary to open the portcullis for she could easily speak over the top. This she did and said it would be out of the question even to ask Mr. Shaw to pose—in fact, most of his time was spent in refusing to be a model for any more artists. Somewhat dejectedly, I left.

I could not melt the stony heart of Miss Patch; it was vulcanized. I had to get to the great man himself and move him not by pity but by humor. What would he have done under similar circumstances? Knowing that modesty is one of Shaw's salient characteristics, and that his apparent blatant conceit is nothing but an inferiority complex combined with the keenest wit and humor, I concocted the following letter after much trouble. I knew that I had nothing to lose and that it might just strike the one unprotected spot in the Achillean armor of reserve. On July 1, therefore, I wrote to him as follows:

"My dear Mr. Shaw:

"Years ago I remember you said that the only reason you posed for Rodin was because you felt that it was the one way in which you would gain everlasting fame.

"That is quite true as far as Europe is concerned, but as for America, with true Shavian modesty I may say that immortality will not be yours there until I have drawn you.

"That is one of the reasons I came to London—to obtain immortality for you in America.

"And when you think it will cost you only one-half hour of time—that is a very small price to pay."

When the following note came the next morning I was the most surprised person in the world:

"I now have considerable experience as an artist's model; but my terms—about $3,750 an hour—are prohibitive. Also, I shall not be disengaged for at least a year to come. G. B. S."

I now felt sure that the proper response would bring results. It was the third of July; the letter had to be timely, it had to contain in itself a reason for being written; in other words, it must of necessity be a reply to his note, so, on July 4, I sent him the following:

"My dear Mr. Shaw:

"Your price for posing is acceptable to me. My price for a drawing is the same amount.

G Bernard Shaw
4ᵗ July 1927

George Bernard Shaw

"You do not have to be disengaged while I draw.

"I am leaving on the eighth. When shall I come?

"If you could pose this afternoon and sign the drawing to-day, think what it would mean to the American people to have two vital documents signed on July 4."

That afternoon I received a phone call; Mr. Shaw's name could go down in history with John Hancock, Thomas Jefferson, and others.

After meeting and talking with him, or rather listening to him talk, for two hours or more, his surroundings count for little in my mind. I dimly remember making a mental note of his dining room, furnished under a decidedly Chinese influence, with a gorgeous Eastern yellow rug, a wonderful open sideboard filled with multicolored Oriental pottery, and on the mantel several Chinese dragons. Behind me was a bookcase, containing, among other volumes, Gibbon's "Rome," Wagner's complete works, and Balzac's novels.

On the light green wall hung Augustus John's portrait of Shaw, which Mrs. Shaw told me she had not liked at first but now felt was one of the best portraits of him in existence—not one absolutely of the man in flesh and blood, but a monumental work of him and his aims.

It was in Mr. Shaw's living room, out of the windows of which one had a long, unbroken view of the Thames, that I drew him, while he sat on a large chintz sofa and talked.

He had a visitor, an economist from Australia, who was interested in little theaters. And when the visitor introduced himself as an economist Shaw remarked: "That's what I am; playwriting is just a pastime."

He went on: "Of the moderns I particularly like Pirandello and Strindberg. Their plays are not logical developments of themes and, after all, I am such an old hand at the business that a logically developed play cannot possibly contain any surprises for me. I know what will happen from the beginning and accordingly lose interest. But when a play goes along without any apparent plan and when at first no consecutive development or plot appears evident, I am at once intrigued into discovering the purpose and outcome. Naturally, if the author is mad the play becomes all the better. And as for Strindberg, of course he was mad. He had an idea he was a mortally ill man. I remember visiting Stockholm and I felt that it would be an act of international courtesy for me to call on him. Accordingly I dropped him a line telling him I was in the city and that I would not like to leave without paying my respects. I received a reply that Mr. Strindberg was too ill to receive any one. But the next day, without any further action on my part, a note reached me saying that he would be home that afternoon. I went. For an hour he was charming. Suddenly he pulled out his watch, looked at it for a moment and in a fearful voice said, 'In twenty minutes I shall be a grievously ill man.'

"To this day," continued G. B. S., "I do not know whether this was the result of my visit or of his diseased mind.

"Of course, it is economics that has taken up most of my time, though—and this may seem strange to you—music has always played a large part in my life. Both my father and mother were musical and I was reared in an atmosphere of music. In fact, harmony I have always sought. Classical music, Beethoven and Bach, were so much a part of my infancy that it really took me some time to learn to appreciate the lighter forms of music, and it was only after an effort that I could find pleasure in the waltzes of Strauss.

"Most people don't know that it was an American who really turned me to sociology. When I was a young man Henry George came to London and lectured. I was carried away by both the man and his ideas. His revolutionary theories appealed to me. And I may say I still see the truth in his Single Tax.

"From George I went to Marx, and his 'Capital' swept everything from me and I was a Socialist. Of course, I was young. In those days I was ready to grasp at everything new. It's strange how men change. At that time I refused to believe a word of the Bible and was ready to accept every new theory any scientist offered. To-day I'd rather believe the story of Jonah and the whale than a fact almost proved by a scientist.

"But to get back to Marx. I was his devout follower and remained so until Jevons showed me certain fallacies in his theory of values. Not that I discarded Marx; I accepted him with reservations, and it was due to the Fabian Society that his theories were made popular in England. Marx was a strange chap. I never met him but I have learned much about his personality from people who had. One of the most delightful stories I heard about him was told me by a lady whose husband had been one of Marx's intimate friends—a fellow-Socialist.

"For years they had been close companions. But one evening, as both were leaving a party, the friend by mistake took Marx's hat. It fitted him and Marx, who prided himself on the tremendous size of his head, from that day never spoke to his former friend."

Shaw's delightful manner, the charm and sonorous tone of his voice with its faint suspicion of a brogue, his interest in the subjects on which he spoke, and the amusing twists he gave to his conversation made it extremely difficult for me to work. I wanted to drop my charcoal and just listen, but I could not. Accordingly, in order to finish my sketch, I had at times to concentrate on my work rather than on his conversation. Various remarks of his come to my mind with the result that I am unable to remember the exact way in which he led from one subject to another.

How he came to speak of his religion, I forget, but in some way or other religion was touched on and he said.

"I have the same religion as Dean Inge. We are both Quakers. We don't believe in set prayers. When we want to talk to God we use the same language as we ordinarily use, not prayers composed for us by other people, and we do not need a church in which to hold communion with Him. I remember that some time ago a movement was afoot to afford more protection to St. Paul's against fire. A meeting was held and various people attended, some advocating more fire extinguishers, others special fire brigades. In fact, countless schemes were devised and discussed. When every one had finished the Dean had proposed nothing. Some one asked him how he felt and he answered: 'Let it burn.'"

And then in some unremembered way the subject of human affection was introduced, and Shaw was asked whether it was not the one compelling thing in the world.

"Human affection," said he with a quizzical smile, "is the one great curse of mankind, the principal obstruction to its progress. Take myself, for instance; all my life affection has been showered on me, and everything that I have done I have had to do in spite of it."

The sketch was finished and I prepared to rearrange the furniture, for in order for me to be comfortable Shaw had removed a picture from an easel that stood in the corner and wheeled it out for me to use. The economist by this time had departed.

I "fixed" my drawing so that it would not rub, and asked him to sign it, which he did, though he said that he felt that it was unnecessary as any one could tell who it was without the name. But I still delayed my going. Shaw had spoken on Socialism, on playwriting and even on religion, but I wanted more.

I had been unable to turn his conversation to the subject of art. Behind him on a desk was the bust Rodin had made of him years ago—the one referred to in my first letter. I mentioned it again and asked if Rodin had required many sittings.

"Yes, quite a number," he said, "and the strange part of it was that in the course of its making that bust went through a complete development of the history of art. At the end of the first sitting it was a work of the very earliest Greek period—archaic smile and all From that it embodied the Greek and Roman styles and at one time it was a perfect example of the sculpture of the twelfth century, a masterpiece of that period, and it kept on evolving from one century to the next until it was finished."

Rodin seems to be one of Shaw's heroes. He showed me numberless photographs of him, which he keeps around the living room—photographs made by Coburn, whom he had sent for from London particularly for that purpose. He also showed the famed "Nude Photograph" of himself and told how it came to be taken. Coburn and he were discussing Rodin's "Thinker." He had tried to assume the pose but he could not, so he undressed to see if he could get into the pose unhampered by clothes. Coburn snapped him. But Shaw told me he was not leaning forward far enough and that the absolute pose cannot be assumed by anybody.

There were other photographs, some thirty or forty years old. The thing that struck me was the apparent change in his skull formation, which I mentioned. He assured me that it was a fact that as a young man his head was broad, rather than long, but that in later years his entire skull had lengthened.

At last I ventured, "And, Mr. Shaw, what do you think of modern art?"

"What do I think of modern art? I have been practicing it seventy years," he replied with a delightful smile, "but seriously I suppose that there must be something good in it. I do feel that any number of incompetents are using it as a cloak for their shortcomings. But take Matisse for instance; from the surety and beauty of his line I know the man can draw in an academic way should he so desire. I will acknowledge that at first his works seemed strange to me, but I have looked at them so much that now I see their beauty without permitting their apparent strangeness to interfere with my appreciation of the part that appeals to me. I don't think the goal has been reached, but there must be forerunners to every great movement. It doesn't matter whether it is religion or art. Cézanne, Van Gogh, Matisse may be only prophets or John the Baptists.

"But the thing you must admit whether you want to or not—look at these pictures often enough, have them in your home, and they will make you feel that the work of their predecessors is dull, drab, monotonous and lifeless."

As I was going he asked me if I would leave the drawing and call for it later, for Mrs. Shaw was out and he wanted her to see it. Here was the man who had laughed at all human institutions anxious for his wife to see a drawing of himself.

There was a simplicity and hominess about the entire place that did not seem to square with one's ideas of what his household would be like. It was the same spirit which I afterwards found in the comparatively small apartment in which Professor Einstein lives.

IV

HOMINESS was more to be expected from the dreamy German philosopher who remains at heart the simple bourgeois and does not attempt to startle with an epigram or surprise by a phrase.

He was no easier to get to than was Mr. Shaw. I had tried numerous leads, none of which went anywhere. I had even wired Emil Ludwig who at that time was in Switzerland, but received a reply that he did not know Einstein well enough to give me a letter of introduction and suggested that I see the Professor's son-in-law. I did this and the young man acted much as a secretary would. He was very discouraging but asked me to leave a portfolio of my drawings which he promised to show to his distinguished father-in-law. When they were returned to me the next morning with word that the scientist would not pose I noticed that the package had not been opened.

My chances of approaching the propounder of relativity seemed very remote as I stood in the courtyard of the building that houses the printing firm for which Professor Einstein's son-in-law works. There was no one else to whom to turn who knew him, and I decided there was but one thing left for me, to go to his house direct and try to see him. A man's privacy is to be respected, but there seemed no other way out, or rather in. I felt, too, that even if a door were slammed in my face, it would not be the worst thing that might happen to me,

Albert Einstein

and accordingly I took a taxi to Haberlandstrasse. It is in a comparatively new part of Berlin, a section built up within the last twenty-five years. About it no halo of history glows. It is a residential quarter of the upper middle class—broad streets, well-kept trees and apartment houses, with vine and awning-covered balconies jutting out here and there in haphazard fashion. There is a home-like atmosphere about the vicinity, a feeling of substance, well-being and contentment, but it can boast of nothing else. The neighborhood does not fulfill one's ideal of the surroundings of a man who has overturned the fundamental ideas of the universe. There is something entirely too tangible about the place; no remoteness, no suspicion of fourth dimensional incomprehensibility.

Einstein's house is surrounded by the homes of well-to-do people, satisfied with the world as it is. Even the statue of St. George and the Dragon which stands temporarily beside its broken pedestal in the center of the small square on which the house fronts, is a Teutonic St. George wearing a smile of complacency, with no hint of prophetic vision—a smile reflecting the feelings of the people of the neighborhood.

In fact, the apartment breathes no more of the extraordinary than the neighborhood in which it is situated. The dull-looking porter in the blue denim jacket and apron who turns the key in the lock and sends the crawling elevator up to the top floor is like hundreds of other attendants in similar flats. The polished brass plate above the bell with "Professor Einstein" on it is identical in every respect, except for the name, with others in the same building. And even within there is nothing about the place that differs essentially from the majority of German homes.

Had a maid opened the door to my ring I am quite convinced that I would never have succeeded in getting either my drawing or my article. As it was, one of Einstein's daughters answered it and to her I was able to make my purpose clear. She was interested in my drawings because she herself is a sculptor, and she promised to do what she could. When I left her I felt that perhaps I was on the way to obtaining the sitting. Next morning, however, when I called up it was Mrs. Einstein who came to the phone and she told me that she was very sorry but although the Professor liked my work he would not give me the time. He abhorred publicity, she said, and it was this that made him refuse. When I replied that even if he desired to avoid newspaper notice, I could not believe that a man credited with having such a kind heart as the Professor would refuse to see some one who had traveled over three thousand miles to meet him, she weakened. She asked me to hold the wire, and the Professor himself came to the phone. After a little preliminary talk he finally consented to pose, but I had to promise him not to publish the drawing.

I arrived very early the next morning—in fact, owing to the German method of designating the time, I was half an hour too early. There was a smell of wax throughout the apartment and the maid was still going over the polished floors with a heavy brush.

The library, with the green wallpaper and porcelain stove, with its built-in bookcases, ornate and filled with novels, histories, and two gigantic copies of the Bible; the corner cabinet, on which stand two statuettes and a half model of a sloop that Einstein's friends gave him; the desk, primarily a home piece and evidently used by the entire family—none of these things gives any evidence of being the surroundings of genius.

Nor does the living room reflect anything of the personality of the head of the house. It is livable and cheerful, but it might be the home of any one of millions of Germans, for there is something decidedly Teutonic about it. Its flowered yellow wallpaper, its family pictures prominently displayed, the portrait of Frederick the Great with his two dogs, the piano with its stubby legs, the three violins in cases under it, and also the heavy wood music stands—these things, together with the Biedermeyer furniture, are characteristic of a nation rather than of an individual.

It was Mrs. Einstein who greeted me—a sweet, motherly woman, whose attitude toward her distinguished husband is that of a doting parent toward a precocious child.

"I am so glad," she said, "that you have managed to get him to pose. He does not want publicity. Last week there were a few photographs of him in the paper and he was so disturbed that for two days he did no work.

"Have you ever seen him?" she asked, and before I could answer she added: "Has he not a wonderful head?" And as she spoke of him there was a suspicion of a tremor in her voice.

"Look at this," she said, and going to the bookcase drawer she pulled out a thin volume, a collection of Einstein's sayings and poems which his friends had collected and had bound as a souvenir of his fiftieth birthday.

There was the sound of bare feet, and, holding a black and white bathrobe about him, apparently oblivious of his surroundings, Einstein entered.

Although he is about average height, his head with its mass of gray hair appears large for his body. His forehead is not high but is distinguished by its curious formation, and his eyebrows grow, not as usual on the upper part of the orbits of the eyes, but above, thus giving a perpetual quizzical expression to his face. His mustache remains almost black, as does a fringe of hair about the back of his neck.

His eyes are large and dark and soft, and in them there is a note of sadness which remains even when he smiles, which he does often in a quiet embarrassed way. In fact, about his entire manner there is a bashful and malleable quality that is almost childlike, and this is accentuated by his wife's attitude toward him

Though he loves the outdoors and spends what time he can spare in the country, his appearance is that of a man who has passed most of his life indoors. He is physically flaccid, in fact, almost fragile, and even his handshake, though cordial, leaves one wondering as to whether there are bones in his hand.

As he stood there, saying he would be ready in a few minutes, it was easy to understand why his home showed so little of his personality. It is doubtful if he even knows what is in it. Detached and remote, he is one of those persons whom it is impossible to comprehend fully.

Talking, he appears to be thinking of other things; gazing, he does not appear to be seeing the object at which he looks. In fact, these peculiarities are so marked as to appear almost abnormal. His mind apparently works of its own accord along certain lines, and when his attention is diverted to something external, one can almost feel the effort that is required on his part to interrupt his natural train of thought.

Patting him on the back, his wife told him to get dressed, and as he left the room she said with a smile: "He is terribly hard to manage."

In a few minutes he returned. His brown suit needed pressing and on his feet he wore, over wool socks, a pair of open-work sandals. His coat collar was half turned up in the back, and when we started to go upstairs Mrs. Einstein fixed his collar and arranged his hair.

As we walked up the one flight of short steps that led to the top floor, he said: "Remember, I have your word that this picture will not be printed. You may use it for exhibition purposes, but I am heartily sick of my portraits being published. That is all right for a theatrical prima donna who wants advertising.

"The people are so inconsiderate in their demands. For months a photographic company was after me to pose playing my violin. The next thing is that they will be wanting me to pose standing on my head."

We reached a door, a wooden one painted white, which he unlocked. At the end of a passage of four or five feet was another door. This he likewise opened and I was in his study— an attic room about fifteen feet square. Under the sloping alcove window is a table which stands on a dais as does an upholstered armchair with an antimacassar on its back. A round table, covered with a red and white cloth, is littered, as is the other one, with papers and pamphlets. Two ladderback chairs, with straw seats, and bookshelves filled with pamphlets complete the furnishings. There are no pictures on the whitewashed walls, no more evidence of observance of surroundings than on the floor below.

Professor Einstein seated himself in the chair on the dais, and before I had arranged my materials, he had taken from his pocket some scraps of paper on which there were figures, and also a black fountain pen, and, as if he were absolutely alone, he began jotting down notes. As far as he was concerned, I was not there.

His legs were crossed and the paper rested on his lap. In his mouth was a small meerschaum cigarette holder, not the kind that is used to-day, but one of the old-fashioned type which holds the cigarette perpendicularly, and which he removed every little while, holding it pipe-fashion.

The previous night I had been in a chess room, of which there are a number in Berlin, and, as he sat slowly puffing, but not inhaling the smoke from his cigarette, now and then changing a figure on the paper before him, or else twisting one of the curls on the back of his head, he reminded me of the men whom I had seen bending over the chessboards, trying to solve problems which they got from the newspapers. It was impossible not to feel that he was engrossed in working out a puzzle and that the ultimate results of the solution did not interest him at all.

To talk to him would have been out of the question. He was too far away, and it was not until he looked up and asked how the picture was progressing that I had an opportunity of speaking to him and asking him something of the history of the development of his theories.

"The general trend of my thinking," he said, "was present in my mind from the beginning, but as I went on the later ideas came to me gradually. Twenty-four years ago I published my first pamphlet and two years later I formulated the general theory of relativity. Since then I have been constantly working on developments."

In reply to the question as to how he came to work along the particular lines he did, he replied:

"First I was struck by the fact that experiments showed that the velocity of light is constant; that it travels at the same rate of speed whether sent out by a source at rest or in motion.

It was while thinking over this that my first theory of relativity came to me.

"The experimental fact that the material mass of a body is the same as its gravitational mass set me thinking along lines which ultimately resulted in my later work."

According to Professor Einstein an infinite number of theories can always be devised that will describe natural phenomena.

"We can invent," he said, "as many theories as we like, and any one of them can be made to fit facts. But that theory is always preferred which makes the fewest number of assumptions. Among the innumerable theories which can be constructed to fit the facts of science we choose, naturally, the theory which starts off with the fewest of these assumptions."

His smoke was finished, and as he laid his holder on the table beside him, without speaking I offered him a cigarette.

"No," he said, "I have just finished one, and everything, including smoking, must be done slowly." Then he went on:

"Of course there are several kinds of theories in physics. Most of these are what I should call constructive, for from some relatively simple propositions they build up a picture of complex phenomena. Thus when philosophers say they understand any certain group of natural phenomena, they mean that they have evolved or built from simpler propositions a theory which explains and embraces the complex ones."

He uncrossed his legs and looked down at the paper in his hand. With his fountain pen he added several figures. Then he looked up again and in his soft voice continued:

"The theories which I have worked out are of a different character. They are theories of principles and are the result of

[39]

an analytical rather than a synthetic method. Their starting point and foundations are not hypothetical constituents but empirically observed general properties of phenomena, no matter how complex, from which mathematical formulae were deduced, formulae of such a kind that they apply to all cases which present themselves."

I realized that very shortly I would be beyond my depth and when he stopped I referred to his violin playing.

"Yes," he replied, "I get a vast amount of pleasure from it. When I am too tired to read or work I find that music rests me. Much has been said of my playing but I am sure that I am the one who gets the most amusement from it."

When the drawing was finished he got up to look at it. From his expression I knew he was pleased, and among other things, he said that I might use it anywhere I saw fit, and then he asked if he might have a photograph of it. Two or three days later I returned with the photograph. Mrs. Einstein was entertaining some relatives, some of whom were back on a visit from their homes in America. Around a small side table in the dining room they sat and in a few minutes the professor entered, wearing the same unpressed brown suit, and with the same far-away look in his eyes. Absent-mindedly he ate a sandwich, and then the subject turned on America and he spoke of its vastness and of the deep impression it had made upon him when he had visited it.

The conversation became general and turning to me he asked to see the photograph. He looked at it for a few minutes and then got up and left the room, walking much quicker than usual. Suddenly from the other room came noises, and Mrs. Einstein quickly arose asking me to come with her. "I know what he is doing," she said.

As we entered there he was in the library trying to take down from the wall a tremendous painting of himself.

"I have told you a number of times to take that down and now I am going to do it." This was said in an excited tone, a tone that no one would suspect he could use. The calm professor, the quiet, removed, methodical thinker had disappeared and in his stead was the temperamental artist.

"And what's more, if I see it around I'll put a knife through it."

I had to help him but finally he got it down, put it into a corner and once more with his usual quiet manner he returned to the dining room.

It was time for me to go and as he saw me to the door I asked him what he considered the best formula for success in life. He smiled, that same awkward bashful smile and thought for a minute.

"If A is success in life," he replied, "I should say the formula is $A = X + Y + Z$, X being work and Y being play."

"And what," I asked, "is Z?"

"That," he answered, "is keeping your mouth shut."

As I left him and jumped into a taxi with my portfolio his last remark rang in my ears. The association of ideas is curious. There was I driving through the streets of Berlin but I did not see them. My mind had gone back to a little snow-covered town in New England where I had heard somewhat the same thing.

V

GENERAL CLARENCE EDWARDS lived in Dedham, Massachusetts. During the war he had commanded the Twenty-sixth Division, with which I had been for some time. While passing through Boston, it was but natural that I should visit the old commander in the near-by suburb.

Edwards was a blunt, matter-of-fact soldier with absolutely no tact. Whatever came into his head was immediately said, and it was due to this outspokenness that shortly before the Armistice he was relieved of his command and sent home. This very fact, coupled with his fatherly solicitude for his boys, had made him extremely popular in New England, and when Calvin Coolidge was running for governor of Massachusetts, he had asked the former commander of the Yankee Division to accompany him on some of his speaking tours.

"On one of our trips," the General told me, "we had to travel about thirty miles by motor. Mr. Coolidge was in one car, I was in another. When we reached our destination I jumped out of my machine and went over to the automobile in which the candidate for governor and his wife were. Mrs. Coolidge looked bored.

"'What's the matter,' I said to her as a joke. 'Has the Governor been talking you to death?'

Calvin Coolidge

"Mr. Coolidge looked up at me. It was evident what was in his mind. 'Well, General,' he said, 'the things I don't say never get me into trouble.'"

But Mr. Coolidge never seemed a silent man to me. The first time I saw him he was spending the summer in the Adirondacks. I had made a hot night journey in a sleeper in order to reach Paul Smith's the next morning.

The President's camp was six miles or so from the hotel and its surrounding cottages. One of these had been converted into a summer executive office. Here the President came every morning and here he saw the representatives of the press two or three times a week. On one of these days I arrived and I met a number of newspaper men whom I knew. The general talk was that he had been particularly short with them. About the entire place was a feeling of repressed awe, which was intensified when I met Everett Sanders who told me that he could not possibly ask the President to pose for me but that I might make some sketches when he was holding his public talk. Accordingly, I was prepared to catch him, as it were, on the wing, while he answered the questions of some thirty or forty men who were covering his doings that summer.

A few minutes after he had entered the room, he saw me sketching. He turned to me and said, "Don't do that now. Wait and I'll see you afterwards."

"Afterwards" turned out to be an hour or more, despite interruptions by nervous secretaries who entered the room every now and then, for the evident purpose of bringing the sitting to a close.

During that time he spoke of art, he mentioned the names of painters little known to the public, and in every way displayed a side of himself that as far as the public was concerned never existed.

This drawing of the President, however, was not what I had really gone after. At that time he was first displaying his interest in fishing and what I wanted was a sketch of him at his favorite pastime. Moreover, even photographers had been banned from the camp, so except for one or two pictures that had been taken before he had moved in, the public did not even know what the place looked like.

After I had been working for fifteen or twenty minutes he left the room to see a senator and told me to wait as he would be able to get rid of him quickly. On his return I broached the subject of going to the camp to make some drawings. He looked at me with a quizzical expression.

"You know I have kept all reporters out of the place," he said. Then he arose and came over and looked at my drawing.

"Would you like to make a picture of Mrs. Coolidge?" he asked. "If you were to come up to do that and should happen to make other sketches, I do not think any one would stop you."

That afternoon I went there. The President took me over the place and showed me the various rooms. Then he said that he was going fishing and led me on to a dock. While he stood and cast from a bridge I sketched him.

Later, on an eminence that overlooked a lake, I made my drawing of Mrs. Coolidge. At the time a well-known publicity seeker was staying at the hotel with his new wife. At every opportunity he spoke to the reporters who were "covering" the summer White House and even handed out photographs of himself and his young bride with the hope that they would find their way into the papers.

While I was drawing Mrs. Coolidge the newlyweds were out on the lake in a canoe and she displayed great interest in them.

"Do you think," drawled Mr. Coolidge, "that if you persuaded them hard enough, you might be able to get them to consent to pose for a picture to be published in the papers?"

The name of a certain statesman came up and a visitor who was there remarked:

"You know, Mr. President, he is really a very able fellow. He went off on a tangent about Socialism but he has completely recovered from it."

"When did he come into money?" inquired the President.

His humor is sharp and dry but is always in evidence. I remember that once when I was drawing him he suddenly turned to me and said:

"I am afraid I am hard to draw. You know I think I would be a much better subject if I had chin whiskers like the Smith Brothers."

He is very particular about his personal appearance. He is one of those people who even on the hottest day appear cool and immaculate, one who looks as if he had just stepped out of the bathtub. Despite the fact that he was born and brought up on a farm, he seems to be more in place in offices than in rural surroundings, and his well-pressed double-breasted suit was much more appropriate behind a desk than when he stood on a bridge with a fishing rod in hand.

His hands, small and well kept, do not look as if they had ever handled pitchforks. He is proud of them. He told me that when he was posing for the portrait by Laszlo which now hangs in the White House, the painter at the end of one sitting had said the picture was finished.

"But," explained Mr. Coolidge, "I did not like the hand and so I sent him a note telling him that I would be glad to give him a couple of hours more to work on it.

"I got a note back from him thanking me but telling me that there was nothing more to be done on it."

He told me the story because he admired the artist's independence. He was amused at his writing that way, not to Calvin Coolidge, but to the President of the United States, and expressed regret that many men in public life were not so sure when they had finished their jobs.

In addition to his humor there is a kindliness and consideration that most people do not realize. I have been ushered into the President's office in the White House and found him sitting with his feet on the desk. In that office he has asked me to remove my coat because it was a very hot day, and he has regaled me for half an hour or more with all the details of the last sickness of one of his white collies.

All in all I found him to be one of the most human people I have ever met. He is reserved, yes—but it is the same reserve that one finds among most of the natives of New England. And with this Yankee quality goes an extraordinary softness of heart.

He demanded respect, but instinctively one felt that it was for the office which he held rather than for himself personally. Indeed, about him is an almost old-fashioned point of view in his regard for the nation. One of the first things he showed me at his camp was the flag with its marine guard.

Of course, he is peculiar. Who is not? It amused me to see him take a leather key case from his pocket, open a drawer in the desk in his office in the White House, take out a long black cigar, carefully insert it into a cardboard holder, put the box back and again lock the drawer. Suppose he has a certain New England thrift; he has also the same keenness and clear understanding about things that go with it. It is those very peculiarities that made him so popular with the men who had to write about him. Will Rogers has chuckled with me about them. Yet that shrewd observer of human nature loves him for his very foibles.

There are a few more memories of Coolidge that remain vivid to me.

"How is the drawing coming?" he said to me one time when he was posing.

"I am pleased with it," I answered.

"Well," said he, "when I do a job and please myself one person is satisfied anyway and when I try to please other people the chances are that no one is satisfied."

My last drawing of him was done shortly after he had made his "Do not choose to run" declaration. No one had succeeded in getting him to amplify it and considerable uncertainty existed as to exactly what it meant. As he sat for me we were frequently interrupted by his secretary entering with papers for him to look at.

Probing, to find out for my personal benefit—for the President cannot be quoted—how he felt on the matter, I asked him if he would not be glad when his term of office expired and he could retire to private life.

He looked at me very keenly and for a few minutes said nothing. Then the Coolidge that the public knows came to the fore and his answer was "No." But the monosyllable was full of meaning.

I have always felt that his statement was taken too literally to please him, that though he did not "choose," he could have been persuaded to run. However, perhaps I put too much store on that one word which he said to me while he was still in office.

He is such a clever politician that it is hard to believe that had he really desired another term he could not have managed to obtain it.

VI

THERE is but one man who seems almost to approach Coolidge in political strategy. Yet their methods are distinctly different. Coolidge is reserved; Al Smith is effusive. The former president weighs his words; the former governor "speaks out." Both are acute, but one's wits were sharpened amid the cracker barrels of the village store; the other learned his lessons on the city's streets.

Politics for Governor Smith has been no passing fad, no relaxation from other affairs. Brought up in poverty, the welfare of the poor, particularly of widowed mothers and of orphans, became almost a fixed idea with him. But with the sincerity of this champion of the unfortunate and oppressed goes an inborn keenness and a surprising care for minute details.

Some years ago I was with him when a talking movie was being made and a pitcher of water was placed on the table beside him. Dr. de Forest, who was making the picture, suggested that in the course of the speech he stop a minute and pour out a glass of water and drink it.

He made the speech before the camera and microphone, but took no drink. When he was finished he remarked: "Did you notice I did not pour out the glass of water? Do you know what would have happened had I done that? When they were showing the film some one in the gallery who had had a drop too much would have yelled out: 'Say Al, ain't you sorry that's not beer?' and that would have queered the film."

When I observed that he had to think of everything, he replied: "In this line of business nothing is too small to be thought of."

This "infinite capacity for details" and a genius for quick appreciation of circumstances are two of the strong attributes which he brings with him into business life. I remember one occasion after he had retired as governor. There was a stack of letters on his desk to be signed, the ever-present cigar was in his mouth. When I asked whether he liked business he took up a round silver lighter and set the cigar going again.

"Sure I like it," he replied. "I like anything that requires the working out of some problem. It does not matter whether it is the question of a budget or of amalgamating two or more state departments or finding the best methods of raising a bond issue or putting up a big building. So long as there are difficulties to be overcome, plans to be worked out, I am interested. The harder the solution, the more interested I am.

"There is no use in going off half cocked in anything. But after your plans are made, sailing becomes easier. Now, to my way of thinking, running a family, a business, and the state have many points in common. There has to be a head to each of them and problems come up upon which decisions must be made. But before any conclusions can be arrived at in any walk of life, a clear understanding of the confronting problems must be grasped.

"Here I have taken up what is to me a comparatively new business and I have to make a thorough survey of it before I can go ahead. Previous to my becoming Governor I had been in the Assembly and I had also been a member of the state convention for the revision of the Constitution. So I was just called upon to execute the laws which I had had a part in making."

Alfred E. Smith

I asked him once whether he thought politics was good training for business.

"I can't answer that question, for it all depends on the individual," he said. "Politics may be for some and for others it is not. In my long experience in politics I have seen business men take up public affairs and become tremendous successes. On the other hand, I have seen them flat failures, and, *vice versa*, I have seen politicians turn into successful business men. That's all personal."

While Mr. Smith had been talking he had been signing letters, his long cigar in a corner of his mouth. Rarely was it removed. His voice is harsh, almost gruff, but as he spoke he looked up every now and then and his eyes twinkled through the tortoise shell-rimmed glasses which he uses when he reads.

His smile is contagious and his expression continually changes as he speaks. In order really to appreciate what the man says it is as necessary to see him as to hear him. That is the reason his campaign talks over the radio were not successful.

Humorous as he can be, his manner is ordinarily earnest. One feels that he takes life very seriously. Speak to him but a few minutes and it is easy to understand why practical workers for social improvement have gathered around him, why professors of economics and government have regarded him as a leader. Intensely practical, he has the faculty of reducing complex problems to comparatively simple ones, of making academic questions popular ones.

I asked how the duties of a business executive compared with those of a governor.

"The business executive has a cinch," he pointed out. "It's much easier to run any organization by common sense than it is by law. The head of a business makes up his mind to do something. He says 'Go ahead and shoot,' and the thing is done. But it's a very different thing in public office.

"A certain friend of mine, employed by a big corporation, came up to Albany while I was Governor and put up an entire building while the State was digging foundations for one that was absolutely needed to carry on the State's business. Why was that? Because every time he wanted to do something he did not have to send over to the Attorney General's office to find out whether he had a legal right to do it. In business every one is working for the benefit of the concern; there are no legislators of a different party who selfishly retard measures for improvement in order to advance their own ends."

A sincere strain of sentiment explains many of his actions. In his office hangs a large, engrossed resolution which, decorated with faded photographs, names him "Commodore" of the Ned Harrigan Club. Beside this relic of an older New York, there is an early lithograph of State Street, Albany, and a dim, framed newspaper clipping with a picture of his mother.

All that is in evidence of thirty years of public service is a high-back mahogany desk chair with a silver plate on it, the chair that he used for the years that he was in Albany. Nothing else gives an inkling of the fact that the man with the tanned complexion, the hair that is rapidly becoming white, and the cold blue eyes, is the man who has had more stanch supporters and more bitter enemies than any other man in public life in a generation.

His faculty of remembering the past, with his eyes looking toward the future, is characteristic of him. As he plans the latest skyscraper on Fifth Avenue he does not forget South Street and Dover Street and Oliver Street. As he whizzes up in an elevator to his modern office, the creaks of the wooden stairs that led from the little grocery and candy store his mother kept in a basement still sound in his ears.

These memories of the past—the hardships, the squalor, the patient suffering of the poverty-stricken, the primitive conditions under which many of them lived, the constant struggle for the barest necessities—were a mainspur in his actions to secure the welfare legislation which was passed while he was in Albany as Assemblyman and Governor; they prompted him to accept the chairmanship of the Housing Association of New York.

I have been with him in his office when he has stood at a window which overlooked the city and pointed out changes that he thought would occur. It has been dramatic to see this product of the city speak with an almost prophetic vision of its future growth. But though he indicated great developments in business structures, it was the improvement in the living conditions of the poor in which he was most interested.

There was real feeling in his voice as he said one day: "Here we have the greatest city in the world, with the latest improvements in every branch of the mechanical and building arts. We give billions every year for philanthropic purposes. We spend hundreds of thousands to study crime and delinquency and disease; yet we do nothing to remove what has been pointed out again and again as the fundamental cause of them—bad housing. We have foundations for orphanages and schools and colleges, and do nothing to provide wholesome homes from which the students are to come.

"Why, we are building new skyscrapers, great factories department stores, and although the employees go to work in new subways, or over new bridges and along newly widened streets, many of them, through the stress of financial conditions, are compelled to live in unwholesome dark rooms, in unsanitary conditions that are beyond description.

"The people of this city have hearts, and this makes it more of a surprise to me that for so many years our municipality has permitted such conditions to exist as obtain in many of our tenements."

He resumed his seat. A fresh cigar was in his mouth. "But," he continued, "after all, that's New York. It's always on the go and always changing. The novelty of to-day is the ash heap of to-morrow morning. When I think of what I have already seen in the way of changes, it's almost foolish for me to make predictions.

"Thirty-five years ago I saw a cow grazing at Nineteenth Street and Fifth Avenue. To-day there is block after block of large apartment houses in sections of the city where, when I was serving jury notices, there were rocks with squatters living on them. Had any one at that time predicted the changes that have taken place up to now, he would have been looked upon as a visionary.

"Yes, New York has changed in many ways since I was a boy. There's no more swimming in the East River, or hitching of sleds on the backs of wagons. The old neighborhood spirit is gone. You can live for years in an apartment and not know the man who lives on the same floor."

"What about bringing up children in the city?" I asked.

"A great many people have done it," he replied with a smile. "As a matter of fact, I do not think it is such a bad place to do that. There is a lot of talk of how much better off youngsters are in the green fields and the open air.

"About fifteen years ago, if you remember, we had an epidemic of infantile paralysis. At that time I was in the

【 58 】

Assembly and represented one of the most crowded districts not only in the city but probably in the entire world. In my district we had exactly two cases of the disease.

"And the people over in that part of town had a hard job, for no matter how clean the housewife is, many of the old buildings are so dirty that there is a constant struggle to keep the flats clean.

"There has been a lot said, too, about the danger of immorality that exists in crowded conditions. Well, I would be willing to back the young people in those crowded tenements any day against those living in villages and towns."

I have seen Governor Smith under many circumstances. I first met him when his presidential aspirations were dim and hazy. I saw him at the Democratic Convention in New York when John W. Davis was nominated for the Presidency, and when Smith, entering that hot, sweaty Convention Hall, proclaimed his allegiance to the party. I was with him when he himself was running for the highest office, and I have sat with him after it was denied him by the votes of the people. Out of countless meetings one little incident comes to the fore. Perhaps I am somewhat sentimental, perhaps I read thoughts into things where they do not exist. But it seems to me that his remark when I spoke of a photograph of one of his grandchildren is most revealing of the real man.

"You ought to see him," he said, "a natural blond—one of the finest looking boys you ever saw. Why, a couple of weeks ago I had him down on the beach and we took a stroll and would you believe it—everybody turned around to look at him."

I am sure that it never occurred to him that it was he at whom the crowds looked.

VII

IT HAS often struck me how frequently the public fails to recognize in the flesh even the most famous people. I remember distinctly riding on a Sixth Avenue horse car (which in itself tells how long ago it was) with Chauncey Depew. He was a senator at the time, and it was on a Christmas Eve. He got on with his arms filled with bundles, for life in those days was simpler in New York. Though his face adorned a cigar box, hardly one person in the car recognized him.

I remember also walking through the Capitol with Mrs. Longworth when a very provincial looking woman stopped us and asked her if she knew the way to the Senate Chamber.

Again another picture comes to my mind. I have had a number of talks with Professor Robert A. Millikan. Once I had to see him as he was passing through New York and he wired me to meet him at the Commodore Hotel. There we sat for fully an hour in the crowded lobby while not a soul paid the slightest attention to him. In a way, this is not so surprising, for, eminent as he is, his portrait has not been universally printed and, besides, he looks like a successful business man.

About him are none of the eccentricities which are usually attributed to men whose lives are devoted to abstract sciences. His white hair is closely cropped, his face is smooth shaven, and no one upon meeting him would suspect that he is the man who literally smashed to pieces the entire atomic theory, upon which a large part of modern science is based. For doing

Robert A. Millikan

this, by isolating and measuring the ultimate electrical unit, the electron, he was awarded the Nobel Prize.

His experiments, however, have not been confined to this little world of ours; the entire universe has been a subject for him, and it is in his blue eyes that one sees the far-off look of a poet, an imagination to fathom not only the most hidden secrets of the earth, but also the mysteries of the stars.

Dr. Millikan was born of New England ancestry and it is probably that lineage which accounts for the peculiar combination of practicability and poetry that seems to be his prime characteristic. He is a Coolidge and an Emerson rolled into one. There is the calm, cool New England thoroughness, and there is likewise the prophetic, seerlike sensitiveness. This may be accounted for by the fact that his father, who was a Congregational minister, was descended from a long line of farmers whose lives had been spent in getting a scanty livelihood from the stony soil of New England, while his mother, an Andrews, a common name in that section of the country, came from a family who for years had sailed the Seven Seas.

They met in Oberlin College where both were students, and when his father obtained a church in Morrison, Illinois, they married and settled there. It was there that Robert Millikan and his five brothers and sisters were born.

"We lived there," he said on one occasion, when he was posing, "until I was about seven years old, when we moved to Maquoketa, in Iowa. It was there that I first went to school. That was about fifty years ago, and it is interesting to look back and see how much more universal knowledge is to-day than it was at that time. I went to primary school there, and also to grammar and high schools. Naturally reading and writing were both taught well, as was mathematics; but the man from whom

I first learned the rudiments of physics in the summertime, made extra money by locating wells by means of a forked stick.

"When I was graduated, my parents wanted me to go through college; in fact, they saw to it that all their children had good educations, and it was but natural that they should send me to the college to which they had both gone.

"At Oberlin I was especially good in Greek, but at that time had absolutely no idea of specializing in physics." It was then that he told me it was an accident that he had made physics his life work.

"It came about," he said, "through the instructor of Greek asking me at the end of my sophomore year whether I wanted to teach physics. At that time all I knew about it was what I had learned from the gentleman with the forked stick. But I had to help pay my way, and that was as good as any other method. So that summer I gathered together all the textbooks I could find and studied the subject in order to be prepared to teach it the following term.

"While there are facts of heredity against which it is utterly futile to inveigh, on the other hand I am a great believer in the fact that eventually man gets to love what he is compelled to do. I became absorbed in the work. Up to that time I had read Aristotle on account of my fondness for Greek; now I read him on account of my interest in physics."

During his last two years at college Dr. Millikan continued to teach and likewise study physics; then he went to Columbia and studied there for his Ph. D. and from there, on the advice of Dr. Pupin, he went to Germany and spent a year at Berlin and Göttingen.

"Upon my return from abroad," he continued, "I was appointed to the Chair of Physics at the University of Chicago, where I remained five years, and from there I went to the California Institute of Technology, where I still am."

I was interested in Dr. Millikan's ideas on religion, and accordingly I asked him whether his scientific studies had shaken his religious faith.

"Religion," he replied, "is one of the most striking possible examples of evolution. In so saying I am uttering nothing that is in any way heretical, nothing that is not said or implied in every theological seminary of importance in the United States. For no fact stands out more clearly, even in Bible history, than that religion, as we find it in the world to-day, has evolved up to its present state from the crudest beginnings.

"Religion, as I use the word, has always dealt with two groups of ideas, first with one's conception of the meaning of existence—that is, with one's conception of God, and second with the conception of one's own responsibility in this world. These two ideas have always been associated in all religions. But these conceptions of God and of duty change as man learns more and more and gets farther from the earliest stages of his development.

"Primitive man finds himself on the one hand surrounded by human enemies, who kill and enslave him, to whom if they are stronger than he, he is obliged to surrender the best that he has. On the other hand, he also finds himself surrounded by the forces of nature, which seem to him as capricious as his human enemies.

"Under these conditions, what does he do? The only thing possible for a man in his stage of development. He personifies nature. He sees a spirit in the storm, a god like his powerful enemy in the thunder, a nymph in a stream, a Pan in the woods, and every mysterious happening in nature he attributes to the caprice of these spirits, or if he happens to be a believer in one god, to the caprice of one Great Spirit.

"He begins to appease Nature, to try to get his god or gods in a favorable mood. To do this he begins to sacrifice.

"Then comes the first forward step in the evolution of religion. Somebody arises, somewhere, somehow, who begins to do a little reflecting on his own account. In the Bible it was Abraham who began to wonder whether Nature was after all just a powerful cruel vengeful brute, whether the real God was a being who could be propitiated by the sacrifice on the part of a father of his only son. And he answered 'No!' and decided then and there to break with the past.

"The Bible says, 'God spoke to Abraham.' How he spoke we know not. I cannot explain that fact. But the amazing thing is the fact that a mind to hear God has got here at all. 'Created out of the dust of the earth'—this is the Bible phrase and science can find no better one—a mind that begins to think for itself. Where do our ideas come from? Science does not know. All that we know is that we are here and that new conceptions lead us on to better things. And so with the abolition of human sacrifice the first stage in the evolution of religion is passed.

"Time goes on, millions of people have lived in the world, and though they no longer believe in human sacrifice, their conception of God is still extraordinarily manlike. Their God is a being who takes pleasure in the smell of the sacrifice of beasts, a being who can condemn whole families and nations to destruction."

Dr. Millikan arose from his chair; he put his hands in his pockets and walked up and down the small room in the hotel in which he was staying. Then he continued:

"And then a divine event occurred—divine just the same as the last. A new idea comes into human thought and life. It came in a limited way through Mohammed, in a much larger way through Buddha, in a big swelling tide through Jesus—a new conception of God.

"Jesus struck the most mortal blow that has ever been struck at all childish literalisms, when he changed the interpretation of the Jewish scriptures, the anthropomorphic conception of God prevalent up to his time, and saw in God no longer a powerful human being, but a being whose qualities transcended all human qualities; when he cried 'It hath been written . . . but I say unto you'; when he taught God is a spirit, when he said 'The kingdom of heaven is within you'; when he for the first time in the history of the Jews conceived a God who was not interested in Israel alone, but whose sympathies, whose benevolence stretched out through all the world; when he also changed man's conception of duty, for this must always change with the change in the conception of God, and when he focused attention on the Golden Rule rather than on sacrifices and burnt offerings."

I interrupted to ask whether science played any part in the development of religious ideas.

"About fifteen hundred years after Jesus," he replied, "another new step begins to be taken. If one is to connect this step with any one name, it is with the name of Galileo that we must associate the introduction as a ruling principle in life of the scientific mode of thought.

"Remember, he lived in an age when people altogether naturally followed the teachings of Aristotle with respect to the relations of force and motion, but Galileo, like Abraham, began to question the correctness of the conventional belief. That is how he came to make the famous experiment at the Leaning Tower of Pisa, as a result of which the formula which had been accepted for two thousand years could be accepted no longer.

"But not content with disproving, he sought to replace the old erroneous conception by a correct one, and did so as the result of a lifetime spent in patient research.

"Jesus had gone a long way toward destroying or refining man's primitive idea of God. Galileo's method, worked out through the following centuries, took a step in the same direction. It began to show a universe of orderliness and of beauty, a universe that knows no caprice, in a word, a universe that works through God.

"Here was another divine event in the evolution of man's conception of God, and as an inevitable consequence, of his conception of duty. The monasteries of the Middle Ages testify to the old idea of God and duty; the insistent activity of a Maxwell, a Pasteur or a Kelvin to find out the laws of nature and to turn them to the amelioration and enrichment of human life, testifies to the new.

"The new God was the God of law and order, the new duty to know that order and get in harmony with it.

"Of course," he continued, "the thoughtless and undiscerning are divided into two great groups. One is the conventional crowd which passes on without change, and the other is the red mob, the devotees of the next, easiest and cheapest philosophy, the philosophy of 'knock.'

"Religion is affected by it. There are immense crowds that hang behind, that cannot break from the past, and there are others who want to break completely with it, who call it a pack of lies. Neither of them has any conception of what it is all about.

"It seems to me there are but two possible points of view to be taken with respect to the entire question of religion. One is that of the dogmatists, and the other is that of the open-minded seeker after truth.

"Personally, if I were compelled to be a dogmatist, it would be easier for me to be a fundamentalist than an atheist, for I believe with Voltaire that if God did not exist it would be necessary to invent Him.

"Charles Darwin, against whom some religious dogmatists rage, said, 'No man can stand in the tropic forests without feeling that they are temples filled with the various productions of the God of nature, and that there is more in man than the breath of his body.'

"Fortunately I am not obliged to be either a fundamentalist or an atheist, for there is another kind of religion—a religion which keeps its mind open to new truth, which realizes that religion itself has continually undergone an evolution, that as our religious conceptions have changed in the past so they may be expected to change in the future, that eternal truth has been discovered in the past, that it is being discovered now and will continue to be discovered. That kind of religion adapts itself to a growing, developing world. It is useful in such a world, while both kinds of dogmatic opinion seem to me useless.

"Such a religion will be with us so long as man hopes and aspires and reflects upon the meaning of existence and the responsibilities it entails."

VIII

IT is hard enough to get the Englishman on his native heath. It is doubly hard when he happens to be a scientist who comes to this country for short stays in many cities.

I had thought it was difficult to see Bernard Shaw, but at least I knew where he was to be found. When Sir James Jeans was here, I could not even locate him. Telephone calls and frantic interviews with his publishers failed to unearth him. It was only when some one suggested that I try sending a wire in care of his brother-in-law, Senator Bingham, that I managed to get on his trail and obtain his consent to give me an hour just before he sailed.

Now at last I sat with him in his hotel room. As he talked about intangible things, the magic of his words made them seem more real than the gaudy furniture and silken walls of his Louis XVI drawing room. Puffing clouds of smoke from his briar pipe, he pointed out that for three thousand years man has been attempting to find an answer to the mysteries of his being and his surroundings; three million years hence man may still be on the quest.

As I sketched and he spoke, it was inevitable that the pictures of two others—workers along the same lines whom I had also drawn—should come to mind: Professor Einstein in his attic room in Haberlandstrasse in Berlin working on equations which have shaken the beliefs of years; Professor

Sir James Jeans

Millikan at the California Institute of Technology in Pasadena, delving into the mysteries of cosmic rays.

There is a remoteness about Einstein that is almost mystic. Though Millikan's eyes are turned toward the heavens, his feet are firmly planted on the earth. Jeans, the Briton, combines the poetry of the German philosopher of mathematics with the rationality of the scientist of New England descent, and Pegasus always accompanies him on his mathematical flights to the farthest realms of the universe. Though his handshake is as unresponsive as Einstein's he has not the abstraction of the dreamy-eyed professor, and despite the fact that he is as keen as Millikan, he has not the latter's businesslike manner.

In appearance Jeans is typically British, rugged and solid, and mingled with his evident tenacity of purpose is something that recalls gardens filled with flowers, thatched roofs, and wide stretches of countryside. Into dull but learned institutions he brings with him the air and joyfulness of the huge rhododendrons that surround his home·in Dorking. He is a simple, unostentatious man about whom a note of boyishness still lingers.

Of Scotch descent, he was born in Lancashire; when he was three years old his family moved to London. After entering school he expected to make the study of the classics his life work. But a new era of discoveries in science was dawning, a decade which he has called greater than the period begun by Galileo or that which Newton inaugurated. It was the epoch which saw the isolation of the atom, the discovery of radioactivity and cosmic radiations and also the Einstein theory of relativity.

Perhaps it was the ancient philosophers who first interested him in science; perhaps, like Millikan, who had also intended to become a classical scholar, he first read Aristotle for his language and later became more absorbed in his theories; or again, perhaps it was the rumble of the fall of Victorian materialism which resounded in his ears. At all events, before he was graduated from Trinity College, Cambridge, he had determined to give up Latin and Greek in favor of mathematics and science.

While still a fellow at college he began his teaching career. Over a quarter of a century ago he came to this country to occupy the chair of applied mathematics at Princeton at the invitation of Woodrow Wilson, then president of that university. He was here for five years and married an American woman, the niece of Donald Mitchell who, under the pen name of Ik Marvel, wrote the "Reveries of a Bachelor" and "Dream Life," books that were extremely popular in the sentimental eighties.

However, when his alma mater called him, Professor Jeans returned to Cambridge and taught mathematics there. Later he was appointed secretary of the Royal Society, but he has resigned from that post and is now spending all his time on his own scientific problems.

"It is but a natural step," he explained, "from applied mathematics to astronomy, but what many people do not understand is how a man who is an astronomer can find ample occupation outside of an observatory. If I am asked where my observatory is, my usual reply is Mount Wilson, for as a research associate of that observatory, a position which I value very highly, I have access to all of the data collected there.

"The day is gone when the astronomer's work is carried on only at the eyepiece of a telescope. Naturally, observations must be made, but these must be recorded by men who are trained for the purpose and I am not one of them. Photographs are taken from which valuable knowledge is obtained, but many of the astronomers of to-day are mathematicians whose work consists of handling mathematical equations rather than telescopic instruments.

"For instance, Percival Lowell accurately predicted the existence and position of the planet Pluto long before it was actually discovered. It is possible that he was not quite correct in his estimates of its weight, but that will not be positively known for perhaps fifty years, when its position will be such as to make it possible to determine that.

"To take another example, Professor Einstein is not an observing astronomer and none of his work has resulted from any observations which he himself has made. His contribution to our changing ideas of the universe has been the working out of mathematical problems. 'Nature's great book is written in mathematical language'—these are Galileo's words and they are so true that in my opinion no one except a mathematician need ever expect fully to understand those branches of science which hope to unravel the fundamental nature of the universe."

As he has explained in his books, Professor Jeans holds that the Great Architect of the universe begins to appear to be a pure mathematician—a controlling power which has something in common with our own minds, though, so far as we can at present see, it is without emotion, morality, or esthetic appreciation. I asked him how this conception affected his feelings concerning the universe.

Sir James smiled and drew from a sheaf of papers one sheet.

"Here," said he, "is a poem that I heard but a day or so ago. It is by Walt Whitman and it so impressed me that I made a copy of it. It answers your question:

"When I heard the learn'd astronomer;
When the proofs, the figures, were ranged in columns before
*   me;*
When I was shown the charts and the diagrams, to add, divide
*   and measure them;*
When I, sitting, heard the astronomer, where he lectured with
*   much applause in the lecture room,*
How soon, unaccountable, I became tired and sick;
Till rising and gliding out, I wander'd off by myself,
In the mystical moist night air, and from time to time,
Look'd up in perfect silence at the stars."

Sir James's voice is deep, and as he read he put the expression of an actor into the poem.

"The mathematician," he continued, "does not only see nature through the mathematical blinders which he has fashioned for himself; indeed he can often find a real note of poetry and reverence in his abstract studies of the universe. Moreover, astronomy is a science in which exact truth is stranger than fiction and about which one could hardly be prosaic if one tried.

"Of course, scientific ideas have radically changed. In a radio talk in England I pointed out that fifty years ago the universe was generally looked upon as a machine. It was held that the final aim of science was to explain all the objects in the world, including living bodies, as machines, as mere jumbles of atoms which would perform mechanical dances for a time under the action of blind purposeless forces and then fall back to form a dead world.

"Modern science gives but little support to such materialistic views. When we pass to extremes of size in either direction—to the cosmos as a whole or to the inner recesses of an atom—the mechanical interpretation of nature fails. We come to entities and phenomena which are in no sense mechanical. To me they seem less suggestive of mechanical than of mental processes. The universe seems to be nearer a great thought than to a great machine. Such is the view I feel inclined to take at present, while fully conscious that at any time the pendulum may swing back again as our scientific knowledge increases."

Asked if this meant that the universe is one of thought, he replied: "I would say, as a speculation, not as a scientific fact, that the universe and all material objects in it—atoms, stars and nebulae—are merely creations of thought—of course, not of your individual mind or mine, but of some great universal mind underlying and coördinating all our minds. The most we can say is that scientific knowledge seems to be moving in this direction. For myself I find almost any system of idealistic philosophy preferable to the materialistic and mechanistic views held two generations ago; but—who knows how things may look two generations hence?"

I inquired if this were not a rather uncertain stand. He got up and looked for his tobacco to refill his pipe; then he sat down again and replied: "Yes, it is; and there is a reason. We on earth have been thinking seriously about these things, for, shall we say, three thousand years. After three million years our descendants will still probably be thinking about these same things. If they make equally good use of their time they ought to know a thousand times as much then as we know now. Yet even then, so far as we can foresee, human life on earth will only be in its infancy. Our race cannot expect to understand everything in the first few moments of its existence.

"Our ancestors of a century ago read their origins in the Book of Genesis, with 4004 B.C. printed in the margin against the account of creation. To-day we trace our origins back to a far greater antiquity. We believe that the earth is merely a tiny fragment of the sun, which got splashed off, almost by accident, something like two thousand million years ago. For hundreds of millions of years it remained uninhabited, until at last life arrived and, after passing through many forms, culminated in man. The upward ascent was a devious one; life followed many dead ends before finding its final road which led to man. We know that man is an absolutely new arrival on earth and has possessed and governed it for less than a thousandth part of its existence.

"The early Christians believed that the world would end in their lifetime; their founder had said so, and they devoted their whole attention to the living generation. To-day, few, even of our religious teachers, expect the world to end in our time. For more years than we can imagine, it is likely to remain in much the same physical condition as now, and so will provide a suitable home for the human race.

"Whatever our views on a future life in another world, we recapture the old Jewish concept of an immortality in this world—or something which is effectively as good as immortality—enjoyed not by us but, through us, by our posterity. Our problem is no longer merely to muddle through for a few more generations. We see ourselves as the architects of a tremendous future, with science giving us the power to build for good or evil.

"I do not worry overmuch about abstract philosophical problems, nor do I trouble much about questions such as finding a logical or rational basis for ethics or morality.

Sayings of Christ—'It is better to give than to receive' and 'What shall it profit a man if he gain the whole world and lose his own soul?'—take one into regions where logic and science are at present unable to provide any guidance.

"We of the present age know very little—almost nothing; we are rather pioneers setting out to explore a new country. We have the thrill of ever-changing views; now and again we reach a ridge or summit which opens up new and unexpected vistas; of necessity our 'point of view' must change. Those who come after us will live in a very different world, which they will understand far better than we understand our world to-day. They may find it far more wonderful than anything we can imagine; on the other hand. it may prove unspeakably dull.

"In either event, they will not know the thrill of the pioneer. And, unless human nature changes vastly in the meantime, we may be sure they will regret the 'good old days' in which we are now living. They will think of our age as the golden age, the glorious morning of the world. And I, for one, do not regret the fate that has cast my life in it."

As I left him the porter was taking out his luggage to have it sent aboard a ship which would reach England in less than five days. The telephone had rung and Sir James was speaking to some one in California. Outside, the streets were crowded with motors, and the plane from Boston passed overhead.

His words, "the glorious morning of the world," were fresh in my mind and I could not help wondering what its midday would be like.

IX

O NE encounters many religions. Scientists, explorers, business men and artists have talked to me of their beliefs. Yet ordinarily one does not expect to find dogmatic fervor in a diplomat. Perhaps the fact that this diplomat is a poet as well explains the apparent incongruity.

I am thinking of Paul Claudel as I write this, a Frenchman whose conversation is as whimsical as Shaw's without the Irishman's striving; whose aphorisms are as unusual as Wilde's without their artificiality; but beyond, and as a basis for all, is Paul Claudel's almost childlike trust in a Greater Being, a devoutness which accepts without questioning and casts a charm of simplicity over him. But the French Ambassador's belief neither warps nor twists; it has its foundations in the apple tree covered slopes of Picardy where he was born and it found itself on Christmas Day eighteen years later in Notre Dame, when in an instant his heart was touched and he believed—believed so firmly, so convincingly, he himself said, that no reasoning or vicissitudes could shake or even touch that belief.

It was in an artificial, amorous and agnostic Paris that Claudel found his faith—the Paris of Zola and the younger Dumas, of Gérôme the painter and Bernhardt the actress; a Paris in which Banville—a Horace and Mæcenas combined—wrote his criticisms, and in which Verlaine sat at the "Soleil d'Or" or before the doors of "François Premier" and sipped

Paul Claudel

his absinthe with Rimbaud at his side. It was here also that Claudel, a boy from the Aisne. studied at the École des Sciences Politiques.

Veiled and occult as his writings are, the man in his personal appearance has nothing of the esoteric poet. Of middle height, with a tendency toward heaviness, his florid complexion, gray mustache, and broad but not over-high forehead give no inkling of the faculty that has produced free verse comparable with that of Chateaubriand and Rimbaud.

Nor in his clothes does M. Claudel display any of those affectations so characteristic of poets. A stiff collar, a plain four-in-hand tie, and a conservatively cut suit, all go to make the Ambassador look more like a healthy French bourgeois than the diplomatic representative of a great European nation and the author of dramas of mystery and poetry of imagination.

Indeed, it is difficult to accept M. Claudel as either a diplomat or a poet, for he at once displays a sense of humor so keen and so incisive that it is impossible to imagine him taking even himself seriously—a seemingly necessary requirement in the profession of either a poet or a diplomat. But his humor and his conversation are subtle. He glides almost imperceptibly from one subject to another; he states facts in so unusual a form that they seem almost fantasies; and he so presents fantasies that they seem to be facts. He mixes truth with romance, and does it in a language in which he is not altogether at ease, thus showing that it is the power of his ideas and not the play of his words that captivates.

"My first diplomatic post," he told me as he sat in a room high up in one of New York's towers, "was as vice consul in

Boston; and after a few years there, I got my first taste of the Orient. For fifteen years I was in China.

"And, incidentally, speaking of China reminds me of one of the strangest portraits that was ever made of me. It was done by a native artist. He sat facing me, and surely and quickly with a brush loaded with water color he drew one-half of my face; then he deftly folded the paper in half and the wet paint was transferred to the other side of the paper and completed the portrait. It was Oriental efficiency, but it was more than that—it was evidence of that love of conventionalization that is so characteristic of Chinese art."

From China M. Claudel was sent to various European countries, then to Brazil. Later he became Ambassador to Japan, where, as in China, he learned the language. Incidentally, he wrote two Japanese ballets, collaborating with a native musician in writing the incidental music and with an artist in designing the settings.

"Too few people," he said, "know anything about the Japanese art of to-day. Hokusai and a number of his contemporaries are well known, but they are dead, and the great artists who are working there are not appreciated in the West. They still retain the old method of drawing that gives such charm to the older pictures; but from the West has come a certain influence that has made itself felt and introduces a new element into their works.

"Those artists of the East have a clear idea of art; they realize that it is not imitative, that it must be the expression of an emotion—an emotion that in a sense may result from a rational idea. What they put down on their paper they put down quickly, but they do not begin until they have thought out carefully what they are going to do.

"I think this is true of most good art. The actual result is achieved quickly, no matter how long the tortures of creation have previously endured."

As he was speaking, the telephone rang, and he answered it; but though he speaks English well and understands it perfectly, he had difficulty in finding out what the person at the other end of the wire wanted, and asked me to talk. It was a photographic news agency that wanted to take a photograph.

M. Claudel refused to pose—he said he hated photographs, and inadvertently I thought of Al Smith who, when I told him I wanted to make a drawing of him, said: "What good are drawings anyhow? Photographs are better."

"That is the trouble with the world to-day," the Ambassador continued, as he resumed his place in the chair. "We are all becoming too mechanical in our ideas. The advantages that we gain from our great mechanistic inventions make us lose sight of the real beauty and worth of those things that are not purely utilitarian and labor-saving.

"If I want to see what the men and women of an earlier period looked like, I do not get out a lot of photographs. I can gain more knowledge of a man's character from a drawing or painting or bust of him than I can from all the photographs of him that were ever made.

"Do you know the work of Carpeaux?" he asked. "Have you seen any of his portrait busts? He did that group of dancing girls to the right of the entrance of the Paris Opera House, and the bust of Garnier, architect of the building, is also by him. His busts give you a better impression of the people than any photographs; they embody the spirits of his subjects.

"You know," he continued, "they show, too, that our idea that the height of the forehead is a token of intelligence is not altogether right. The eyes, the nose, the mouth or the chin can show mental capacity as well as the brow.

"Most statesmen, for instance, have long noses," he went on. "But I suppose that is very lucky, because most of them cannot see further than the length of them, so that a statesman with a short nose is handicapped by nature."

He chuckled.

"But, seriously, there is a strange fact that always impresses itself upon me whenever I look at the portraits of any number of men of one particular epoch; and that is, that for some reason or other there is a certain resemblance among all of them.

"Do you remember how many men looked like Lincoln during the period in which he lived? You do not see any to-day. It is the same about other periods in the world's history. There is always a predominant type.

"Have you ever noticed the spirit of Bismarck that is present in most of Lenbach's portraits—I mean those of other people? That fact interests me. The reason for it does not. If it is because at that time God felt that that type of man was essential for the welfare of Germany, that is beside the question. The same thing that is true of all the men painted by Lenbach is just as true of any other period of the world's history. How many old Roman busts have you mistaken for Julius Cæsar? Don't you recognize an epochal resemblance among all the Dutchmen painted by Hals or Rembrandt? And assuredly all the men drawn by Ingres have something in common in their looks."

I asked how he accounted for this.

"I do not know," he replied. "And, moreover, as I said before it does not interest me. That is the trouble with the age in which we live. Scientists are ruining the world searching for causes. An artist has no desire to find them out. He is contented with the results.

"When I look out of this window and see the sun glowing on the huge piles of masonry that rear upward into the sky, I am satisfied with the majesty of the scene. The reasons for which the buildings were erected, their cost and their housing capacity do not interest me. Nor do the causes that were at work to produce a fine painting hold any attraction for me. A scientist looks at a painting, and for him it is certain earth or chemical colors dissolved in water or oil, and laid on a piece of canvas; his eyes do not see the soul of the picture."

As he spoke about these things I could not understand why he had given up the greater part of his life to diplomacy. I mentioned this to him. He smiled.

"You Americans also have had authors who did the same thing. There was Irving and also Hawthorne, and in France we have had many men who have combined literature with government work. There are Chateaubriand, Lamartine, and Morand, to mention only a few of them.

"After all, art—and by art I mean painting, sculpture, music, literature and the allied crafts as well—in a way binds all people together, and makes for a better understanding among the various peoples upon this earth; so that even those artists who did not go in for diplomacy have done their part in cementing friendships and smoothing away miscomprehensions."

X

PAUL CLAUDEL's words had seemed strangely familiar to me as he spoke of peace. They recalled for me another Frenchman and a warm summer day in Paris three years before. The bookstalls on the walls of the quay were all open and doing a lively business; the floating baths in the river below were crowded; and as I passed the Chamber I noticed a throng of serious, stiff-collared Frenchmen, interspersed here and there with tourists, waiting for admission to hear the proceedings of the Deputies. A soldier directed me to the almost hidden, steep staircase in the courtyard which leads to the waiting room of the then Minister of Foreign Affairs, the office of Aristide Briand.

This room is bare save for a row of chairs along one wall and a table with periodicals, in the center. I had come in from the bright sunlight and it was a few minutes before I discovered the source of the low rumble that I heard as I entered. In the shadow, at the head of the table, sat, or rather reposed, an attendant. As gently as possible I tried to waken him. I moved a chair but the rumble continued. I coughed. I dropped one of the magazines on the table. There were no results. Undisturbed, he continued to sleep. At last, becoming desperate, I shoved the table. This had the desired effect and, waking, the attendant smiled guiltily, assuring me that it was very warm.

When I explained that I had an appointment with M. Briand he stretched himself, got up in a leisurely way and

Aristide Briand

went to the closet in the corner of the room. From this he took out a tail coat edged with gold braid, on the front of which hung a number of medals. Carefully he brushed it. Then he removed the worn garment he had on and got into the gorgeous one that he had taken out of the closet. With a knowing wink he left me alone, but returned in a few minutes and ushered me through a labyrinth of halls into the presence of the Minister of Foreign Affairs of the French Republic.

Although he comes from Brittany, there is something of the southern Frenchman or even of the Spaniard about Briand's appearance. His wavy black hair, now mixed with gray, his brown, crinkly mustache, his dark skin, with decided redness in his cheeks, through which tiny blood vessels can be seen, all tend to make him resemble a portrait by Velasquez. As a matter of fact, there is a certain resemblance between him and the portrait of the Admiral by that painter that hangs in the National Gallery in London.

His prominent eyebrows are not mates, one being considerably higher than the other, and from beneath them gleam two dark blue eyes that are so deep in hue as to appear black. A deep cleft between his eyes and a mustache, drooping at the corners, give a formidable expression in repose, though when he is speaking this expression rapidly changes and his face is suffused not only with kindness but also humor.

To his personal appearance he apparently pays little attention. In fact, there is a story current in Paris that when he was Premier he went on a walking trip in Brittany and was arrested as a vagrant. At Geneva he was the most carelessly dressed man in the Assembly.

No less vital a personage than Clemenceau, Briand radiates a note of sincerity that seemed lacking in the older man. Compared with him Poincaré looks flabby and soft. Poincaré is more interested in theories than in humanity. And it is humanity that appears to be the one thing in which Briand is completely absorbed. It is for humanity that he has acted the part of the peacemaker of Europe. He has great political ideals coupled with indomitable courage, but he is politician enough to realize that at times those ideals must be compromised, not abandoned, for the sake of peace.

As a young man Briand worked as a journalist. After service on several papers he finally became editor of *La Lanterne*. In those days he was an ardent internationalist, and although some of his ideas have changed since then, nevertheless to-day one discerns in his appeals for the unity of nations the same ideals that he preached and wrote about in his early years. At Locarno, turning his back on Chamberlain so that he might look directly at Luther and Stresemann, he said: "Our people have fought against each other with equal heroism. Has not the time now come for us to work together for European peace?"

He likes to talk about his early days; his law studies, his contributions to the anarchist journal *Le Peuple*, how he founded *L'Humanité* with the Socialist Jaurès. Those were wild days—days of studying, writing, and founding labor unions; nights of card playing, when if luck was against him he would take off his shoes and put them on the table, hoping that they might bring him better fortune.

In speaking of that period he told me a rather amusing story of the time he was connected with *La Lanterne*. One column of that paper was reserved for scandals involving the Catholic clergy. It happened that one day, through the carelessness of the man in charge, there appeared under the heading, "A Contemptible Padre," a story of how a priest had rescued two little boys from drowning. That oversight cost the editor his job.

"But," said Briand, "it was an accident that it was ever discovered. For I am an old enough newspaper man to know that the thing that counts in a newspaper is the headline, not the text beneath.

"That is the great trouble with the press," he continued. "Very often the hastily written words of an incompetent reporter will sway public opinion. I remember after Locarno, the English, the German, and, yes, the French papers also, all acted in practically the same way. In Germany there were headlines saying that the Germans had been imposed upon; here in France I was looked on as a dupe, and in England it was said that I had put Sir Austen in my pocket. Of course, Sir Austen wittily replied that my pocket was not large enough to hold him; nevertheless, there was chance that these hastily written articles might do irreparable harm.

"What the papers should do is to spread a feeling of better understanding among nations—that rather than enmity."

It must not be assumed from these remarks that Briand is a visionary. To see him slouching in his chair, one shoulder considerably higher than the other, his eyes peering from under his mismated eyebrows, and the butt of a half-smoked cigarette drooping from his mouth, would soon dispel any such idea. He is a very real person, keenly alive not only to the better qualities of humanity but also to its weaknesses. He knows that men are neither as good nor as bad as they are painted. Accepting the world as it is, he is confident that it can be made better. With the Nationalist he has no more sympathy than with the red-flag-waving Internationalist.

"The Nationalist," he said, "declares that Germany is a horrible, bloodthirsty country whose sole desire is our destruction and whose very industrial plants are constructed for the sole purpose of furnishing military supplies. Accordingly, we must irritate that dangerous country and make it hate us more. England is trying to ruin us and, therefore, we should be on the worst possible terms with her. Italy is a nation of mandolin players and we cannot take them seriously, while as for America—you can imagine what they say of her.

"It sounds like a joke, doesn't it? But that is the pith of their remarks. They, however, are not a bit more ridiculous than is the rabid Internationalist who wants to wipe out all boundaries and is willing to commit any atrocity so that the lion and lamb may lie down together.

"There is good and there is bad in all of us, though I will acknowledge that it is a little harder for me to see France's faults than those of another country. But that is because I am a Frenchman.

"There is only one thing that wipes away boundaries. Look around you," said he, pointing to some Gobelin tapestries. (Is it any wonder that Claudel's words called Briand to mind?) "You know who designed them—Rubens. The originals are in the Louvre. He was not a Frenchman, but his work is as dear to us as to the people of his native country. And now let me tell you a secret. After one of my most strenuous days at Locarno I returned to my hotel utterly exhausted. An old friend of mine was there waiting for me. I knew that he played the piano, and I felt that I must hear some music. Shall I tell you what I asked him to play? Wagner's 'Walküre.'"

When I left Briand that day in his office on the quay I did not know that I should see him again amid very different surroundings within a few weeks.

There was a council meeting of the League of Nations at Geneva. Into a glass-walled room, that at one time might have served as a conservatory, pressed a crowd of hot, perspiring newspaper men and a host of intense women intent on improving the world. So numerous were they that they hardly left room for the delegations of the nations of the world: Chamberlain, diplomatic and suave; Stresemann, blunt and uncomfortable; Scialoja, captious but humorous; Briand, bored to death. For two days, hunched in his chair, with his cigarette perilously near his crinkly mustache, he said nothing while the council listened to reports on "The Settlement of Greek Refugees," "The Traffic in Women and Children," "Methods to Make It Easier for States to Apply Economic Sanctions," and other similar subjects.

The dowagers in taffetas, with yellow badges on their bosoms, sighed: "Marvelous!" Flat-chested females took notes in loose-leaf notebooks. The correspondents wrote columns on how the world was becoming a better place in which to live. But Briand developed eye trouble and left.

Did that mean that he was not interested in the League of Nations? Assuredly not. But he realized that it was not there that he would have an opportunity to play his part of the peacemaker. He waited.

Then came the Assembly Meeting and he saw his chance. Above all other things a public speaker, Briand intuitively senses the feelings of his audience and puts them into words. I shall never forget him as he arose in that meeting. There was an expectant hush as he began his address. His voice, resonant and under perfect command, rises and falls at will, so that in fact he has been called "Old Baritone" and "Gypsy Cellist." Using that voice to the best of his ability, and speaking, as he does most of the time, without notes, he made another plea for the World of Peace.

"I desire," said he, "to make an act of faith in the name of my country and to say that we have faith in the future of our work of peace. We are prepared to persevere. We have suffered. France has been crucified in the past. We cannot forget our sufferings and we are determined that we shall not allow such sufferings to take place in the future."

XI

Briand had spoken to me of peace with all the emotional fire of a Frenchman. It was in more measured language but with no less depth of conviction that the president of Columbia University once expressed similar views.

"To-day the whole world is thinking what that old prophet Jeremiah long ago called thoughts of peace. The mind of the world has been turned from a backward-looking and forward-fearing mind to a forward-looking and backward-fearing mind."

These are the words of Dr. Nicholas Murray Butler. As he spoke, he was posing for me in his office on the second floor of the library of Columbia University. There, in the middle of a large room, the windows of which overlook the Hudson, at his desk sat the man under whose guidance and direction Columbia has grown to be one of the two largest universities in the country.

The Morningside section of New York is a city in itself. It has its own essential characteristics and in many ways it is entirely different from the rest of the city. But it has none of the sleepy atmosphere of most college towns. The subway pours out its hordes there as it does in other parts of the city; the surface cars clang their bells just as loudly and the automobiles whip by at the same speed.

To the north of the university rises the tower of the new Riverside Church, a tower which would have taken years to build in Oxford or Cambridge.

The pulsing throb of the metropolis is not halted by the aggregation of buildings of learning; they are a part of it. The golden Alma Mater with outstretched hands bids welcome to her students and her alumni and alumnae to a campus where Pan plays his pipes to the accompaniment of electric riveters and she bids them to pore over tomes no longer dusty but vacuum cleaned.

Just as the university of which he is the head typifies a combination of present-day life and all learning, so does Nicholas Murray Butler stand for the man of learning taking an active part in the life of the times.

There is nothing of the absent-minded professor about this well-groomed man as he sits in his office. Former presidents of King's College look down on him from their highly burnished and ornate frames, and on a bookcase stands a head of Victory. They are but his background, and are in shadow; he looms out of them, not inseparably detached, but more prominent.

There is a certain fumbling attitude about most college professors. Though Masaryk has attained the Presidency of his native land, on meeting him one feels that he is still looking for a piece of chalk to demonstrate some problem on a blackboard. About John Dewey there is a careful hesitancy. Even Woodrow Wilson, after eight years of the presidency, still remained a teacher.

But this is not so of Dr. Butler. It would be impossible to imagine this former Professor of Philosophy going out forgetful of the fact that he had no hat; in fact, one would be certain that his hat, were it not a silk one, would be a derby.

In other words, he is not the dreamy scholar who, secluded in his library, does not see the actual present. With scholarship he combines executive and business ability. He is living in a rapidly changing world and his eyes are open to the changes

Nicholas Murray Butler

that are going on about him, and although he has been connected with the university during practically his entire lifetime, he has never lived, so to speak, within the campus; he has never permitted the college walls to obstruct his view of what has been going on outside.

For this reason, in addition to being the head of Columbia, Dr. Butler has taken an active part not only in city but also in national and international affairs. On the other hand, in these days of specialization, he does not believe that a man can succeed by turning first to one thing and then to another, but that, though his interests may be diverse, he must stick to his chosen work.

In speaking of a certain man who had attained some prominence in various lines of endeavor, he said:

"Had he only stuck to what he started out to be, he would be much more successful to-day. He came to New York too late in life. This city is the graveyard of village reputations. Men comparatively well known come here and are lost in the crowd.

"On the other hand, it is quite a different thing for the country boy," he continued, "for as Cardinal Newman said years ago, a city is by its very nature a university."

"Naturally the city draws to itself men and women of all kinds. It is the home of great collections of art and science and it affords abundant opportunities to come under the influence of the best music and the best literature of our time. The great city, and especially New York, is intensely cosmopolitan and contact with its life for even a short time during the impressionableness of youth is in itself a liberal education.

"It is this same rubbing of elbows, as it were, of the various peoples of the world, that will go far toward making the dream of a lasting peace real.

"It would be impossible to think of a war being declared to-day," he continued, "in the same way that it was fifteen years ago.

"The revolutionary psychological change among men began while the war was still in progress.

"Post-war unhappiness, problems and perplexities halted it for a while, but when Briand, Stresemann, and Chamberlain had their momentous meeting at Locarno, the beginning of the end of the old order was in sight.

"There remained the carefully stimulated naval rivalry between the two great branches of the English-speaking family. Hired trouble-makers and, I might add, unscrupulous newspapers did what they could to make the era of international war and its dark and costly shadows last a little longer. They did this by playing upon the credulous ignorance of public men and public opinion. But these actions have now been laughed not only off the stage but off the front page as well."

The winter sun was quickly going down behind the Palisades on the other side of the Hudson. It threw an orange glow over his strong features. He appeared rapt in thought for a few minutes and then turned abruptly around.

"After Locarno," he said, "came Washington. The Prime Minister and the President, face to face and in kindly confidence, crowded into four days' conversation and understanding forty years of formal diplomatic procedure. Those three foreign statesmen with their associates at Locarno and Mac-Donald and Hoover at Washington have done the business for which a weary world was waiting with bated breath.

"The change that has taken place in the way that international business is conducted can best be shown by the amazing contrast between meetings such as these and those of former times.

"Just about seventy years ago, on a bright summer's day, one of the chief personalities of Europe left Geneva; he left in disguise, bearing a false name and armed with a false passport. That was Count Cavour, Prime Minister of the government of the Kingdom of Piedmont. Secretly, and, I might say, on tiptoe, he made his way to Prombieres in the Vosges. It was the height of the season when he arrived, but instead of going to any of the fashionable hotels he took quarters in a small chemist's shop. There amid the smell of drugs and surrounded by blue and red and green bottles he waited until a summons came, and in the dark he was escorted into the presence of the powerful reigning monarch, Napoleon III. These two men of high place and vast responsibility did not confer together; they conspired as to how they might bring about a great war.

"That was only seventy years ago, but there was no legislative debate, no popular appeal, merely two high-placed and powerful dictators, with all the arms and apparatus of two governments, together with the peace of Europe, in their four hands.

"But two generations later—a very short time in human history—a Prime Minister of State, who wields the vast and responsible authority accorded to him by a great people living under free and democratic government, starts across the sea. He dons no disguise, he carries no false passport. His own countrymen acclaim his going. The daily press of the world records his every act and word. His very voice is carried right into the homes of millions, when in six days' time he reaches the welcoming and hospitable shores of another land.

"The enthusiasm of genuine affection is showered upon him, both for himself and on behalf of the great people for whom he has come to speak. He goes to no upper story of a chemist's shop, but to the White House, and then, as the personal guest of the President of the United States, to a simple cabin in the foothills of the Blue Ridge, that there, quiet and undisturbed, they may speak together of the great issues and the little ones which divide peoples and which bind peoples together.

"This is no conspiracy to organize war. It is a conference to build peace. There is the difference.

"Public confidence has succeeded in displacing secrecy, conference has routed conspiracy, and the authority of free peoples and their public opinion is underneath, behind, and all about what the Prime Minister and the President have done."

I asked what part the Paris peace pact would play in avoiding wars.

"On August 2, 1928," Dr. Butler replied, "the civilized world through its organized governments formally and solemnly condemned recourse to wars for the solution of international controversies, and the several governments renounced war as an instrument of national policy in their relations with one another. They further agreed that the settlement or solution of all disputes or conflicts of whatever nature or of whatever origin which may arise among them shall never be sought except by pacific means.

"This declaration, applauded from pole to pole and the whole world round, is of so stupendous importance that it is even now most imperfectly understood.

"In his haste, the Psalmist said, 'All men are liars.' Unless all men and all governments are liars, national policies will, without delay, be adjusted to the new international life that has been so gratefully brought into being.

"Gone is the fear for national security; gone is the argument for compulsory military service and huge standing armies; gone is the plea for the protection of sea-borne commerce and a navy as powerful as any in the world; gone is the haste to build bombing planes and to store up vast supplies of poison gas; gone is the whole gospel of preparedness for a war which is promised never to be fought—gone are all these unless all men and all governments are liars!"

It was dusk. The pink sky with its purple clouds was luminous behind the massive buildings in which lights began to appear. The unfinished tower of the new church loomed vast and graceful and tall.

"Then," I asked, "you think the last war has been fought?"

Dr. Butler looked serious, and then, in the half-darkness, he replied:

> *"They have no pact to sign—our happy dead,*
> *But if, O God, if we should sign in vain,*
> *With dreadful eyes, out of each narrow bed,*
> *Our dead will rise again!"*

XII

THOUGH Dr. Butler has never held political office, he has for years taken an active part in public affairs and has even run for the vice presidency. But not many men in political life have been drafted from our colleges. Although in Europe the college professor and the writer are often engaged in political activities, in this country, with but few exceptions, the political leaders have come from other professions.

Wilbur L. Cross of Connecticut is one of those exceptions, for Dr. Cross had no sooner resigned as dean of the Yale Graduate School than he was nominated for governor. Naturally the election of a college professor to the governorship immediately calls to mind the career of another Democrat.

Yet there is little in common in the personalities of the Governor of Connecticut and the late Woodrow Wilson. The former President was a little more cosmopolitan in manner, a little more given to theatricalism than the deliberate, slow-going Yankee who still likes to use the homely language of the country in all his conversation.

Tall, almost awkward in his movements, and with a quiet shuffling walk that is characteristic of men who have spent their lives in libraries, Dr. Cross, in distinct contrast with Dr. Butler, at first impresses one as a scholar rather than a man of affairs.

There is nothing formal about him, nothing that smacks either of a desire for effect or regard for the impression that he

Wilbur L. Cross

is making. Everything that he does, from lighting his cigar to dipping his steel pen in the inkstand, is done without haste, but no matter what is done one feels instinctively that it is done thoroughly.

Although a tyro in politics, he has managed to hold his own against the seasoned politicians. His easy-going manner has irritated his opponents, and his classical allusions have confused them. His presumable innocence of political wiles, however, has proved misleading and a source of strength, and men who have pulled wires all their lives are puzzled by this professor of English who, after an academic career of almost half a century, made a three-minute speech at a clambake and, as a consequence, became a candidate for governor.

But his acts as governor might well have been predicted from his characteristically individual campaign for election. He mixed stories of "settin' hens" with quotations from Chaucer and, while his listeners understood all about the former, they thought the latter was a farmer "living out Wethersfield way." The shrewdness of much that he said pleased his audiences. They liked his manner and his nickname, "Uncle Toby," which he had acquired at Yale, even if they did not understand its allusion to the candidate's admiration for Georgian literature. And because he had edited Stevenson's "Travels with a Donkey," they thought he had written an important history of his party.

However, the inhabitants of Connecticut have always been keen. They quickly saw that here was a candidate who was not trying to sell wooden nutmegs, nor could he be sold one. They respected him for both his honesty and wisdom. And, accordingly, when the votes were counted on election day, the sole survivor on the Democratic ticket was this benevolent, humorous, white-haired professor.

Although he laid aside the cap and gown to take up the reins of government, a man cannot easily abandon the habits of a lifetime, and so into the towered Capitol at Hartford he has brought with him the restfulness of the elms of New Haven. Sitting in the Governor's room, with its golden oak furnishings, its paintings of Putnam and Buckingham, and a relentless electric clock whose hands jump noisily every few minutes, he, by his very presence, has apparently transformed the room into a library. His desk is as cluttered as was his office of the *Yale Review*, but although the volumes of literature which covered it have been supplanted by law books, a literary air still surrounds the Governor. Formality is foreign to him, and the unaffected manners of this Connecticut Yankee are in direct contrast with those of the brass-buttoned, gold-braided messenger who, big and bearded, resembles an African monarch and supplies the pomp and circumstance that surround the gubernatorial chair.

But it is not only he who provides a contrast. The uniformed police, the clerks rushing through the tiled halls, the air of officialdom in the huge building dominating the hilltop, all make the Governor appear more unassuming. The difference between these surroundings and those of Yale where he seemed to fit so perfectly into the almost colonial atmosphere of the college town, prompted me to ask how he regarded the change in his occupation.

He leaned back in his chair and smiled. "There are not so many differences as one would imagine," he said. "Now let's see, as dean of the Yale Graduate School I had to deal with thirty departments of study all the way from the fine arts and literature through the natural, social, and physical sciences to engineering and clinical medicine. I met men very unlike in nature, from the hard-headed engineer engrossed in figures to the temperamental artist ready to fly off at a tangent at any minute. One must be politic, to say the least, even in a college, in dealing with such varied types.

"Since I have become governor, I have had to transact business with about the same number of major departments of state, running from banking and insurance into labor, aviation, and highways. It is again largely a question of temperament in different professions.

"Of course, the men one runs across in a college have all been brought up in about the same way; the majority of them come from the same type of families. Most of them are young, with hopes and aspirations that have not been dimmed or altered by contact with the world, and all are eager to make a name for themselves. As governor I come in contact with different kinds and classes of people, not all actuated by the same motives. In this way a governor's field of observation is broader and for that reason more interesting than that of a college professor. He rubs elbows with the world, but in a capitol more elbows are threadbare than in a college."

"It is unusual, however, to find a scholar entering politics," I remarked.

He smiled. "Yes, I suppose it is. In this country the term politician has taken on a distinctive meaning. Often it is used as an epithet of opprobrium. Perhaps that is because there have not been enough scholars in politics to give it a good name.

"In Europe this is not the case. Many professors enter public life. Here we have an idea that law is a particularly fitting prelude to public office. Why this is so I do not quite understand. For to-day, owing to the rapid changes in social ideas, the duties of public office are becoming increasingly complex, and a large part of the work is extraneous to a knowledge of law. Great social, moral, educational, and economic movements now animate the public as never before.

"All about us we see these movements at work, in the churches, in labor organizations, in chambers of commerce, in both business and professional clubs and always in colleges and universities. As a matter of fact, many of the latest theories in sociology and economics have been born within college walls.

"Of course," he continued, "while not many teachers have gone into politics, a number of statesmen, after they had made their names in politics, felt that they were progressing when they became teachers. I have one in mind who preferred to go down in history as the father of a university rather than as President of the United States.

"Speaking seriously, however, it is a fact that in the university affairs politics rarely, if ever, enters; while in state affairs it is always in the background.

"When a man enters public life it is a foregone conclusion that he will become embroiled in disagreements. However, there are disagreements in other professions, too. In the administration of college affairs everything does not always run smoothly, but the differences arise from an honest variance of opinions. In politics they often spring from opposition of political parties, so that instead of partnership in government we have partisanship.

"But it seems to me that the people are becoming convinced that government is likely to be good in so far as it is separated from politics in a narrow sense. I believe in the two-party system. I believe in it so much that I felt that the Democratic party needed building up, and so I said I'd run for governor if they would let me make a few changes in the organization."

From his vest pocket the Governor took a cigar and lighted it deliberately. For a few minutes he seemed wrapped in thought. Then he continued.

"When you come right down to brass tacks, the principal business of government is to further and promote human strivings, and in state house as well as in college one encounters them. Who learns more of them than the instructors at institutions of learning?"

"How long," I asked, "have you been connected with such institutions?"

"From the time I first went to the little red schoolhouse on the hill in Willimantic, which was a good many years ago," he answered. "When I graduated from the high school there I had to work my way through Yale. Then I began to teach. For a time I was a member of the faculty of Sheffield Scientific School; then I became dean of the graduate school, and while still filling that post I was appointed editor of the *Yale Review*. Each time I made a change my friends told me that I was making a mistake, that I should stick to what I was doing. But I have different ideas. I do not believe a man should continue doing precisely the same kind of work too long. He must progress; that is the law of nature. To keep on doing the identical thing for years tends to fossilize any one.

"Up to the time I became governor, although my work was always along more or less the same lines, it had slight variations. For instance, before I received the nomination I had retired from my position in the University and had determined to go to Europe to deliver a series of lectures on English literature at a number of universities there; instead I am now here in Hartford as head of the State."

I asked him how he became interested in politics.

"You must not forget," he answered, "when I was a boy there were no movies or radios. Men's thoughts naturally turned to politics as a diversion, and in the long winter nights instead of listening to Amos 'n' Andy or watching Charlie Chaplin, men congregated round the red-hot stove in the store at the crossroads and engaged in political discussions.

"I can remember the vitriolic arguments which took place when Greeley and Grant ran against each other and when the boys who were Republicans dressed in blue and those who supported Greeley wore tall gray hats. Those were the days of flowery orations, of torchlight parades, of debates, and brass bands. It is not surprising that a youngster growing up in such surroundings should become interested in the affairs of state and, as soon as he was able to vote, that he should affiliate himself with one of the political parties, usually the one to which his father belonged. I think politics followed paternity more closely in those days.

"When Cleveland declared that 'public office is a public trust,' it made a deep impression not only on me but also on the rest of the students. I became so enthusiastic and vociferous about it that my classmates nicknamed me the 'Senator,' and although Frank Brandegee actually became one, I still am called by that title by many of the men whom I knew at college.

"So you can readily understand that although I have been a teacher most of my life, I have nevertheless always retained an interest in politics. But it was not until I resigned from the graduate school that I felt free to enter politics practically."

But public life has not separated him from his literary work. He is still editor of the *Yale Review*. He still reads every article before it is accepted and he goes over the proof. I asked him how he found the time to do this.

"By getting up early in the morning," he replied. "I have discovered that a tremendous amount of work can be done before most people think of getting out of bed. Then there are Sundays also, when one is not likely to be disturbed and when a great deal can be accomplished.

"It would be difficult for a man who has always devoted a great part of his time to reading to be compelled to give that up, so that even now I continue to re-read my old favorites.

"The writers of the eighteenth century have been those whose works I have most thoroughly studied, and the development of the English novel has always held a great interest for me. As soon as I have a little more time I intend to bring my book on that subject, which was originally published over thirty years ago, up to date.

"In the meantime, as I sit here in my office every day I meet characters who seem to have walked out from the pages of books I have read. Tom Jones and Roderick Random, Tristram Shandy, Major Pendennis and Micawber—to mention but a few—are still roaming our streets. Here I am having a most wonderful time renewing old acquaintances and meeting again, after a lapse of years, old friends whom I last knew in some favorite novel."

XIII

INTERVIEWS do not always turn out the way one expects. Once I had gone to Washington especially to get Senator Borah's ideas on Russia. I did not get them. But instead I obtained a much clearer picture of the man than I would have, had he spoken on the subject that I wanted.

When I first saw him he said he would think the matter over and the next morning he called me up and said, "I don't believe I can say anything about Russia that is not already known but if you care to come over and hear my ideas on literature I'll be glad to tell them to you."

There is another side to this "lone wolf" from the stern political aspect which the public knows. And yet the first impression that Senator Borah gives is the remarkable likeness that he bears to his portraits. There are people whose faces are familiar in pictures and yet, when seen for the first time, an uncertainty arises as to their identity, and there are many people of whom no two photographs are alike; but not so Mr. Borah. His square head, his dark eyebrows almost meeting above his short nose and shading his penetrating but kindly eyes, his long upper lip and firm mouth, his strong chin, with its well-defined cleft in the center, his thick hair parted in the middle and allowed to grow rather long at the back—all are unmistakable.

Mr. Borah's coloring is as characteristic as his features. His eyes are blue. Their black pupils give them a vividness of

William E. Borah

expression and a surprising degree of intensity. His hair is dark brown with a trace of gray above the ears, while his complexion inclines toward the ruddy and betokens health and strength. His voice, though not deep, is mellow, and as he speaks, one feels that he has given time to the study of elocution, for he knows the value of a change of tone.

Had he not gone into politics it is possible that he would have become either an actor or a minister. Some people appear to belong only in their own epoch; others seem out of place, while there is a third group that can be imagined in any period. With all his native Americanism, Senator Borah is one of those who might have been at home in the Forum at Rome; he might have been one of the Puritans who left England for these shores; it is easy to picture him boarding the ships that carried the tea into Boston Harbor, or as a contemporary of Webster, or a member of Lincoln's Cabinet.

In his character the fanaticism of the preacher is combined with the emotionalism of the actor. Imbued with the righteousness of an idea, he clings to it irrespective of party principles, no matter how it may harm him politically. He feels deeply and shows his feelings; there is no Yankee reserve or reticence about him. His moods change rapidly, not because they are not intense, but rather on account of their intensity. I saw him change in less time than it takes to tell from sincere sorrow over the loss of a friend to an earnest discussion of foreign affairs, although it was evident that his grief was just as deep as his interest in the condition of Russia.

His humor is sharp and sarcastic, but it carries no lasting sting. Once when I saw him Mr. Coolidge's attitude toward accepting another nomination was still uncertain. I asked whether he thought the President could be persuaded to run again, and he answered with a twinkle in his eye: "That presupposes that some one is going to try to persuade him." And again, when it was suggested that the Russian peasant had little to say in the conduct of the Soviet government, the Senator remarked with a smile: "About as much as our farmers have in ours."

To understand Senator Borah it is necessary first to remember his start in politics. Born the year the Civil War ended, he was brought up in a county in Illinois which was, as he puts it, "a hotbed of politics, where one year the Democrats polled a tremendous vote and where the next year the Republicans had startling majorities." The result was that before he was old enough to vote Borah was a seasoned political orator. In those days there were no independents. Feelings ran high, factional fist fights were not infrequent, and a voter was either a Republican or a Democrat. Even the Mugwump was unborn. Reared in this atmosphere, he of necessity allied himself with a party, although at heart and by temperament he is not a party man.

A Democratic president is attacked by members of his own party in the Senate, and Borah, a Republican Senator, thunders out a defense in the Senate Chamber. President Coolidge appoints a member of the Morgan firm Ambassador to Mexico. There is much criticism, but Borah, the foe of big business, approves of the selection.

"I eliminate personalities in determining policies," says the Senator. "The individual means nothing to me. In fact, I will travel with the devil if he is going in my direction."

Of all the men in Washington in the public eye, Borah is probably the least conspicuous in the social affairs of the capitol. No man of his prominence attends fewer dinners.

Outside of horseback riding he is supposed to have few recreations, but there is another Borah who is almost unknown to the public—a side he has managed to conceal.

Most of his evenings are spent in his library. It is there that he finds rest and relaxation. Naturally, as Chairman of the Committee on Foreign Relations, he has a vast amount of reading to do, but aside from this the Senator employs his leisure in reading for enjoyment.

"At the risk of being called an old fogy," he began, "I still follow Carlyle's example and each time a new book is published I read an old one. And right now I may as well confess that I am vitally interested in novels. To my mind the majority of modern novels might better be classified as textbooks of physiology and psychology. I read solely for pleasure; I am interested in people, but I do not care for the dissecting table. When I tell you that one of my favorite novelists is Hawthorne you will see that I do not shrink from morbidity. As a matter of fact, Hawthorne's morbidity appeals to me; but after all it is, if I may so call it, a healthy morbidity clothed in an almost poetic form. It is all right to call a spade a spade in a book on sewers, but for my part I am not interested in sewers as a literary subject.

"My other favorite novelist is Balzac. I like Dickens and Thackeray, but Dickens I find given a little too much to caricature and Thackeray a little too English to appeal to a Middle Westerner. But Balzac's characters are real. They are French, it is true, but they are human beings first. I feel their humanity rather than their nationality. Take Rastignac and his friends, who are found in a number of novels—why, I know a crowd of young chaps right here in Washington whom Balzac might have been describing when he wrote of those Frenchmen. Then there is the 'Country Doctor.' Disregarding his monarchistic ideas, I know scores of doctors out west who might have served as a model for him, striving as he did for human betterment."

"Do you also read poetry?"

"Oh, yes," he went on, "but here again I am old fashioned. I suppose I ought to tell you that I am interested in free verse, but I am not. The three poets whom I most admire and whose works I read and reread so often that I can quote pages from them are Shakespeare, Milton, and Dante. So you see, in some things I am not as radical as I am painted. Whatever I can say of any one of them would seem very trite, but how true and applicable are many of Shakespeare's characterizations, and how well some of them fit some of our public men to-day!

"There are two more writers whom, if I am speaking of my favorite authors, I must necessarily name; they are Emerson and Swift."

As he mentioned the latter I involuntarily smiled, for I immediately recognized a resemblance in outlook on life between the Dean and the Senator. He noticed my expression and grasping almost intuitively the reason for it, he continued: "Yes, other people have felt the same way as you, but I am flattered at the comparison. After all, even if he was somewhat of a cynic, whatever weaknesses and frailties he saw in human nature and in governments he tried to cure rather than increase. And his imagination and quaint humor permitted him to point out those weaknesses in a manner that entertained at the same time that it instructed.

"As for Emerson, nobody knows the amount of inspiration and comfort that I have received from his essays. Many a night, after a terribly trying day in the Senate, when everything has seemed to go wrong, when I have doubted even my own convictions, I have gone home and after dinner have taken up a copy of Emerson and turned to his essay on 'Self-reliance.' It has put new life into me, made me look at things in a very different way, and often when I have been on the point of giving up, that work has kept me sticking to my guns."

XIV

I THINK that Emerson has been mentioned more often by people who have posed for me than any other author. The effect that this sharp-faced old New Englander has had upon succeeding generations appears to be deep and lasting. In a way it was not so surprising that he should influence the Senator from Idaho; what did startle me was the day I saw a copy of his essays lying open upon the desk of Georges Clemenceau.

I had received a letter the previous evening saying that M. Clemenceau would pose for me the following morning at nine-fifteen and I did not know exactly what to do, for I had an engagement with another French statesman. I was particularly anxious to draw Clemenceau; so I decided it would be best to go to his house, explain matters, and ask him to fix another time.

At an early hour, with portfolio and charcoal, I jumped into a taxi and told the driver to take me to 8 Rue Franklin. We drove in the direction of Auteuil, past the statue of Benjamin Franklin, and finally entered a rather narrow street filled with apartments and shops; by no means a smart street, and so distinctly Parisian that it was the last place in the world imaginable as the residence of one who was supposed to love the countryside. Number 8 is one of those typical French apartments with a small courtyard and a *concierge* and several baby carriages whose noisy occupants cast doubt on the statement that France's birthrate is declining.

Georges Clemenceau

Here Clemenceau lived. One expects some sort of homage to be paid to fame; and I confess that when I asked the *concierge* (at the moment busy with her baby) which floor was M. Clemenceau's, I was somewhat startled when, without raising her eyes, she told me it was on the ground floor in the rear.

I was ushered through a dark hall into Clemenceau's library. Here I was in the room in which he spent most of his waking hours, a room which, if inanimate things can reflect a personality, must more than any other be representative of Clemenceau himself.

The room seemed to be cluttered with things of all sorts, so crowded that the memory of it brings to mind no individual objects but a jumbled mass of furniture and bric-a-brac. On three sides were bookcases, the tops of which were filled with vases and statuettes, and above these, photographs, drawings, and prints. In the middle of one wall was the inevitable white mantel and mirror so characteristic of all French rooms, and here all sorts of knick-knacks had accumulated. A sofa took up the remaining side, while in the center was a large kidney-shaped desk piled high with papers, books, and pieces of African pottery. A number of chairs helped fill the remaining space and aided in furthering the crowded effect.

With the exception of two sketches by Monet, the pictures appeared to have been selected for their subjects rather than their artistic worth. But beside the mirror and in one of the most prominent places hung a large water color drawing of a woman with red hair, a profile with delicate features—not French, I thought, and immediately I began to wonder if perhaps it was a drawing made long ago of that Stamford girl, Miss Mary Plummer, who afterward became Mme. Clemenceau, but with whom her husband had not lived for some time previous to her death.

I imagined him sitting at his desk and looking up at the picture as he was writing and living again the years in America when he taught French in that young ladies' boarding school in Connecticut. The entire room evidently belonged to a man living with his memories. Things were there not for themselves, but for the associations connected with them.

As I look back now, I realize that all these impressions were crowded into a space of time much less than it takes to record them, for I had hardly seated myself on the couch when I heard the patter of feet and two strange little gray dogs trotted in. Short and squat, with long hair covering their eyes and hanging over their mouths, they were appropriate heralds of the short little gray man who came in after them.

This was Clemenceau! Dressed in gray—gray slippers on his feet, gray silk gloves on his hands and a modification of the poilu's hat, likewise in gray, on his head. All of this grayness accentuated the darkness of his skin and gave it a ruddy hue which scoffed at almost four score and ten years.

The active little dogs were no more vigorous than the vital little man who followed them.

Before I had a chance to say anything he began, "You are twenty-five minutes late; I wrote to you to come at a quarter to nine and now it's ten after. I do not like to be kept waiting. The sand runs too rapidly through the glass."

I explained that his letter had said a quarter past nine and I had another appointment at nine-fifteen, but that I would come at any other time he would name.

"There is no other time; I have arranged to give you this time, you are late, but I will pose for you now—otherwise not at all."

Clemenceau spoke in English, very good English with a French accent—a rather sharp incisive speech with a rising inflection as he finished each sentence. But his manner gave a note of finality to what he had to say, so that I immediately felt there was no use arguing about what time his letter named or in endeavoring to change the hour of the appointment.

I accordingly told him that I would draw him then and there and the Tiger drew in his claws and purred. He literally purred, for with the slightest suspicion of a grunt of satisfaction he dropped his gruff manner and became a charming, beneficent old gentleman.

He tried several places in the room in order to get the best lighting, he made sure that I was comfortable, and when everything was arranged satisfactorily he began to pose. Unlike many other busy men I have drawn, he gave me his undivided time and neither read nor wrote as I made my sketch, but, seated at his desk with his hands clasped in front of him, he looked straight ahead of him into space. The light from the window fell directly on him and brought into strong relief the well-modeled head. The light was not complimentary; it did not soften the wrinkles, nor did it blur the marks of age. But after all, it was the right kind of light in which to draw this rugged old Frenchman, most of whose life had been spent in fighting.

Though we were in the heart of Paris, none of the noise or bustle filtered into the high half-lighted room in which Clemenceau sat.

Neither of us said a word. I wanted to speak, but he seemed so engrossed that I hesitated. As I drew I tried to read some of his thoughts, for politician though he was, his face was no mask and his expression changed and seemed to betray what was passing in his mind. At one time the faintest suspicion of a smile appeared to cross his face, while at another I thought I detected the trace of a watery film over his eyes. Once I was almost sure that he was living over the days in Montmartre, when, as a young doctor, he had treated, gratuitously, the poor of the neighborhood. I saw him go through the fearful strain of war again, and later, when a peculiar look of sadness came over him, I was certain that he was wondering why the one gift that he had really wanted had been withheld from him by the French people. Like the Romans, they had caused to be placed in each schoolhouse of the nation tablets recording the fact that Georges Clemenceau was deserving of the thanks of the Republic; but the thing that he wanted was the presidency and this had been denied him.

Suddenly catching hold of himself, he turned and smiled a half-guilty smile, as if he felt that I had overheard his thoughts. And in that eloquent silence I am sure that I had. But the spell was broken and I knew that whatever he would say could not be half so revealing as the reflections of his inner moods which crossed his face as he sat there in silence.

One of the little dogs that had been asleep on a newspaper that was lying on the sofa got up and shifted his position. Clemenceau looked at me as if he felt that he had given enough of his time. I took the hint.

"The drawing is finished. Will you sign it?" I asked, showing it to him and at the same time offering him a piece of charcoal.

Putting on a pair of horn-rimmed spectacles, he looked at it a few minutes, and then muttered to himself, "*C'est moi.*" But instead of taking my charcoal he used his pen, saying, "I can handle the pen better than the crayon."

I left with the decided impression that Clemenceau was, like Mark Twain, a very lonely man, and in spite of his fame not an overhappy one, for about him there was a note of inexplicable sadness. Almost all of his intimates had gone.

"At eighty-six," he had said to me, "one does not make new friends and the old ones have gone to keep appointments that cannot be broken."

But although Clemenceau has now gone to keep those appointments, he is in but one sense of the word dead. To the men who worked with him or fought against him he is almost still alive. There was something so vital about the grim old warrior that it is hard for them to realize that the roar of the Tiger has been forever hushed.

XV

I HAVE noticed that the country breeds a certain freedom and unrestraint. Men who are cautious in the city will speak their minds freely and become more friendly when removed from urban influences. Although I have met Winston Churchill only once, our encounter was at his country house, and as a result of that visit, I feel that I came to know the man much better than many others whom I have seen more often.

Chartwell Manor is in Westerham, a little Kentish town, with a quaint Wren-inspired church steeple, heavy-walled cottages, and air redolent with flowers.

The drive from the station is past gardens and through woods—gardens filled with larkspur and hawthorn and gigantic rhododendron bushes, and woods damp and earthy, with heavy elms and beeches and oaks. There are not many cars on the roads; more often a horse-drawn wagon that serves as a home for a roaming family moves slowly over the dirt pathway. There is a sleepy air of indolence about the section, and plodding horses seem much more a part of the place than scurrying motors. One feels a remoteness from the present and a loneliness that has made the North Downs region an ideal setting for the opening scenes of numberless romances.

Indeed, as I drove through this typical English country I had a feeling that it was on exactly such a road that Kipling's traveler pedaled his bicycle as he suddenly came upon that

Winston Spencer Churchill

house in which "They," those more than human children, played and were loved.

A sharp turn and, seemingly out of nowhere, appears the Churchill home. Its grayness, its ivy, and its hungry moss all proclaim a static condition, a slow growing out of the earth that makes it as much a part of the place as the trees around it. There is not a note about that jars, that does not belong. Accentuating the unity of the building with the landscape, the flagstones that are before the main entrance do not stop at the vestibule, but continue right over it into the main hall.

An Admirable Crichton ushered me in, but before he would go to Mr. Churchill he wanted to make sure that I had an appointment. "For," said he, "Mr. Churchill is down at the lake and I do not want to get him all the way up here unless he expects you."

I assured him that I was expected, and so he went, while I waited in a small reception room furnished with that English chintz-covered furniture so characteristic of country homes. On the walls were a portrait of Nelson and some paintings that I first thought were by Sargent. French windows opening on a stone piazza occupied almost one entire side of the room, and through them could be seen a broad expanse of rolling country.

As I was taking in my surroundings I heard quick footsteps in the hall, and then into the room strode Winston Churchill. Somewhere Richard Harding Davis—whom in many respects Mr. Churchill recalls—wrote that although, strictly speaking, a soldier of fortune was a man who for pay or for love of adventure fights for any country, in a bigger sense he is a man who in any walk of life makes his own fortune. As my host stood before me in a baggy soiled suit and battered hat, and as I looked into those clear, blue eyes and remarked the high forehead, the stubby nose, the thin upper lip and the heavy lower one, the face covered with light freckles, I felt that he fitted this description perfectly.

A seventh grandson of the original Duke of Marlborough, he has in him undoubtedly something of the spirit of that old adventurer and military genius; but Winston Churchill is not what he is because of this old bewigged victor of Blenheim, nor because he is a son of the late erratic Victorian statesman and the beautiful American, Jennie Jerome. In the walk of life in which he was born he has made his own way. His forebears were often an obstacle rather than a help. Had he not been Lord Randolph Churchill's son it is doubtful whether there would have been a question in the House of Commons when, as a young subaltern, he ran away and joined the Spanish Army. Every one thought he was in a mess, instead of which, having been awarded a medal for gallantry by the Spanish Government, he left the army and became a newspaper correspondent.

Almost at the very beginning of the Boer War he was taken prisoner, after a thrilling skirmish in which many of his companions were killed. For almost any man this would have been the end, but not so for Churchill, to whom every tragedy seems, by a strange quirk of fate, to bring a happy *dénouement*. Within a few weeks he had managed to scale the prison walls and escape, and after a lapse of silence, when every one thought he had perished in the South African wilderness, he turned up, by luck, in the house of the one Englishman in a hostile village. Again, as a combatant and also as a correspondent he found laurels in an undertaking which at first had promised to lead nowhere.

It has been the same all through his life. He went to Africa with Kitchener, and in a book that he published after that campaign he attacked the commanding general unmercifully. Once more every one thought that he was done for, but within a year he was defending "K. of K." against still more violent attacks in Parliament.

When he was thirty-one, some one said of him, "He has ridiculed those in high places, he has insulted his cousin and patron, the Duke. Without political friends, without the influence and money of the Marlborough family he is a political nonentity." Yet at thirty-two he was Under-Secretary for the Colonies and one of the most popular of the younger men in England's public affairs.

To-day there is the same enthusiasm about him, the same devil-may-care laughing at conventions as there was thirty-five years ago when he returned from Cuba and discovered on his first night in London that the Empire Music Hall had closed its bar. Arising, he made a speech, and the audience was more entertained by the wit and charm of the handsome sandy-haired boy, with his aura of romance, than by the paid entertainers. He called upon the crowd in the hall to storm the barricades, which they did, and once again glasses clinked and corks popped.

I made my drawing in his library, a room filled with Georgian furniture and dominated by a portrait by Orpen of the master of the house, and there he spoke of those early escapades and laughed over them.

"It is hard," he told me, "to find time to do all the things that I want to, and now that I am living here I fortunately can do some work that interests me.

"Those little paintings in the other room are some copies that I made of sketches by Sargent. Come on upstairs and see the drawing that he made of my mother."

He arose and led me to his bedroom in which there was a four-poster bed and a desk. Over the desk hung the well-known charcoal sketch that has been reproduced so often.

"There is more color in that," he remarked, "than there is in any number of paintings that I have seen. Is there any one except Sargent who would have dared to put that heavy outline against the light side of the face? And yet how perfectly it models."

When he had started to pose again, I asked him how his present life compared with that as a Cabinet Minister.

"There is one thing that appeals to me strongly now," he answered, "and that is I am my own master. I am accountable to no one for what I do, and the success of what I am doing depends solely upon my own efforts. When a man is in the Cabinet, no matter how strong he may be, he is bound to take into consideration public opinion. He may advocate measures that he firmly believes are for the public good, and he may see them work harm through the failure of someone else to carry them out properly. But the blame falls on the proposer's head, not upon the dullards who did not understand.

"In this life of ours I am sure there is but one way to find any true happiness, and that is to get some fun out of work, irrespective of the results. The artist or even the dauber who gets a thrill out of putting paint on canvas, the man who is enthralled by trying to write a sonnet or a play, or even the little craftsman who gets real pleasure from turning a lathe—any one of these men, can he make but a bare living, is getting paid for doing something from which he derives joy.

"Now look at our poor millionaires, worried to death over their affairs, and getting no pleasure from their work. After they have been successful, they spend their lives endeavoring to learn some way of obtaining happiness by spending their money.

"While in public life there are many recompenses to the cares of office, nevertheless there are many heartaches also. Here I keep busy doing all the things I want to do. I can write, paint, or lay bricks, whereas in other places I have often had to do things I did not care about."

When my drawing was finished he took me downstairs and showed me some large still lifes that he had painted. They were pitched in a high key and formed marvelous decorative spots on the walls.

"Now I'll show you some more of my work," he said, and we went out on the terrace.

"See that wall," he indicated. "That is my doing also. You cannot imagine the amount of fun I had in building it, for apart from the actual pleasure of seeing it grow, I think that I planned out a couple of books while I was laying the bricks."

Then we went to his studio, a one-story affair about two hundred feet from the house.

"I got some new ideas from a painter friend that I am working out now," he said as we entered the room, which was lighted from the north, and had little in it except a table, a chair and countless canvases.

"A painting," he explained, "consists of two essential elements—form and color. If you go out to paint a landscape and try to embody both, the light has changed by the time the form is looked after. So this is the idea. I go out and when I see what I want I snap it with a camera, at the same time making a rapid sketch, disregarding the form largely but endeavoring to put down my impression of the color.

"Then I have a lantern slide made of the photograph. I darken the studio and put the slide into this lantern and then project the picture on the canvas and paint it in monotone. In this way I have the form. Then with my color sketch before me I put the color in the picture."

He was like a boy of eighteen as he described the process. He darkened the room and did everything just as if he were painting a picture. He showed me any number of his canvases, some done by this method, and some more spontaneously, and when I suggested that I preferred the latter, he declared: "So do I at present; they are not quite so mechanical."

From the studio we walked over the grounds and he pointed out some lakes he was literally moving to improve the landscape. When I remarked that he had numerous interests, he replied: "These are my toys, and I believe that as long as a man can play with toys, that long will he remain young. When you meet a man who can derive no enjoyment out of doing something, you can make up your mind that that man is old, no matter what his years are."

As I was leaving I expressed the hope that I would have an opportunity of meeting him again in London before I sailed for America. I was in the motor by that time, and I noticed that he had picked up a paint box which was in the hall as he came out to say good-by.

"I fear not," he replied. "It is a marvelous time of year to paint here in Westerham. I go down to the city only when I must, and then I come back as soon as I can. Moreover," he added with a smile, "there are a great many walls that must still be built on the land."

I drove off, and as the car turned into the road I caught my last glimpse of him. A silhouette on a hilltop, the sun behind him, he stood looking out across the fields.

XVI

MANY laymen still have the idea that artists are irrational beings whose works are produced with no sense of rhyme or reason. As a matter of fact, the names of two men, both leaders in their respective arts, immediately come to mind—Henri Matisse and Ignace Paderewski, both of whom I found tremendously sane and methodical.

About no one in modern art has a greater controversy raged, nor has any one had a greater influence in directing its trend along certain lines than Matisse.

It was on his first visit to this country that I saw him. He was on his way to Tahiti, that island made famous by another French painter, Gauguin, and it was by accident that his name was discovered on the passenger list of the Île de France. No sooner was he landed than he was whisked mysteriously away and remained in seclusion for the short time that he was here, preferring, as he himself said, to remain "incognito," so that he might enjoy the privilege of seeing New York without distraction.

Indeed, it required more detective work to discover where he was staying than it did to find Sir James Jeans, and it was infinitely harder to get him to pose. He finally made an appointment to sit for me at a gallery, where some of his paintings were on exhibition. It is small, gray and modern and reminds one of the little intimate show places on the Left Bank in Paris, rather than of the more pretentious *salles* that face the column in the Place Vendome.

It is comparatively easy to interview an authority on a subject about which one knows nothing. His statements, no matter what they are, call forth no mental reservations on the part of the interviewer. On the other hand, here I was waiting for a man who had almost literally brushed away all the conventions of the art upon which I had been reared, and before whose canvases I stood in perplexed wonder.

I was puzzled by his pictures. To me they appeared signally dead and drab compared with the sunshine and the people on the street. I was standing before one which revealed three figures, each drawn in a different scale, and amply filling a large canvas. Six eyes suggested by six gobs of dark brown paint glowered at me, as if shaming me for lack of understanding; hands were neglected and bodies slighted.

Suddenly the door of the gallery opened, and Matisse walked in. His vitality and alertness seemed to me in sharpest contrast with the figures on his canvas. He wore a brown overcoat and a bright yellow muffler which repeated the color notes in his tawny hair and beard. His head is massive, his features large, and he wears glasses with lenses so strong that it is practically impossible to see his eyes behind them. He is quiet and reserved, and there is nothing of the poseur about him; in fact, it would be easier to imagine him bending over a microscope in a physiological laboratory of a German university than setting the art world agog over his paintings.

We went into a little room in the rear of the gallery, and as I followed him there it was like going with some old family doctor into his office. There is a certain deliberate, scientific air about him which one does not ordinarily associate with an

Drawn by
S. J. Woolf

merci -
Henri - matisse

Henri Matisse

artist, especially a French artist. He inspires a feeling of confidence and immediately conveys an impression of deep sincerity and earnestness. In his presence one must of necessity be ashamed of not liking his paintings, so evident is his devotion to art, so intense is he in his work.

He had just visited the Metropolitan Museum, and hardly had he seated himself upon a great gray corduroy sofa, which was placed immediately under a skylight, than he began to talk of the pictures there. He mentioned Rembrandt, Manet, and Cézanne.

I asked him whether he liked Rembrandt.

He smiled condescendingly at me.

"Like Rembrandt?" he said inquiringly. "Of course, I do. Two years ago I made a trip to Amsterdam that lasted six weeks just to study him and some of the other Dutchmen.

"He was one of the great modern painters of his day. He painted light.

"Many people talk about modern art as if it were a separate and distinct thing in itself, as if it were a sudden break, a new mode of expression, rather than an orderly and rational development of what had gone before.

"A direct line of descent can be traced from Rembrandt. I mention him because you spoke of him, but in reality it begins with Cimabue and Giotto, goes down to Cézanne and those who came after him. There is no hiatus, no sudden jump, everything is orderly and progressive.

"Every art is a reflection of the time in which it was produced, it is the logical result of its own surroundings. The gray skies of Holland are reflected in its pictures just as the sunshine is reflected in Italian pictures. But in addition to the geographical conditions, the surroundings and thoughts of the people as well as their activities all have their effect on the canvases of their painters.

"When I sailed up the bay and saw the skyline of New York, when I went up to the top of the Woolworth Building and got a glimpse of the city, I felt that all of these things must of necessity influence the painters. Here is a different civilization from that of Europe. I have seen any number of photographs of New York and countless cinema pictures, but no one can grasp its majestic grandeur until one sees it. Its vastness is beyond all comprehension. The avenues appear to have no ends, they seem to go on to infinity, while the tremendous buildings are awe inspiring.

"Now compare conditions such as these with those of fifty or a hundred or more years ago, and you will understand why such an apparently radical change has come over painting. It is the age in which we live which differs more from preceding ages than the painting of to-day does from that which has gone before."

His manner became that of the scientist. His suit was brown, his tie was brown and his shirt was tan; beside him on the sofa were his overcoat and muffler, the latter the only spot of color in the room. Coolly and dispassionately, like a naturalist dissecting a specimen, he analyzed the present-day tendencies, while through a crack in the door I saw a group of art students, who, by their very gestures, showed they were discussing "moods" and "nuances." Their idol seemed wonderfully sane and keen as he removed his thick glasses and polished them with a light brown handkerchief as if preparing for a further examination of the object under observation.

"A few days ago," he said, "I was in Paris; in a few more days I shall be in the South Sea Islands. Think of that and compare it with the period when a journey from France to Italy was a matter of months. Overhead men are flying, on the streets they are rushing around in automobiles, the wheels of industry are humming all about. Is it any wonder that these things are reflected in what is being painted?

"Swiftness and celerity are the dominating characteristics of the day and they must find their expression in its art. But though this is a mechanical age, that does not imply that emotion must be absent in modern painting, sculpture, or music. Indeed, it means, if anything, that there must be more emotion, and the artist of to-day, surrounded by machines, must have more emotion to express.

"By mechanical means an image is now fixed on a photographic plate in a few seconds—an image more precise and exact than it is humanly possible to draw—and so with the advent of photography disappeared the necessity for exact reproduction in art.

"Cézanne no longer painted an individual apple, he painted all apples. Van Gogh's 'Postman' is a portion of humanity."

"Does that mean," I asked, "that you do not use models?"

"I most assuredly do," he replied. "It means that I no longer believe in a literal rendering of what is before me. A camera can do that better than I.

"It means that, as well as the object, an emotion must be expressed and that with the aid of a model a certain amount of surface must be made interesting by means of a design; that an arm is not only an arm, but also a component part of an entire canvas, which must have as much beauty in one part as in another."

As he spoke it was easy to understand why he rarely goes out, and why it is that, in his little studio in Nice, with colored draperies on the wall, high model stand and a low seat for him to sit upon, he finds his greatest joy in life.

His talk was straightforward, there were no evasions, no confusion of terms, no mysterious allusions to metaphysics. Sitting there with the strong light beating down on his forehead—a forehead heightened by his receding hair—there was not a trace of the iconoclast in either his appearance or his conversation. A statistician could not have been more precise, an academician more apparently conventional.

Knowing that at one time he had painted very academic pictures, and remembering particularly a still life of a candle with some old, brown, leather-covered books, I asked how he had happened to change his style so completely.

"Because I could not help it," he replied. "I started out in life to be a lawyer. In fact, I was twenty-one before I seriously began to study art. That is just forty years ago. I studied under academic masters and I painted academic pictures.

"I married, I had three children and I had an arrangement with a dealer whereby he took all the still lifes which I painted at four hundred francs apiece. It was not very much as things are now, but it meant a livelihood for us all.

"One day I had just finished one of my pictures. It was quite as good as the previous ones and very much like them, and I knew on its delivery I would get the money which I sorely needed. I looked at it, and then and there a feeling came over me that it was not I, that it did not represent me or express what I felt. There was a temptation to deliver it, but I knew that if I yielded to it that would be my artistic death.

"Looking back at that time I realize that it required great courage to destroy that picture, particularly as the hands of the grocer and the baker were outstretched waiting for money. But I did, and I count my emancipation from that day.

"It meant," he continued, "suffering and deprivation, but then who has not suffered? Why, think of it, I bought a painting by Cézanne for three hundred and fifty francs. To-day, if I wanted to sell it, I could get one million francs for it, but the picture is no better now than when it was painted.

"I shall never forget the first time I saw it and inquired its price. Much as I wanted it I did not feel that I should spend that much money. It was called 'The Bathers,' and it showed some men in a river. Shortly after that I went down to Toulouse to see my family, and I went for a walk on the river bank. There in the water were a number of soldiers from a near-by cantonment, swimming. The sun on the water, its movement, and the actions of the swimmers brought back but one thing, and that was Cézanne's painting. I felt as if I had already viewed the scene, and I realized that an art that was so great that nature seemed but a reflection of it must be something worth while. I could not afford that picture then, I did not have enough money to pay for it all at once, but nevertheless I bought it."

"And in what does its greatness lie?" I inquired.

"In its color, its design, its swiftness and sureness, and its sincerity," he replied. "Every piece of that canvas is a part of a perfect whole. It was done quickly, but that is immaterial. People say that my canvases do not look finished. I consider that a compliment, for then I know that I have well concealed the labor and the effort, that I have stopped when the séance was over, and not turned a labor of love into one of torture."

I showed him my drawing. He said it resembled him, which in the light of his former remarks I did not consider very complimentary. Then I asked him to autograph it. He hesitated. He feared, he said, it might be mistaken for one of his, so taking my pencil I signed my name first, whereupon he put his under mine.

I left him standing in the middle of the little room, the top light playing strange pranks on the heavy lenses of his glasses, and as I walked down the gallery filled with modern paintings, through my head ran those lines by Kipling:

> *And each in his separate star*
> *Shall paint the Thing as he sees It*
> *For the God of Things as They are.*

XVII

ALTHOUGH Paderewski is surrounded by an air of romance which harks back to those days when kings sought musicians' favors and painters served as monarchs' emissaries, nevertheless his approach to art is also sane. Many pianists have come and gone since those days in the early nineties when a young, slim, ascetic Pole startled Paris, Berlin, and London by his magic artistry, but the glamour that surrounded Ignace Paderewski at that time has not been dimmed or lessened. In fact, if anything, there is about him an added glory, for, putting aside his art, he closed his piano for five years in order to serve his country as its first premier.

And yet no one typifies so much as he the mauve decade. He is a contemporary of the *Yellow Book* and Aubrey Beardsley; Burne-Jones drew his haunting profile and used it in several paintings, and young women put down their copies of Du Maurier's "Trilby," shocking book, to hasten to St. James's Hall to hear him play. Kipling was at the height of his powers and Sherlock Holmes was still solving the "Study in Scarlet"; Oscar Wilde was the smartest playwright in London, Gilbert and Sullivan were crowding the Savoy Theatre with their operas, and Anthony Hope was a young genius.

To-day, Paderewski, nearing seventy, is the same popular figure, the same force in the world of music that he was forty years ago when, as a young man with flowing auburn hair and low white collar and soft tie, he carried all before him in Europe and America and became the musical sensation of the dying Victorian era.

Many changes have come about. Mechanical music has been developed, radio has been discovered, jazz has beaten its way over three continents, but none of them can drown the clear-cut tones that this artistic descendant of Chopin and Liszt brings forth from the piano. It is a personality, expressed not only in his music but in his every action, that has risen above all else and that persists. This is the secret of his greatness. The piano has always remained for him only a means whereby he might express himself. Indeed, even the compositions that he plays become subservient to his interpretation of them.

I had an appointment with Paderewski at six-thirty one evening and when I arrived an armchair, a cup, and a pot of tea awaited his coming. He was a few minutes late, and as he rushed into the room, apologizing for having kept me waiting, little did he appear to be a man who had almost lived the allotted three score and ten.

His once auburn hair is silver, but about those small keen eyes, almost hidden by the heavy lids, were the interest and enthusiasm of youth. His high but sloping forehead is his most characteristic feature; domelike, it dominates the remainder of his head, and in comparison with it the lower part of his face seems small. His mustache and goatee still retain their reddish hue and help to give him a leonine appearance which is further accentuated by the height and formation of his cheekbones.

There is nothing of the faraway musician about him. He is neither removed nor remote. His manner has nothing of pose or abstraction. When he speaks he is vitally interested

Ignace Paderewski

in his subject, and one immediately senses that he is no one-sided artist whose knowledge and thoughts are limited to his art. With a magnetism that compels, an enthusiasm that enthralls, he speaks on all subjects. His English is perfect and he has the aptness for coining phrases that belongs to the writer, so that he plays with language as with a musical instrument.

It was the traffic that delayed him, he told me as he sat down before his tea. The chair was a large one, but he did not recline in it. He poised on its edge, as if he were playing the piano, and as he spoke he continually moved and gave emphasis to his words with gestures.

I mentioned the drawing of him by Burne-Jones.

"He made three on that day. None of them was entirely finished, but the next morning he sent me the one that you probably know. I was always most anxious to be drawn by Sargent, but, although we made a number of appointments, they were always broken by one of us."

He spoke about a painting which Zuloaga had done of him. He referred to the character in people's hands, and as he did so he raised his own. It was not the thin nervous hand one would expect to see. Firm and powerful, its fingers blunted at the ends, it expressed strength and force. It was the hand not only of the pianist but also the Prime Minister.

I referred to modern art.

"Art," he replied, "has been on an orgy. Some few years ago it went wild for color. Line was forgotten in a mad desire for vivid hues. To-day music is still in the state that painting was in some years back. Color is the god before which all modern composers are worshiping, but they forget there are other gods than that. They have blinded their eyes, if I may so express it, to the beauty of the simple lines of the classicists and endeavor by effects of color to attain beauty without line. Light and shadow and the glow of color are wonderful, but they must have outlines to bound them, otherwise they are formless masses. And then, too, while I have been speaking of painting and music in similar terms, after all color is not music.

"Indeed, music is not the handmaid or slave of any other of the arts. It should not be made subordinate to poetry or painting, a mere decoration; it should have its own form, its own meaning, its own *raison d'être*."

I asked him to what he attributed these tendencies in all the arts.

He leaned farther forward in his chair. His soft, loose collar and his white four-in-hand completed the picture of the romanticist.

"We are living in a strange age. Economics and inventions and discoveries have held the public attention for some years. I do not underestimate the value of these things. They may make for physical comforts, but with them they bring attendant evils that kill creative genius in art. For genius is a tender plant which will not thrive in all soils or surroundings, and the quiet and peace that are essential to it have been driven out by the haste and the desire for change and challenge that mark this era.

"Individuality and originality are being killed by the increasing necessity, I might almost call it, for collectivism. The day of the lonely craftsman has passed. One man rarely produces any finished product to-day. It is the result of many hands, and while perhaps better automobiles may be produced in this way, surely better poems or paintings or sonatas cannot. And it is this spirit which is pervading everything.

"For great art, though it is the creation of one man, is the product and the result of the time in which he lives. Bach could not have written his works in a skyscraper any more than Michelangelo could have decorated one of the modern temples of industry."

The shades were but half down and the tall lighted towers of the city could be seen. They rose majestically into the night sky, but they appeared to be resting on the open piano which stood before the window, crushing it. From the street came the drone of the heavy traffic, thousands rushing through the streets. Suddenly from the sky came the whirr of a plane.

He heard it, and continued:

"But despite all, men are not happy to-day. Throughout the world, in politics as well as in all the arts, there is an anxiety to get away from existing conditions.

"In art there is a striving for originality. Men are endeavoring to create something new. Nothing new was ever created consciously. True originality has its foundations in the soul, not in the mind, and when there is an effort to create something different it is usually a failure. Beethoven or Schumann or Chopin did not try to be original. They were original.

"However, this craving for originality, this desire to get away from old forms, this pulling down of the old-time gods is typical of this period of the world's history.

"Men feel the same dissatisfaction in regard to politics. Throughout the world there is an undercurrent of unrest. For years the so-called parliamentary system in government had been looked upon as a panacea for all ills. It was felt that when the man in the street was represented in a legislative

〖 157 〗

body then that man had something to do with making the laws and with the management of his country.

"But ideas in regard to this are changing. People are beginning to see that this system is not altogether what it promised. Indeed, it has been my experience that in most bodies of this kind a tremendous amount of time is wasted in useless and futile talk. Hours are used up in listening to speeches of no import or value. In times of economic distress long discussions in parliaments only irritate. A hungry man's appetite is not appeased by words. What he wants is food. And when he sees that the words do not give him food he becomes dissatisfied with that system of representation which does not provide him with necessities, let alone comforts.

"It is this spirit of dissatisfaction with things as they are that has caused both the artistic and political restlessness throughout the world to-day."

He stopped for a minute and took a gold-tipped cigarette from a silver case. He inhaled deeply and continued.

"As a matter of fact, it is only when a nation is enjoying not only comforts but luxuries that a great art develops. Contentment, mental and bodily, and leisure must be present. For although the individual artist may not be prosperous, it is when a country is passing through an age of luxury that art flourishes. When Greece was mistress of the world under Pericles its masterpieces of art were produced. Italy at the height of her power during the Renaissance gave us her greatest works."

The drawing was finished. I left. As I was walking down the hall of his suite I heard the tones of his piano. Stopping, I listened. He was playing a polonaise written years ago by another romantic Pole; the poetic outburst of a national feeling.

XVIII

A RUDDY-FACED man in the sixties, with dark brown hair and reddish beard rapidly graying; sunlight falling on stucco walls; paintings by Arthur Davies; purple chrysanthemums; poetry recited as if it were a prayer—these are some of my memories of AE.

It was in the early morning that I made a drawing of him, and it was well that it was so. There is something of the earth breath of early morning about him, something that transports and invigorates, a quality of sympathetic exuberance.

There he sat, comfortably at ease in a Windsor chair, his kindly blue eyes twinkling behind his gold-rimmed spectacles as he told of his plans for improving the conditions of the agricultural folk of the world so that the countryside would become a place from which nobody would willingly emigrate. For he believes that the great danger which threatens all modern states is the absorption of life in great cities.

It is difficult to say exactly what George Russell is, for one cannot call a man an economist when he has written some of the best known poems of his time, nor can one limit him by calling him a poet when he has exhibited paintings of recognized genius, and also edited one of the most influential papers in his native country.

"I wanted to be a painter," he said as he puffed at his pipe and the smoke, blue and light, curled about his head in fantastic shapes, "but my family was poor. Art meant a long course of study in schools, it meant that during that time I would have to be supported, so I gave up the idea. Indeed, I did not take up painting until I was forty. What I did was to go to work in an accounting office.

"But I do not think that I could have been very good, because I did not see the dry, uninteresting figures on the page before me. As I look back at that time now I can remember how I would sit for hours with my eyes on the ledgers and I would be miles away in my fancy, hiding in caves filled with sprites, climbing the tallest of the Himalayas, fighting with dragons, or searching for the banshee.

"How I ever stood the work the length of time that I did I do not understand. But in the evenings, sitting by the light of a lamp, I would let my imagination have full play. I became a poet, or at least I began to write poems. I did not have the technical skill to draw the pictures that I saw in my mind, so I described them in words.

"It was through my poetry that I became an economist, for I published a book of poems which Sir Horace Plunkett saw. At the time he was the head of the Irish Agricultural Society, and it was he who grafted a slip of poetry upon an economic tree. I do not know whether he expected a hybrid, but my books on that subject are not economics in his sense of the word, nor are they poetry in my sense."

It was at this period that George Russell became AE. For the accountant dreamer wanted to hide his poetic yearnings under a pseudonym, and signed his poems Aeon, but unfortunately his handwriting was none too legible, and the typesetters on the papers to which his first efforts were contributed, unable to read the signature, printed only the first two letters of the nom de plume.

George Russell (AE)

"So you see," he said with an impish glint in his long, oval eyes, that at times looked as if they might have been Pan's, "I was labeled AE, which some people seem to think means agricultural economist."

And then, apparently forgetting my presence, he began to recite a poem, a poem of the earth and the man who tills it.

"That was the first poem in the book, the one that prompted Sir Horace to invite me to join his society.

"You may think it is strange that a poet should be asked to aid in an economic movement. But I do not think it will seem so incongruous if you will stop and think for a moment.

"In the history of my own country it has been the poets who have given vision, imagination, and warmth to all of its political history. In fact, some of them have died for it. After all, it is only one man in about every hundred who can see just a little more than the other ninety-nine. They are the poets, the artists, the writers, the statesmen, and the philosophers of this world. They must be the leaders of any movement that takes place. They are the people of vision.

"It is to interest such men as your Robert Frost, Vachel Lindsay, and Carl Sandburg in this movement that I have come to your country."

I asked him to explain exactly what this was.

"Up to the present there has not been much deep thought given to the life of the country man, the man who is compelled to live far from urban civilization. This is evident if we compare the quality of thought which has been devoted to the problems of the city, state, or the constitution of widespread dominions, from the days of Solon and Aristotle to the time of Alexander Hamilton, and compare it with the quality of thought which has been brought to bear on the problems of the rural community.

"Yet it is on the labors of the country man that the entire strength and health, indeed, the very existence, of society depend.

"The disease which has attacked the great populations both in Europe and here is discontent with rural life. Thousands of farms are overgrown with rank weeds, and the young people who should be working them in many cases are living in great cities in fetid slums and murky alleys where the devil has his mansion.

"The details of our modern civilization are all wrong. In wide areas of all countries there are stagnation and decay. This is especially true of the rural districts. It is so general that it has often been assumed that there was something inherent in country life which made the country man as slow in mind as his own cattle."

AE got up. Although he is not very tall, he is built on large proportions. Without being ungainly there is that massiveness about him that Boswell makes us attribute to our mind pictures of old Samuel Johnson.

"But this is not so," he continued. "There is no reason why as intense, intellectual, and progressive a life should not be possible in the country as in towns."

"Why does it not exist?" I asked.

"Because," he replied, "the country population is not organized. Because a new social order must be created, and that is what we are trying to do.

"It is the business of the rural reformer to create the rural community. That is the precursor to the creation of a rural civilization. But it is not enough to organize farmers in a district for one purpose only—in a credit society, a dairy society, a fruit society, or a coöperative store. All these are but beginnings, but if they do not develop and absorb all rural business into their organization they will have little effect on character. No true social organism will have been created.

"The specialized society only develops economic efficiency. The evolution of humanity beyond its present level depends on its power to unite and create true social organisms.

"It is our object to unite the average men or women in the fields and to convince them that the noblest life will be possible for them. For if you do not provide for people the noblest and the best they will go in search of it. Unless the countryside can offer to young men and women some satisfactory food for soul as well as body it will fail to attract or hold them and they will go to the already crowded towns. The lessening of rural production will, in turn, affect production in the cities and factories, and the problem of the unemployed will become keener.

"The problem, however, is not only an economic one, it is a human one also. Man does not live by cash alone, but by every gift of fellowship and brotherly feeling that society offers him. The final urgings of men and women are toward humanity.

"It is one of the illusions of modern materialistic thought to believe it is not possible for as high a quality of human life to exist in the village as in the great city. It is one of the aims of the rural reformer to dissipate this idea and to prove that it is possible—not to concentrate wealth in country communities as in cities, but to bring comfort enough to satisfy any reasonable person and to create a society where there will be intellectual life and human interests.

"Now," he said, "you have heard enough of my aims. Let me see what you have done."

I showed him my drawing, and he asked me whether I had not made him look too kindly. "For remember," he said, "after all, I am an economist."

He recounted his first meeting with Shaw. It was in the Art Gallery in Dublin, and he did not recognize G. B. S.; indeed, he mistook him for a retired Indian Government official. "But," he added, "when he began to speak my respect for government officials began to rise."

He recalled Yeats, who, he said, kept on rewriting and polishing his poems until they were ultrarefined and lost their original strength. He declared that it took a Keats to rewrite a poem seven times and have the last version better than the first.

His secretary entered the room and broke the spell, for Mr. Russell had an appointment at a broadcasting studio.

All three of us rode up the Avenue. The poet gazed through the windows of the taxi at the marvels of our greatest thoroughfare. He spoke of the color and the crowds and the sunlight.

"It is magnificent," he remarked, "but think of the glory of a day such as this in green fields and wide spreading pastures."

There was a note of incongruity in riding up Fifth Avenue with this man who was surrounded by an aura of outdoors. Into the heart of civilization, into the very vortex of the mechanistic age, he brought the simplicity of farms and fields and flowers. It would have been better to have walked with him over grassy meads, to have heard him speak in the shadow of a great tree.

XIX

SUCH a setting vividly recalls Ramsay MacDonald. For though I have also seen him in Downing Street, the residence of all Britain's prime ministers, it is not in official surroundings that one gets the clearest picture of Labor's former premier. No matter where this tall, gaunt Scotsman may reside, a "wee sma' town" near the northern tip of Scotland, a little fishing village set among the hills—Lossiemouth, his birthplace, will always be home to him.

It is a dour place, this Lossiemouth; there is a sadness about the long sweeping hills that even the bright yellow broom flowers cannot dispel; there is a melancholy song of the sea as it washes the sandy shores, and as the wind plays in and out among the hillocks the wail of the banshee can be heard.

The houses, too, are drab and the little streets of low granite huts all seem in keeping with the severity of the natural landscape. Nor are the inhabitants themselves a joyous lot. Even the clothes of the younger people lack color and the little children's frocks are black. Cottet might have painted his Breton fishing village figures, with their sad eyes and somber garb, in this little northern town where in midsummer the lingering twilight continues until nearly midnight.

Lossiemouth rejoices in the reflected glory of a native son. It is not a demonstrative gladness. That would be impossible among those tanned, furrow-faced people whose knotty hands show the constant toil that is necessary to win a living from the stony soil and treacherous sea. Mingled with the pride over the honor that has come to their fellow-townsman, there is also a feeling of contrition for the way a large proportion of them treated him during the war. For popular as Mr. MacDonald is to-day just so unpopular was he when he preached pacifism to a fighting country.

MacDonald of Lossiemouth, in many ways, is a very different person from the occupant of Downing Street. There are necessary formalities that go with the office of prime minister which for a man of MacDonald's temperament are unusually irksome. In order to be free from these he must travel sixteen hours northward where he can forget for the time being that he is the real head of the greatest empire in the world and live again the life he led before he entered politics.

The house he occupies in this town is one that he built for his mother not far from the one in which he was born and not very much more pretentious. There is nothing to distinguish it from any of the others on the same street. There are no butlers and no guards about. I entered the little gate in the wall that has not even a bell to announce the coming of a visitor, and before I was aware of it I came upon a porch at the side of the house away from the street and overlooking a stretch of waste land covered with the ever-present broom plant.

Here under the shelter of a wooden roof are a rough table, several old morris chairs, and a bench built along one side of the wall. This serves as a dining place in pleasant weather and here the Prime Minister does some of his work. The house is small and there are no spare rooms. In fact, his modest bedroom, with its mission bed, its family photographs,

Ramsay MacDonald

and pitcher and basin on the wash table, also serves as an office, and a large flat-topped desk placed in the center of the room leaves space for only two chairs.

Dressed in tweeds, his wavy white hair blown by the breezes that come across the fields, his complexion darkened by exposure to the weather, the Premier is a distinctly outdoor type. His features are clean cut, and his dark eyes which peer from beneath heavy brows have a note of sadness in them, for in his expression are traces of the hardships he went through as a young man.

There is the faintest suspicion of the Scotch burr in his speech and this probably accounts for his shyness of foreign tongues, and his refusal to pronounce certain names and words in any but a way that is natural to him.

Seated at his desk in his room in the little house at Lossiemouth, it was evident that he was wholly engrossed in the subject at hand, whether it was an answer to a letter that he was dictating or some little detail of his early life that he was recounting.

This is true of whatever he does. Riding through the countryside on his way to the golf links near Forres he appears to put aside completely the cares of office and to have no thoughts but of the region through which he is traveling. And no one knows more of the legends and stories of the place, no one is more stirred by the beauties of the landscape; for in him there is the spirit of the poet, too, as any one who has heard him read "When lilacs last in the door-yard bloom'd" can attest.

And so it is not strange that he is a good golfer, for when he settles himself for a stroke there is only one thing in his mind and that is his game, and nothing can distract him from it. It is this power of concentration that has made it possible for him to accomplish the tremendous amount of work that he does.

While he was posing for me two secretaries were constantly coming in with letters, the door of the room was open and other members of his household were continually going up and down stairs, but he did not object. When he spoke to me, so far as he was concerned I was the only person in the house; when he was dictating to one of his secretaries, I am sure he did not realize that I was there.

It was difficult to believe as I sat opposite him in a room so small that I had to rest my portfolio on the edge of his desk and had to get up to allow a secretary to pass, that this man, so simple and unaffected, with no sign of "pomp and circumstance," was filling the office once held by the romantic Disraeli and the classical Gladstone, and conducting the affairs of Great Britain from this tiny room in a remote village.

Concerning the political future of the world, the Prime Minister is optimistic. In speaking of the League of Nations, he said that he believed that its influence would depend upon the moral and political power the small states of Europe acquired.

"If they can really exert an influence at Geneva," he said, "it is possible that in the future we shall have something corresponding to a United States of Europe. But if this does not happen, if they do not obtain that influence and the larger powers continue to dominate and use the machinery of the League to carry out their own policies, things will be less hopeful and more confused.

"For the powers will naturally try to maintain peace, but they will be inert and act as an older generation does toward a younger one, telling them what to do and imposing their own will, and that does not make for a condition of stability."

One of Mr. MacDonald's intimate friends, in speaking about him, said: "The trouble with him, if you can call it a fault, is that he is too much of an idealist, and he trusts people too much."

He trusts people because he loves mankind and believes in the rights of the individual. He sees the whole world being apportioned into vast economic fields controlled by powerful syndicates which recognize no boundary lines other than those of markets and which will hold in their keeping the lives of millions of human beings.

"What may be called 'social materialism' is growing vigorously," he said, "and during the coming years it will become increasingly a problem for those who care about individual liberty.

"The self-determination of nations has been the watchword since the beginning of the war; now the cry for the self-determination of individuals will replace it.

"Individuality and personality are supplements of nationality."

That Mr. MacDonald is strongly an individualist is not to be wondered at. Born in the part of Scotland that has always been radical, it is not strange that the spirit of democracy is strongly developed in him. When he was a child the large farmers were turning the people off the land and the hatred the Scotsman has for landlords was taking firm hold.

"We boys looked down practically from the moment of our births upon the people we called 'swells' and regarded ourselves as quite as good if not better than any of them," the Prime Minister said.

After his schooldays he had to do something to make a living, for his people were poor, and with farms all about him it was natural that he should turn to agriculture. He went right into the fields and though the work was hard and tiring he did not mind it.

"For a man," he said, "is never the worse for hard muscular work. Those plowmen were a fine lot. Every one of them knew his Burns as well as his Bible, and nearly all of them composed songs of their own and these fields in the springtime were alive with whistling and singing as we dug our furrows."

His schoolmaster did not approve of his continuing as a farm hand, so he went to MacDonald's mother and between them they arranged for him to return to school at half fee and he became a pupil-teacher.

After holding this position for some time young MacDonald gave it up to be secretary to a man in Bristol, intending to go to the Royal College of Mines, for in those days he was much interested in science.

"But," he continued, "the Bristol experiment was a failure and off I set for London.

"I knew but one or two chaps of my own age, and I spent my days looking for employment, for when I arrived I did not have even the traditional half-crown. I obtained a job at ten shillings a week addressing envelopes, but it was only temporary work and I have known what it is to walk through the streets of London with nothing in my pockets, debts hanging over my head, and nothing to do."

At last he obtained a permanent position as invoice clerk in a warehouse. Though his salary was only fifteen shillings a week he said he lived like a fighting cock, saved money and had a holiday in Scotland, besides which he helped to support his mother and also paid his tuition fees at the City of London College and Highbury Institute.

It was not easy to do these things on his meager salary. It meant that he had to buy his food where it was cheapest; his oatmeal, which to a Scotsman is a necessity, was sent to him from home.

"Tea was too much of a luxury for me to afford," he explained, "but you know that hot water is really quite as good as tea from the point of view of food, and it tastes quite good after you have grown used to it."

For a time his mind was divided between science and politics, but an illness which used up what little he had saved compelled him to take a position as a private secretary, and there he soon realized that he could not go on indefinitely with two divergent interests. It was essential that he make a choice so he decided to go into politics and journalism.

There were hard years before him, and as he recounted some of his experiences he seemed to live them over again. His voice is rich and dramatic and he uses it like an actor. When he is speaking he emphasizes a point by a gesture of his right hand on the thumb of which he invariably snaps his pince-nez.

At the head of the government to-day, he does not forget those early trials, nor does he forget his boyhood friends, many of whom still live in the old town.

I met one of them, a country storekeeper who had called to get his daily order. I was leaving the house and he volunteered to show me some of the older part of the town, including the hut (for it is not much more than that) in which MacDonald was born.

Later, sitting among the fruit and vegetables of his store, he reminisced.

"Yes, sir," he said, "I remember the Prime Minister as a boy. We went to school together. His people were farm folks and lived down below; mine lived up here near the top of the hill. They were sailors. Many were the fights we boys had, for there was constant warfare between the hill boys and the farm boys.

"It happened, however, that Jimmie and I went to the same school. I don't call him that now, but I know he wants me to. When I see him, he puts his arm around my shoulder and asks me how things are going, and to see the two of us together you would never think he was the Prime Minister and I the greengrocer who sold him vegetables.

"As I look back on those times now I should say that Jimmie's dominant trait was his love for his mother, and even on those days when we had sneaked off from school he would constantly keep his eyes on the position of the sun, so that he would not be late in returning home."

XX

I HAVE preserved no order in writing these memories, nor have I attempted any classification. Indeed, it is but rarely that a man in a certain profession will bring to mind another in the same calling. Perhaps it is because they are both Italians that I think of Benito Mussolini in conjunction with Arturo Toscanini. I doubt it, however. I think it is the difference in viewpoint rather than the identity of nationality that links them together as far as I am concerned. Toscanini refuses to permit patriotism to influence his musical judgment, Mussolini holds patriotism above all else.

And yet in America I doubt very much that Il Duce would have gone into politics. In this country he might have been an actor or an impresario or even a sensational financier.

Emotionally, he is essentially Italian; still in Rome he has not done as the Romans do. The result is stupendous. Into a city without sidewalks in many streets, where bicyclists ride in the evening holding lighted candles in their hands, where restaurants send their waiters to nearby fountains to get water, where forums have become the breeding places of cats, where the ruins of antiquity are millstones around the necks of the people, into these surroundings this strange man from the country, unawed by traditions, has introduced modernity, but with it all the trappings of the Renaissance.

We in America gloat over our democracy when former newsboys run for president; but in Italy a man sprung from a similar origin has become a dictator, and little is said of that side of his history by the Italian people.

Remarks on that score are chiefly confined to old ladies with chignons and black velvet ribbons around their necks, who have made Italy their home for years because Elizabeth Barrett Browning wrote her sonnets there; who sit in the cheaper restaurants and, fearing to mention him by name, speak of the mysterious Mr. X. and whisper in Oxonian accents that "this thing is as bad as Bolshevism."

And still this thing, this Fascism, started out as a movement of youth. Even the most radical of them all, the leader of the left wing, the thundering Farinacci, is a big overgrown boy of thirty-five or forty who, laughing, plays a game of matching fingers at lunch.

Youth has gained control of a government and is making the most of it, borrowing from here and there and realizing that the people like a certain amount of theatricalism in the government, but never forgetting "the grandeur that was Rome."

Although youth is in control, it has not discharged age. I found this out when I went to keep my appointment with the Prime Minister at the Chigi Palace.

At the head of a flight of broad marble steps covered with a runner of thick red carpet, I entered one of those over-decorated rooms in which it can easily be imagined that during the sixteenth and seventeenth centuries any number of plots were born. Its painted pilasters and columns, its ceiling on which birds and flowers are arranged around medallions of gods and angels, a marble bust of some early cardinal or pope with a sort of marble halo around his head, all speak the language of another age.

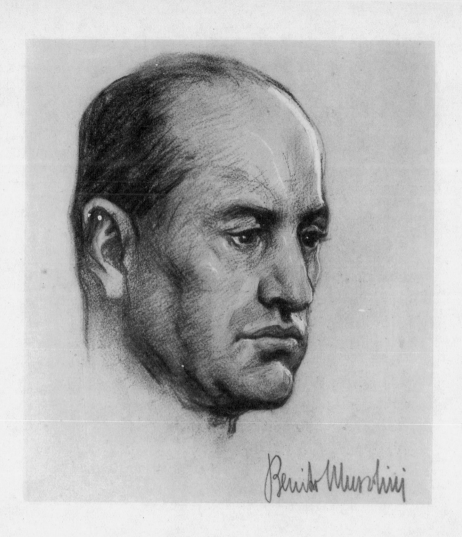

Benito Mussolini

There I was met by an old man well past seventy. The tips of his shoes turned up and his Prince Albert coat hung below his knees. Suspiciously he looked at me over the tops of his silver-rimmed glasses and, although I explained that I had an appointment with the President, as Il Duce is called, it did not allay his misgivings.

He wanted to know what I had in my portfolio and when I opened it and he saw that it contained nothing more dangerous than some sheets of drawing paper, he shuffled off to inform the proper authorities that I was there.

In a short time my name was called and I was ushered into Mussolini's office. It is a tremendous room about forty feet square, and in one corner, placed diagonally, is a large table with a lamp on it. Behind the table, staring, his right hand raised in salute, stood a man. As I entered, the first thing I saw was the white of his eyes, glistening and making his pupils seem intensely black and beadlike. The stare was so intense that it might almost have been the look of a fanatic. It dominated everything in the room.

Not until later did I notice the marble floor with its thick oriental rugs, the two globes—one celestial and one terrestrial, each over five feet in diameter—a table on one side with a model of a Roman galley, and its companion piece against the opposite wall with a photograph of Sir Austen Chamberlain, and also the old tapestries that hung against the brocade.

These things made no impression; they were absolutely effaced by the dominating personality in the corner. Though not nearly so tall as his pictures make him appear, by sheer intensity and vital force he dwarfed the immensity of his surroundings. As a skilled artist by a clever manipulation of perspective manages to center the entire attention of the onlooker on one figure, so on entering the room all the lines of perspective appeared to vanish in this one comparatively small figure behind the table. There was nothing in the room but him.

It was dusk outside. The stream of automobiles on the Corso kept up an incessant din. The lights in the room were on and made shining high lights on his swarthy skin; they struck his forehead, high and well-formed; they shone along the side of his nose; they accentuated the darkness where his face was shaved; and they made his winged collar gleam inordinately white.

Despite the squawks of the horns on the motor cars, despite the electric lights and the braid-bound morning coat and the starched collar, there was more of the feeling of the Renaissance about him than there was of the present. It was fitting that his office should be in the ancestral home of a family that had given the world two popes.

The hand that had been raised in salutation dropped suddenly and, as I advanced toward the table, it was stretched across to grasp mine.

"I am not going to pose for you," he said as he sat down and busied himself with some papers, but there was a suspicion of a smile in those dark eyes as he spoke, "so sit down and get your things ready."

Before him was a portfolio—one of those leather affairs without which no Continental writing table is complete—and in the middle of the table was a green bronze inkstand. Except for these things, a pen which stuck in the stand, and the lamp, the large table top was clear.

For a few minutes he concentrated upon the papers before him; then he looked up with a smile. "Life is very short," he said, "and there is so much to do.

"Life is work," he continued. "You see, my methods and the power that the Fascisti have won have brought to me a tremendous responsibility which means that I have to work about sixteen hours each day.

"But I have always worked hard. I had to. When one's father is a blacksmith, it goes without saying that one must work to live. I studied to be a teacher and taught for a while. Then I went into exile in Switzerland and had a very hard time, in fact I was a mason there. Then I came back to Italy and began writing for a Socialist paper."

Mussolini's English is good, but his sentences are short.

"Then the war came," he went on, "and from it and its after effects I learned many lessons. Books are good to read, but in my experience I find that there is but one book that teaches a man. That book is life.

"The war began in August, 1914, and within two months of that time I was no longer a Socialist. I saw that their theories were not my ideals. But I needed experience to learn that lesson. It was through the war that Fascism had its beginnings."

I asked him how that was.

"That is a long, long story. It means going into too many things, recounting long days of strife and nights of work, of telling about the articles that I wrote for my own paper in order to show the people of Italy that they were being deceived, that the old democracy was a shell and that a new system of government was necessary for us to regain our feet.

"Bolshevism was sowing its seeds here. Strikes were becoming numerous; our money was worth little; and while the stated causes of agitation were always economic, in truth they were political and the aim was to undermine the state's authority with the idea of establishing soviets.

"That ever-growing band of patriots, the Fascists, firmly held their places during strikes, realizing with true patriotic zeal that the real sufferer in all these disputes was the Italian nation.

"At last we got into power, and the world knows what has happened."

From a glass that stood beside him he sipped some water; his black eyes flashed.

"I took over the direction of the state when it was at its lowest ebb. There was a six-million-dollar deficit. Inflation and printing presses created an illusion of prosperity. My policy changed all this, for the Fascist financial policy was a sound one.

"Civil life had to be reorganized, the school methods had to be changed, public services had to be improved, and old bureaucratic methods done away with.

"For six years now I have given up every personal thing and devoted all my energies to effecting these improvements for Italy."

Suddenly Mussolini stopped speaking. He stared at me darkly, almost sinisterly, with the expression of a man who is trying to frighten a child. I endeavored to conceal a smile. He saw my efforts and began to smile himself. There is something childlike about him, a desire to produce theatrical effects, but beyond this is a tremendous sense of humor, and a certain lovable quality that is hard to describe.

From nowhere, apparently, some one had appeared. Words so low as to be almost inaudible were exchanged and Mussolini arose. He stood very erect behind his desk and rubbed his hands together. Slowly over his countenance spread that terrifying stare directed toward the door, but I noticed there was a sidelong glance to see the effect upon me. Some one entered, his hand went up in salute, and the stare became more intense, almost a grimace.

It had the desired effect, for the visitor, evidently absolutely awed, tiptoed toward the table. It was with difficulty that he found his voice and began to speak. Mussolini beckoned him to sit in a large red chair at the opposite side of the table but he himself remained standing. Then began a remarkable performance.

The visitor spoke; for what seemed an interminable time he kept up a continual stream of talk but the President said nothing. His expressions, however, and his actions were more eloquent than any number of words. There was hardly an emotion that was not portrayed by the silent party in those ten or fifteen minutes of the one-sided conversation. During that time Mussolini showed anger and pleasure, disgust, hatred, satisfaction, and impatience. He showed these feelings not alone by the expression on his face, but by his entire body. From an imperious Caesar he changed to a rollicking Falstaff; the eagle of imperial Rome became a slinking cat, and with feline movements and grace almost slid over the table that separated him from his visitor; suddenly the claws were stretched out as if ready to scratch, and as suddenly they were drawn in.

The interview was ended. The visitor arose and as he walked toward the door, Mussolini drew himself up to military attention and appeared to concentrate upon the back of his caller's head. The look was intense, as if he were trying to extract every thought from it. As the stranger reached the door he turned and up went his hand. Mussolini's did likewise, and as the door closed he turned with a half-smile and a sigh, like an actor who appears before the curtain for applause, and then resumed his seat.

As if there had been no interruption he took up his conversation where it had been broken off.

"I have given up everything for the state," he continued. "Except for a horseback ride in the morning and occasionally a little fencing, I have not had time to devote to any other exercise of which I am very fond. My reading has been confined to political papers and works, though it was my usual habit before entering public life to indulge myself in reading poetry and, as an Italian, I suppose it is unnecessary for me to tell you that Dante has always been my favorite as a poet. Even my violin playing has had to suffer, and it is difficult for me to find the time to play my favorite arias of Verdi and Puccini."

I asked him why it was necessary for him to give so much of his own time to the government now that it was running smoothly.

"Because I realize," he said, "that I dominate the party, and it is because I realize this fact that I have the ability to keep the party alive.

"I suppose you wonder why it is necessary to continue it in the same form that it existed when it achieved its victory. History will give you the reason. Force is necessary to make a revolutionary movement legal. New and unforeseen things continually arise. The Fascisti followed me during the trying periods almost blindly. To disband the party and retire would seem impossible to me.

"One of our principal duties is the formulation of a new Italian method of government. In order to do this I have remained at the head of a party that was formed for this purpose, and by my will I have kept the party intact with the same ideals with which it started out. I have seen the political prophets who predicted a short life for Fascism and a return to old principles put to shame, and to-day the party remains untouched by attacks.

"In fact, in order that our aims should not be changed from their original purpose, we have closed our ranks to newcomers, for as soon as the rest of the people in Italy saw that we were successful, they wanted to join. What the admission of too many strangers among us would have effected was uncertain and for that reason we now take no more new members, although we have what we call the Avanguardia which, together with an organization of boys and girls, selects and educates the youth of our country in the principles of Fascism."

Gathering all his papers together in his portfolio, he arose. Silently, his secretary appeared with the evening journals. Mussolini took them with his portfolio under his arm and, putting on his hat and tapping its crown, he turned to me and said:

"It's half-past eight. I am going home."

"Tired?" I asked.

"No," he replied, "I am never tired. Now I am going home to work."

XXI

ABOUT Maestro Arturo Toscanini there is an element of mystery. He has built around himself a wall of reserve that few can scale. He feels that he should be judged by the music that he produces and that his personality can be of no concern to the public. Apparently, to his mind, even the applause that greets the performance of the orchestra under his direction is accorded to the music rather than to him.

His shunning of publicity has given rise to numberless stories about him, some true, others not. He never uses the same baton twice; he does not go to a barber shop; his daughter cuts his hair—many such anecdotes are current. Whether they are true or false makes little difference to him. He leads a simple life, the center of a circle of friends who weigh his every word; who perhaps remark that the maestro is in a good mood to-day, for he smiled, or with awe say that the maestro is in a fury, for the rehearsal did not go well.

There are, in reality, two Toscaninis. One the public sees; the other his friends know. There is the frowning maestro of the rehearsal room, the Napoleon of the orchestra, who leaves his men exhausted yet admiring. He demands almost super-human efforts from them, but, as one of them said after a particularly arduous rehearsal, "By the time he gets through he will make musicians out of all of us." This is the short, dark-complexioned man with graying hair that is thinning on the top of his head, whose every muscle is taut and whose

Arturo Toscanini

every nerve is tense as he walks quickly to the conductor's stand in the middle of the stage. When he appears the men whom he has urged and coaxed and reprimanded arise. It is their mark of respect for a great musician.

Before him there is no music stand, nor any music. He knows by heart the score of every piece he directs. Under his arm he carries his baton as one carries a riding crop. His back is to the public. The applause seems to have little effect upon him. He waits, turns and bows, but apparently his mind is far away. His bow is quick and jerky, his attitude is that of a man who is interrupted in some important work. Again facing his orchestra, he waits for a moment, taps the music stand of the 'cellist who sits before him, and, as if saluting with a sword, brings the tip of his baton up to his head; he closes his eyes and then for a second appears to remove his every thought from anything extraneous. Another tap, more authoritative than the first, and the concert begins.

Toscanini draws melody from his orchestra. The baton in his right hand commands, but his left hand wheedles the tones he desires. That left hand is a study; thin and shapely, with a long thumb that starts very near the wrist, it performs an entire symphony by itself. Tenderly it hushes the strings; commandingly it calls for volume from the brass; it goes to the heart when it wants melody; and, closed into a fist, it compels thunder from the drums.

As Toscanini directs he appears to be playing every instrument in the orchestra. The violins have a leading part, and the delicately held baton moves as a bow through the air over imaginary strings. The trombones take up the strain, and his cheeks puff out until he seems to be actually blowing upon one. Or perhaps there is a choral part in the piece, and immediately he sings, not loudly but as if his voice were one in the chorus.

When the performance is finished the salvos of applause do not move him. He points to the orchestra and signals that it is they, not he, that deserve it. Floral tributes are tabooed by him. "They are," says he, "for prima donnas and corpses. I am neither."

That is the Toscanini the public knows; the man whom, twenty years ago, the directors invited to conduct opera at the Metropolitan. They went to see him at La Scala at Milan, to try to induce him to come over here. In him they did not find a temperamental musician whose head was in the clouds. For, temperamental as he is, he never forgets the demands of his art. He is well aware that although upon the conductor rests the responsibility for the artistic merits of the performance, nevertheless he must have an efficient and coöperative personnel behind him. The fact that Mahler conducted at the Metropolitan was one thing that made him decide to come, but before he gave his assent he insisted that not only the director but also a number of the others at La Scala should be engaged.

To know the other Toscanini it is necessary to meet him away from the scene of his work. Surrounded by his friends, he is an entirely different man from the one who steps before the public, baton in hand. Among them he relaxes. In his home in Milan an artistic and musical coterie finds him a gracious host and a charming companion. In the United States although he keeps out of the public eye, he nevertheless has his group of intimates whom he frequently sees and to whom he speaks freely.

To them he is the simple, unaffected Italian whose parents were so poor that he went to a school at Parma where not only education but living was free. It was there that he studied music and learned to play the 'cello. The discipline at the school was so strict, Toscanini recounts, that one day he was discovered playing the piano and was severely punished for it, because the 'cello was the instrument he was expected to study.

At nineteen he was 'cellist in an orchestra in Rio de Janeiro. The opera "Aida" was to be performed, and the conductor was booed by the audience. Toscanini's fellow-musicians, realizing the young man's ability, proposed that he should direct the opera. "From then on," Toscanini often says, "I have been a conductor, though I have not forgotten my first love, the 'cello."

Although he has given a large part of his life to the conducting of operas, he has expressed to his friends a preference for symphonic music.

"For," he says, "in the directing of symphonic music there are not so many extraneous things with which to contend. My orchestra is, as it were, one instrument upon which I play. In a short time the men who work with me begin to know what I want and they help me to obtain the results that I desire. But in the opera house many other things arise that are in conflict with music, or at least are outside its domain.

"There are, first of all, the peculiarities—I call them that rather than another name—of the singers. Then there are the numberless questions of scenery and stage management. Many conductors feel that these things are outside of their province, but I feel very much as Wagner did, that for an opera to be a work of art it must be a unified whole. To achieve that end, one man must direct the entire production. The general tone of the scenery plays a part in an opera, as well as the general tone of the music. Wagner, if you remember, not only composed the music of his dramas, but also wrote the libretti and made plans for the scenery. He went even further; he designed an opera house for the productions.

"To Wagner I am indebted for much; I often wonder whether many musicians realize the tremendous fund of knowledge there is to be found in his writings. I think that I can honestly say that whatever I am to-day as a conductor I owe largely to what I learned from him.

"What Wagner was to Germany, Verdi was to Italy. He represents the highest point in the development of the music drama in his native country. But aside from his musical genius he stands for everything that is fine and noble in man. Italy could well be proud of him as a citizen had he not written one bar of music."

Great is Toscanini's admiration for these two masters; so great indeed is his respect for Wagner that he has refused to conduct "Parsifal" because he believes that that opera should not be produced outside of Baireuth, except in a church. But his veneration for these composers is exceeded by his worship of Beethoven. In him he sees the superman. The majestic loneliness, the frightful deafness borne with patience, and the deep humility of the man increase his admiration for Beethoven as a musician. To Toscanini the nine symphonies are the apotheosis of all music. In conducting them he feels that in such works man approaches the divine, and that in them is the essence of all religions.

"Many eccentricities," he said, "are being introduced at the present time in the craze for novelty in invention, and many old forms are being modified and exploited as something new. Only recently the question arose as to whether a department of jazz should be inaugurated in a conservatory in Germany. Now, I feel that there is not a well-trained musician in the world—I mean one trained in the so-called old school of music—who need be puzzled by the peculiarities of jazz. Even the much vaunted saxophone has been used for certain effects in the regular orchestras for years.

"Personally, I am interested in jazz—as a matter of fact I have been from its very beginning. It undoubtedly has an element of novelty and has added something to the treasury of music. The unexpected in it appeals to me. But there is a great deal of jazz music that is absolutely worthless. I have a number of gramophone recordings of an excellent jazz band, and I have just bought a number of new disks."

Toscanini has expressed strong ideas on permitting patriotism to play any part in musical judgments.

"Music," he said, "may be written by a German, an Italian, a Frenchman, or an American, but to me that is unimportant. It is either good music or bad music. The nationality of the composer has nothing to do with its merits. The same thing may be said about classical as opposed to modern music. Music is not like wine; it does not improve with age. Nor, on the other hand, is it like an egg that can be spoiled by being kept too long. Occasionally, of course, the true worth of music is not appreciated until years after it is written. There is good old music, and there is bad old music, just as there is good and bad new music.

"The most essential requisite in listening to music is an open mind. When I hear a composition for the first time I try to put myself in the position of the average untrained listener. After all, music is not written for the enjoyment of professional musicians, but for cultivated lovers of music.

I know many musicians who, while hearing a piece for the first time, analyze it in every minute detail. This is a mistake. It is analogous to the act of a critical painter who, on looking at a canvas, examines minor technical details without first getting an impression of the work as a whole.

"Do you know, I believe that there is such a thing as crowd understanding—that the public often grasps the merits of a particular composition which escape the ear of the professional musician.

"The Americans have one great advantage over the people of other nations. This is the meeting place of the entire world. Italians and English, French and Germans, all come here and bring their traditions with them. Those who remain here and become citizens still retain their traditions. This interchange, this mingling of different ideas and ideals is a marvelous thing for music, for although music must be universal in its appeal, nevertheless it is undoubtedly influenced by various elements. You could no more imagine Wagner having written 'Aida' than you could imagine Verdi composing 'The Meistersinger.'

"But in America there is no one single dominating element at work. I notice this in the orchestras here. When I conduct in Milan I am at the head of an organization that is composed entirely of Italians. Here I have men with me from all four quarters of the globe. I get the best from all countries and not all from one country.

"The same thing is true of the American audience. It is so conglomerate in its make-up that no one type of music will satisfy it. This makes for varied programs, which in turn tend to create a cosmopolitan taste.

"Naturally, the hearing of great works of music improves the taste of any people. But of course one cannot present only works of the most exalted standards. There are not enough of them. However, I give nothing in my programs that I do not consider worthy of being heard.

"Although America now hears all that is best in music, that does not guarantee the foundation of a school of music. Gods have been born in stables and musicians have sprung from what would seem to be the most unfavorable surroundings. Geniuses appear in the most unlooked-for places and at the most unpropitious times."

XXII

THE rain was coming down in torrents one Sunday morning when I drove down Unter den Linden and around to the Stresemann house in Friedrich Ebert Strasse to make a drawing of the Foreign Minister. It was dark because of the storm, and the lights in the house were a pleasant contrast to the cold, dreary grayness outside. As I was ushered into the library, the lighted lamps, the round center table and the tall bookcases seemed more than ordinarily "gemütlich."

In the few minutes that I had to wait before I saw Dr. Stresemann I examined the contents of the bookshelves. One entire case was filled with the works of Goethe and books pertaining to him, and the other was largely taken up with works, memoirs, and lives of Napoleon. On the table were more books, among them a life of Hoover in German and a small volume of extracts from speeches and letters of the First Consul, also in German.

Certain passages in the latter book were marked, two of which seemed pertinent and indicatory of the owner's own thoughts. The first was a letter sent to Friedrich Wilhelm III of Prussia. "Were I a beginner in the art of war," it ran, "and did I need fear the tricks of luck on the battlefield, then this letter to your Majesty would be unnecessary. But your Majesty will be defeated, and without a warning you would endanger your own freedom and the very existence of your own people."

Gustav Stresemann

The source of the second quotation was not given, but there were two pencil marks on the margin calling, as it were, double attention to it. "A statesman," it said, "is not created to be sensitive; he is a person who stands entirely alone and whom the entire world opposes."

It was a sparkling room, so filled with lights and furniture that memory of it is an impression of a mass of lights shining like jewels rather than of definite objects. However, the spirit of it is distinctly French, tinctured by a Teutonic influence and this is accentuated by a colored print of a painting of Napoleon, which overpowers a print of Frederick the Great hanging near it. The French Emperor is not depicted as the victorious conqueror; it is a picture of him as a family man, holding the King of Rome in his arms, while seated by the family hearth is Marie Louise. The entire room was one which Menzel might have painted, and how he would have reveled in flicking the brilliant high lights on the polished furniture and the glowing lamps.

Among these surroundings the Foreign Minister in his black clothes of modern cut was somewhat of an anachronism. He was distinctly a present-day type and essentially Teutonic. Augustus John painted him and, by exaggerating the modeling, produced a caricature, but in no way gave the impression the man himself produced.

His head was round and the planes merged one into the other. Very blond, with light blue eyes, his complexion was inclined to pallor and seemed paler in contrast with the redness of his full lips.

His English was good, though it had a trace of foreign accent. At the meetings of the League when he had a paper prepared he invariably read it in English; on the other hand, when he talked extemporaneously he used his mother tongue.

After speaking with Dr. Stresemann for five minutes one felt his chief characteristic was his optimism. It was that trait which carried him through the troubles and the trials he underwent during the last six years of his life, for it was but that length of time that he was in the eyes of the world.

The thing ahead was always the thing that interested him most, and like the majority of his countrymen who since the war seem to have put sentiment behind them, he seemed to be in no way guided by the past. It was the future that interested him. To use his own words, his policy was "marching forward over the graves."

His disregard of tradition played an important part in his career. In many cases this almost proved disastrous to his political future but he never allowed the desire for office to sway his opinions, nor did he ever conceal his beliefs for the sake of political preferment.

He was born in Berlin, the son of a restaurant keeper in very moderate circumstances. His father made great sacrifices to send him through the Universities of Berlin and Leipzig where he specialized in economics and politics. First elected to the Reichstag in 1907, he served there, with but one year's interruption, until 1923, when he became Chancellor and began the policy of reorganization that made him the great post-war statesman of Germany and linked his name with Briand's as an apostle of peace.

The chancellorship was too uncertain a position for Stresemann, and the German nation could not afford to permit so valuable a man to hold so transient an office. Accordingly, he was appointed foreign minister. Chancellors came and went, but he continued to wield his influence for the reorganization and reconstruction of his fatherland. He effected the security pact with France, negotiated the Locarno Treaty, and obtained the entry of Germany into the League of Nations, while in all the conferences incident to the adoption of the Young plan his guiding hand was felt.

Germany's future, he believed, lies in the capability of its citizens for hard work. "There is no sham about them, but a deep-rooted sincerity and a desire for advancement," he said.

The American and German people have many characteristics in common and to this fact Dr. Stresemann attributed the resemblance that Berlin bears to large American cities. In our people he saw the same energy, push, and adaptability that he recognized in his own.

That break with tradition which has always been so evident in American methods he saw as a post-war attribute of Germany.

"It has been demonstrated in a growing measure," he said, "that the German policy of peaceful reconstruction and conciliatory collaboration has nowhere found sincerer recognition than in the United States. In fact, American collaboration stands at the beginning of Germany's reconstruction. America was first among former enemy powers to come out for the principle of constructive economic common sense and fair play for Germany, and to make possible the first fruitful negotiations between the Reich and her former opponents.

"It is due to the decisive attitude of American statesmen and financiers that these negotiations were brought to a positive conclusion and that the reparation problem was removed from the sphere of political passions and ambitions for power and raised to the level of an impartial examination of economic viewpoints.

"On the other hand, Germany's thoughtful attitude regarding the solution of the question of safety on the Rhine, which is the central point of European discord, and its position in negotiations attending the adoption of the Locarno Treaty did not fail to impress America, which is highly interested in the pacification of the European economic body. Nobody can doubt what rôle America is destined to play in developments of the near future.

"That Germany and America have entered into relations of sincere friendship and are following well-defined common aims must be considered one of the pleasantest results of German foreign policy and a promising indication for the future."

Dr. Stresemann's admiration for America extended even to his private life. As he was speaking of the drawing which I had made of Mrs. Stresemann, and saying that he thought I had made her look like an American woman, she entered the room.

Looking at the portrait of her husband, she said that she thought I had done enough, and, turning to him, she continued: "And I think you had better go upstairs now and rest a little before dinner."

"But I am not tired," he replied. (How like Mussolini's words!)

"You never know when you are tired; go up and rest anyway," she answered.

He got up and, with a smile, said to me: "I think you were right; I do believe she's more American than I had realized."

Though I have seen Dr. Stresemann making fervent addresses in the Assembly of the League of Nations, I shall always remember him best not as the man of international affairs, but as the home-loving German in his house in Berlin.

XXIII

MY MOST vivid memory of Elihu Root is of him
walking into the old-fashioned living room in his
home on Fifth Avenue. A spirit of early New York
pervades that home. Although he lives in an apartment,
he has so transformed it that it seems to be one of those
brownstone houses which were characteristic of the city
when horse cars jangled and gas lamps lighted the streets,
when presidents were made or broken on the red leather
lounge in the corner of the marble-floored hall of the Fifth
Avenue Hotel and governors selected before the bar of the
old Hoffmann House.

The walls of his living room are covered with steel and
copper engravings of the seventeenth and eighteenth centuries.
The dun-colored paper, the mahogany bookcases filled with
volumes bound in calf, and the furniture all reflect the solid
comforts of a period when people impressed their own personalities upon their homes. It is a room that is evidently lived in
and its symmetry would not be marred by a misplaced magazine, nor its comfort sacrificed for conventionality.

Black-framed, white-matted prints of the wigged jurists
of England, French actors in Watteau costumes, a tiger by
Delacroix and an old Jew by Rembrandt, all looked down on
me as I sank into a great chair before an obviously much-used
fireplace. Outside the morning sun hit the bare trees in the
park across the avenue, tinted the white marble Museum of

Art pale orange, and made the room which reeked of substantiality seem somewhat somber.

Like another famous lawyer, Mr. Root seems to have discovered Florida's fabled fountain. In many ways his manner and attitude toward life are reminiscent of Justice Holmes. Into old-fashioned surroundings both bring the spirit of eternal youth. The Supreme Court justice is the more humorous of the two. There is a twinkle in his blue eyes that is lacking in the sad eyes of Mr. Root. About both of them is that simple courtliness which Thackeray delighted to describe. In the case of Mr. Root this likeness to one of the novelist's characters is heightened by his appearance: his silver bang and his sparse side whiskers recall pictures of Victorian days. As he walked briskly into the room and stood there, erect and vital, it was hard to believe that this was the year 1931.

This alert man, so many of whose contemporaries have passed to the great beyond, seemed time defying. Atlas-like, he appeared to be carrying another age upon his shoulders, but it did not bear him down. Into the room he brought memories of Grant, of Tilden, of McKinley, of Cleveland, and a host of others who by this time are almost legendary; and here was he who had known them all and who had worked with many of them, strong, active, and absorbed in world affairs. For him the sun had presumably stood still, not for a day, but for years.

He took me into his study. It is a small room, in the corner of which stands a mahogany roll-topped desk cluttered with papers and books. The impression that it left is rather blurred, for my attention was riveted upon him as he sat with the light from two windows falling upon his head, and his surroundings out of focus. I can remember the blue cover of a copy of "Moby Dick" and three pictures hanging above the desk.

Elihu Root

One was an engraving of a jurist of the Georgian period; this was flanked on one side by an enlargement of an old daguerreotype—the portrait of a poetical looking man of middle age with chin whiskers, his head resting on his hand—and on the other by a large photograph of Lord Bryce. I mentioned the pictures.

"The engraving is a portrait of Lord Mansfield," he said, "Chief Justice of the King's Bench during the American Revolution. Lord Bryce you probably recognize. It was sent to me by Lady Bryce after his death. The third one is a portrait of my father."

Mr. Root has been accused of being cold, of lacking sympathy, but as he looked at the picture of his father there was an expression of softness and tenderness in his eyes.

"He was professor of mathematics at Hamilton College in Clinton, which I attended. But that was a great many years ago."

"You have seen many changes in your lifetime," I remarked.

"Yes, a great many." Then there came a moment of silence.

"Ideas and ideals are changing, and I think we are constantly moving toward better things. Gradually men's conceptions of their relations to one another have improved. While this is a slow process and has been going on since the dawn of history, even in my lifetime I have seen evidences of it.

"That is the reason why I can look to the future with hope. When you go back in history and study the condition and character of civilized peoples in each succeeding century, you find an increase in liberty and justice and righteousness. Education has gained ground and men have become generally more intelligent, less cruel, and more considerate of the rights of others.

"Even in my time compassion not only for human beings but even for animals has grown. I distinctly remember that when Henry Bergh founded the Society for the Prevention of Cruelty to Animals he was looked upon as more or less of a crank. To-day a man who is cruel to animals is regarded as a brute. It is this growth of compassion that I would say was the greatest change that has occurred in my lifetime.

"As late as the last century there was an amazing degree of cruelty, of oppression, of immorality, and of corruption which would not be tolerated to-day. A little more than one hundred years ago there were at least two hundred offenses punishable by death in England. Of course, it has been the change in the inner man which has brought about the abolition of these punishments.

"Religion has gone through a metamorphosis. From a narrow dogmatic theology, I have seen it swing to gross materialism. Now, with Jeans and Eddington and other scientists discovering that this materialism will not explain everything, there is a return to spirituality. The men of science are faced by a stone wall and they must stop; they know no more about the ultimate than the most bigoted Fundamentalist preacher."

He paused. For a few minutes he said nothing. Then he continued:

"Our ideas of right and wrong have also changed. In eighteenth century England a man expected to pay thousands of pounds for a cabinet appointment, and it was not a disgrace for a minister to buy the vote of a member of parliament.

"That was the period when the roads of the nation were beset with highwaymen and Dick Turpin and others of his calling were heroes in the eyes of the people. The custom of the country permitted the plundering of wrecked ships; jails were breeding places of pestilence and hospitals and insane asylums were not much better.

"I mention England as an example. The same thing was true of the rest of the world. But when we compare these conditions with those of to-day in England and her dominions and in the United States, or for that matter in all of Europe, we must realize that honesty and humanity have made amazing progress.

"In fact, some of the very evils which the government now frowns upon it sanctioned years ago. In New York State, for instance, a law was enacted in 1814 to raise money for colleges by lotteries. In my youth there was a tradition that the president of one of these colleges bought out the interests of other institutions, which were to benefit by this form of gambling, and thus enriched his college, which was fostering and promoting the morals of the young men of the time.

"In my lifetime I have seen the attitude toward any number of things undergo a radical transformation. For example, there were the objectionable railroad practice of rebates, the questionable management of corporations, and even the abuse of the elective franchise. Of course I mention only a few of the ills which I have seen cured.

"I distinctly remember the frauds, the tricks and devices and acts of violence which worked against fair elections before Federal election laws were passed. In those days there was no registration of voters; the wayfaring man could vote a resident out of house and home and the count of ballots was at the mercy of anybody who managed to buy a local election officer. The ballots themselves were supplied by the party; they were made out and handed by political workers to each voter, who was given one or even more to drop into the ballot box. I have seen a long line of men march out of a tramp lodging house with ballots held high in the air and continually in sight until they were deposited, so that those who bought votes would know they were getting what they paid for.

"Things are by no means perfect as yet in politics," he continued with a smile. "Human nature must still progress. But what I want to make clear to you is that the attitude of the majority of people has changed toward many things. Marcy's declaration 'to the victor belong the spoils' is no longer accepted.

"Of course, there is much still to be accomplished, but I think things have improved," he continued, looking up at the photograph over his desk, "since James Bryce wrote his 'American Commonwealth' a generation ago, when the government of practically every American city was a byword of shame for Americans all over the world.

"Politics in themselves have not changed as much as men's ideas. But in the natural course of events these ideas will ultimately affect politics and improve them. It is a long way from the day of the Greek serf, and although slavery persisted up to a comparatively short time ago, there has been a gradual, steady growth of human sympathy. The words liberty, justice, order, and peace denote the application of moral ideas to the conduct of men in mass toward their fellow men. They mean more to-day than ever before.

"This growth of human sympathy, together with the realization of the advantages of self-control and of working for a common interest, is changing man's attitude toward life. He has come to learn that the progress of the world has now reached a point where society must rely upon that self-control and that common interest for the smooth working of the vast machinery of government. The mere forcible enforcement of law is inadequate, for laws do not effect reforms, nor do they make men better. The improvement must come from man himself. It is not the fear of the policeman or the sheriff that keeps peace among us; it is the self-control of our citizens who conform their lives to the rules of conduct necessary to the common interest. It is upon this spirit that the hope for the permanence of modern civilization lies."

XXIV

IT IS significant that two former American secretaries of
state should be deeply interested in a cause for which the
Permanent Court of International Justice stands as a
worldwide symbol. Mr. Root is one of those secretaries, the
other one is Charles Evans Hughes, Chief Justice of the United
States. It was just before he left to take his seat on the bench
of the Permanent Court that I visited him. He went, not
as a representative of the United States, but as a judge selected
by the Council and Assembly of the League of Nations. For
the United States is not a member of the Court, whose function
under the League Covenant is to interpret treaties, pass on
questions of international law, and settle differences arising
between nations.

Mr. Hughes believes that the Court will aid materially in
preserving peace and that we shall gain something in our
quest for peace if we recognize that war is not an abnormality,
that it is the expression of the insistent human will, inflexible
in its purpose, and that the culture of civilization has strength-
ened, not enfeebled it.

"However," he said, "there are controversies between
nations which should be decided by a court. There are controversies calling for the examination of facts and the application of the principles of law. There are international
contracts or treaties, now more numerous than ever, to be
interpreted.

Charles Evans Hughes

"It is to the interest of the United States with respect to the disposition of its own controversies that the best practicable method of judicial settlement should be provided. We have rights and duties under international law. We are parties to treaties under which we have rights and obligations. And we cannot be the final judge in our own cases; we need the best possible international tribunal to decide them. This is to the interest of every American citizen. It is also to the interest of the United States that controversies between other nations to which we are not a party should be appropriately determined.

"Suppose a citizen of this state should say that he was interested in having a judicial tribunal to determine controversies only between states to which New York was a party, and that it made no difference to him what happened if the question was between Missouri and Kansas.

"Every citizen knows that it is to the interest of domestic peace to maintain a tribunal by which controversies between any two states can be determined. It is equally essential to world peace to maintain a tribunal by which controversies not our own should be peacefully and impartially determined, wherever that is possible."

Mr. Hughes has the happy faculty of simplifying seemingly complex questions. As he talks he emphasizes the point he wishes to make with a smile. It is not a smile of humor, but one with an interrogatory twist which seems to ask whether the listener understands—a smile which assumes the simplicity of the statement no matter how abstract it may be. Mr. Hughes sees but two ways for the settlement of controversies between nations, for a controversy cannot remain, as he put it, "a festering sore." Ultimately the alternative to peaceful settlement is the arbitrament of force.

"The only way to prevent war," he said, "is to dispose of the causes of war, and the desire for peace must be supported by the institutions of peace. Because a court may not be able to deal with every sort of controversy, but only with controversies that are appropriate for a court to decide, is no reason for dispensing with it. There is no immediate access to the millennium, and a demand for the millennium will not prevent war."

The son of a Welsh Baptist clergyman, Mr. Hughes was born and lived the first years of his life in Glens Falls, a village which is filled with Revolutionary lore. While the battle of Appomattox Court House was being fought, and Richmond threatened, he was visiting the cave made famous by Cooper in his "Deerslayer" and seeing Bloody Pond where hundreds of earlier Americans had met their deaths in the French and Indian wars.

When he was but three years old, this country, to use his own words, "was standing aghast at the irreparable loss of the martyred Lincoln and confronted with the suspicions, hatreds, and scandals of the period of Reconstruction."

"In England, the long career of Palmerston had ended and the first ministry of Gladstone had not yet begun," he said. "In France, Napoleon III was endeavoring to conceal the decadence of the empire with a fatuous splendor. In Italy, Cavour had been laying the foundation of Italian unity, but the essential successes of Victor Emanuel were yet to come. In Germany, Bismarck was pressing to the fateful victories of Sadowa and Sedan, and with relentless will was forging the mechanism of German imperial power. Mill's 'Liberty' and Darwin's 'Origin of Species' had but recently appeared, and 'Das Kapital' of Marx was shortly to be published. The electric age was in its beginning and science was yet to win the victories which have given us the practical achievements of the gas engine, the moving picture, and the radio—more revolutionary than political theories."

It was but a short time after this that his family moved first to Jersey City and, after a brief stay there, crossed the river and made their home in New York.

Both parents were deeply religious and looked forward to their son's following in his father's footsteps, but the boy had a will of his own. In fact, when he was but five years old, disapproving of the method of teaching in the school which he attended, he formulated a plan, set it down on paper and under the heading "Charles E. Hughes, his plan of study," presented it to his father. When he delivered the salutatory address in old Public School 35 he had firmly made up his mind to become a lawyer.

There followed years at Madison, now Colgate, and at Brown; teaching Greek and mathematics at Delhi, New York, and a course in the Columbia Law School, succeeded by three years of graduate work.

The professorship of law at Cornell took him to Ithaca where he spent some of the pleasantest days of his life, and then he returned to New York to resume his practice of law.

"Life is only work, and then more work, and then more work," he said, and his entire career has exemplified this idea. To-day with a world-wide reputation, he works as hard as did the young lawyer who was selected by Senator Stevens to investigate the gas and electric companies. He crowds as much into one year now as he did twenty-five years ago, when, having finished with the Stevens Committee, he became counsel for the Armstrong Investigating Committee and made a nation-wide reputation in unearthing the wrongdoings of the life insurance companies. This resulted in his election as Governor of New York, and for the ensuing quarter of a century he has been constantly in the public eye—a period during which he said that he had been more libeled than any other public man by bad drawings of himself.

He gave me a photograph which he thought might help me to finish the portrait I was making of him. He believed it was like himself, but as I looked at it I remembered the quotation from Burns. It was a picture of an entirely different man from the one I saw. The obliterating hand of the retoucher had smoothed away all the marvelous character that was present in the original. Gone were the lines of concentration above the eyes; the beautiful modeling in the well-shaped nose had been removed, and the fire in the eyes had vanished.

Mr. Hughes has changed considerably in appearance since the days when he founded what eventually became the Rockefeller Bible Class, or even since the time he was Governor of New York. The square-cut brown beard which was once the target of cartoonists has turned gray and is trimmed more closely. But there is the same fire in the eyes and the same smile, a smile which breaks suddenly with no warning.

There is something of the air of the medical man about him: there is a finality about his statements that there is no gainsaying, and a positiveness which a diagnostician would employ when he was sure of the conclusions at which he had arrived. And then, too, there is something of the teacher, a didactic manner of expression, meticulous and precise. No consonants are slurred, and sibilants are given their full force.

He is one of the few men whom I have drawn who did not keep me waiting a minute; President Coolidge was another. The moment I arrived I was ushered into his room and he apologized because he had to continue his dictating for a few minutes. When he had finished he turned in the swivel chair behind his desk and faced me. In repose his expression is stern, almost Jovian; it is only when he speaks that it lightens, and then it becomes benign.

For the last thirty years, he told me, he has been doing a daily dozen on arising. These exercises, together with walking whenever he has the time, have kept him in first-class physical condition, and he recalled the long walks he used to take on Riverside Drive when he lived on West End Avenue and when Grant's Tomb was still a novelty.

In reading, his tastes are catholic. On his desk and beside his bed there are always books that may be picked up for a few minutes, but he does not believe that "by the study of books you can obtain the equivalent of contact with men."

"As I observe," he remarked, "the profusion of educational opportunities not only through varied courses of instruction but in the multitude of books and periodicals, of dramatic portrayals by word and picture, I realize that what is needed is not more information but better judgment, not more bulletins but more accuracy of statement and a better assimilation. And as we consider the welter of controversies and the dangerous clashes of interest, we come to place our reliance not upon emotional appeal but upon the processes of reason and the dominance of those who have not lost emotional power but have been able to hold passion in check.

"We live in an interesting world and we must not contract ourselves into some narrow little sphere in which we happen to be placed and refuse to come out and get into contact with the varied interests of the world.

"It is a beautiful world, too—beautiful in nature, beautiful in the works of the imagination, beautiful in the works of art, beautiful on every side."

XXV

STRETCHING along Fifteenth Street between where Pennsylvania Avenue stops on its course from the Capitol to where it begins again as it runs past the White House, stands the Treasury Department. Discolored by dirt and age it appears even darker in contrast with the green grass about its main entrance. There is something very secure about it and, compared with the domed Capitol and the newly painted White House, it has a stern business-like aspect.

In a corner on the second floor is the office of the Secretary of the Treasury—a large room done in mahogany and blue that might be the office of the president of any large corporation. On the walls hang five paintings, portraits of Mr. Mellon's predecessors—Chase, who served with Lincoln; Taney, afterwards Chief Justice of the Supreme Court; Sherman, author of anti-trust legislation; Gallatin, the fourth to hold the office; and Hamilton, father of our governmental financial system. Through the windows one gets a vista of the city and, above the trees, the Washington Monument shoots its shaft skyward.

Mr. Mellon is seated at a desk at the far end of the room. The sunlight that floods the room is reflected by some papers and throws a glow over his head, emphasizing his prominent cheekbones and the strongly defined markings in his face.

A tall, slightly built man, he gives an impression of great nervous energy under complete control. One senses in him a tremendous force, a force of brain, not of muscle; a man whose reasoning faculties are always dominant over his emotions. Mr. Mellon is not robust but he is that thin type which is capable of great endurance under physical or mental strain.

To whatever he undertakes, Mr. Mellon seems to give himself over completely. For more than a decade the subject absorbing his attention has been the Treasury Department, and it is by what he has done there that he wants to be judged. Upon personal topics he lives up to his reputation for shyness. And so the conversation turned to Mr. Mellon's work in Washington and what he as a business man thinks of the administration of government.

"The Government is really a gigantic business," he began. "It should be run, and can be run, on business principles, though there are certain necessary limitations on efficiency, which we are not obliged to contend with in private life. I mean by that such limitations as, for instance, selecting employees from a limited civil service list and paying salaries which are frequently inadequate for the quality of service demanded. There is, too, the political pressure that is constantly applied for the promotion or retention of undeserving employees. Because of the low salaries in the higher positions such as, for example, in the Bureau of Internal Revenue, the labor turnover is very high in the key positions. The housing facilities are often inadequate, though plans are under way for a building program in Washington which will to a large extent eliminate this evil.

"These are some of the disadvantages. On the other hand, there are many compensations and advantages. It has been my experience to find in Washington a sense of unselfish service and a pride in position that have brought the Government an honest, and more faithful class of workers than private industry could command upon anything like the same terms.

Andrew W. Mellon

I know that this is true so far as my own department of the Treasury is concerned."

"How do you feel about getting results? Isn't it slow work as compared with the way in which private business can operate?"

"Oh, yes," Mr. Mellon replied, "but it is necessary to have patience. The Administration and many members of Congress worked for years just to get one idea across—that in reducing taxes it was also possible to revise and reform the tax system, and that just because taxes were high it did not necessarily follow that they would produce more revenue, or even so much revenue, as lower taxes would produce. But eventually we saw that idea enacted into law, just as in time most things work out. The danger is to expect too much of government.

"No government, however able, can change economic conditions overnight or accomplish the miracles demanded of it. All that can be expected is that a government moving with intelligence should give economic forces freedom and help the country to cure itself. In this country we have usually avoided false gods in the past. But new theories and new remedies are constantly presented, and we should therefore analyze carefully the political promises of to-day. When a candidate, in order to bring about the millennium, would start the Government in an orgy of spending, let him submit the details of his budget.

"Our ills, as they arise in our economic system, cannot be cured by magic formulas, but only by the application of well-tried economic principles. The rest can be left to the initiative, intelligence, and good sense of the American people.

"You see," he said with a smile, "such a philosophy of government calls for the same conservative principles which operate successfully in business. That is my conclusion derived from more than fifty years of business experience before I came to Washington."

"Did you say fifty years, Mr. Secretary?" I asked, for his appearance made the statement seem incredible. "Have you really been in business so long?"

"Yes," said Mr. Mellon. "I was in the banking business in Pittsburgh in 1874. At that time banking, along with most other business, was on a very different scale from what it is to-day. Industrial America, as we know it now, hardly existed before the early seventies. Production was limited, and industrial and manufacturing concerns were operated chiefly by individuals or partnerships. The great natural resources, which were to produce such untold wealth for the country, were still lying largely undeveloped, or undiscovered. Such industries as petroleum, natural gas, and cement hardly existed; the steel industry was in its infancy, and the automobile industry was unknown."

I suggested to Mr. Mellon that as well as vast changes in banking and in business in those fifty years, he must also have seen a change in the attitude of the public and the Government toward business.

"Yes," he said, "there has been a change in attitude, particularly in the last decade or so. The distrust of great corporations has largely passed away, as it has become more and more evident that organization on a large scale is necessary in a country as large as this, not only in developing our natural resources, but in producing such things as automobiles, express and freight trains, textiles, electric power, and many other commodities necessary to our present mode of living.

"It is the old story of large-scale production. We have learned that lesson in the United States, and realize that only by achieving a uniform, and, therefore, cheaper production of commodities, and by taking advantage of labor-saving mechanical devices, thus increasing the productive capacity per capita of labor, is it possible to pay high wages and still reduce costs, so that the finished products are within reach of the great buying public. It follows, of course, that, as a result of lower prices, consumption of commodities is increased. This still further stimulates production, and so it goes. In the end, we find that it pays to manufacture in quantity and to make a large volume of small profits.

"It is because this fact is becoming so generally understood that much of the distrust which formerly existed against corporate organizations is disappearing. There is, too, the further fact that corporations are not owned by a few wealthy people, but by millions of stockholders, many of them persons of small means, who find they can secure a surer return on their money through investment in some useful and well-run enterprise than in any other way. There is nothing new in what I have been saying, but it is a fact of great significance that this change is taking place."

"I suppose, Mr. Secretary," I said, "that in the changed attitude of both the Government and the public toward business, there is also to be found an explanation of the changed attitude of the Government toward the banker, whose services are called on more and more in helping to solve governmental problems."

"It is partly due to that," said Mr. Mellon, "and partly to the fact that the problems themselves have changed. This is particularly true since the war. In recent years problems have arisen that are so largely financial and economic in character that bankers have been called upon to help in their solution, even when those problems are of an international and semi-governmental nature, such as were once left to officials and diplomats to settle.

"American banking before the war largely confined itself to financing industrial developments in this country. But now we have become a creditor, instead of a debtor nation; and banking is finding that, just as it earlier became involved in industry and has been obliged to help in the solution of industrial problems, so it must now help in finding a solution for those international financial problems which must be solved if the world is to go forward."

"And now, Mr. Secretary, one more question. You have seen America grow from a comparatively poor nation to a very prosperous one. Do you attribute its present wealth, as foreign critics sometimes do, to its great resources?"

The Secretary deliberated a moment before replying. "In part, of course, it is due to those resources," he said. "But it is due in a larger measure, I think, to the energy and initiative of the American people and to their genius for organization. Those of us who have lived through the economic readjustments of the last fifty years know that the country's dominant position in the world of finance and industry is due to the fact that America has succeeded in adjusting herself to the economic laws of the new industrial era. In doing so, she has evolved an industrial organization which can maintain itself, not only because it is efficient, but because it is bringing about a greater diffusion of prosperity among all classes of citizens than was ever known before in any other country in the world's history."

That, one realized, was a statement of Secretary Mellon's faith in the soundness of America's business system and of the principles underlying the whole American civilization. It was easy to understand; but what was not easy to understand, was that the keen, vigorous man before me, who is in the very forefront of all that is going on in the world to-day, could be the same man who was a business contemporary of Carnegie, Frick, and the other great figures of thirty or forty years ago. Mr. Mellon is, indeed, one of the last of the great business leaders still living, who link us with that earlier era when conditions of life were so vastly different from anything we know to-day.

XXVI

CONSIDERABLY younger than Mr. Mellon, but also a link with that almost mythical past when great fortunes were amassed in a growing country, is Charles M. Schwab. Seated in his library, a large room, its walls lined with carved bookcases above which hung paintings by Diaz and Turner, he told me that after fifty years of business it made no difference to him whether he had one dollar or a hundred million—and I believed him. For he could make almost anybody believe almost anything.

Several days before seeing him in his home on Riverside Drive, I had gone to his office to make a drawing of him. A salesroom takes up the ground floor of the building—a salesroom with the atmosphere of a cathedral, in which salesmen speak in whispers and in which tools are incidentally displayed. As the elevator whisked me by the nine floors occupied solely by offices, I caught fleeting glimpses through the glass-paneled doors, and as each succeeding floor came into view the only things that could be seen were articles made of steel and painted a dull green—steel cabinets, steel desks, and even steel chairs. On the tenth floor the elevator stopped. Here customers were again received, and I entered what at first seemed to be a dimly lighted cloister. As on the ground floor, a semi-religious note was introduced into the scheme of decoration and formed a marked contrast to the snatches of bare efficiency to be seen on the way up in the elevator.

Charles M. Schwab

I was ushered into a small office, and within a few minutes Mr. Schwab came in. There is something all-compelling about him—his voice is such as Homer ascribed to Nestor, "a stream of eloquence sweeter than honey." The only requisites for holding a conversation with him are two words, "yes" and "no," and they should be used sparingly. He has so much to say, he is so anxious to say it, and seemingly finds so much joy in doing so that one hesitates to interrupt. As an evangelist he would make Billy Sunday seem like the veriest tyro; as a politician he would put Al Smith to shame; had he become a criminal lawyer, juries would thank his clients for having committed murder. At his persuasiveness the eyes of needles would open to permit camels to pass through.

While I was making my drawing of him he did not have much chance to tell me anything about himself or his ideas. People were constantly coming in; before they left they were profusely grateful to him for permitting them to do as he wanted. In the few business transactions in which I saw him take part he was always the same—suave, genial, and accommodating.

But in his home Mr. Schwab told me something of his half-century of business life, and it was there that he said that he was tired to death of the laudatory articles that appeared about him and that, like Cromwell, he wanted to be painted "warts and all."

"As I sit and look back over those fifty years," he began, "I cannot for the life of me understand the whole thing. All I can do is to wonder how it all happened. Here I am, a not over-good business man, a second-rate engineer. I can make poor mechanical drawings. I play the piano after a fashion. In fact, I am one of those proverbial Jacks-of-all-trades who are usually failures. Why I am not, I can't tell you.

"When I left Loretto and went to Braddock to take a job in a grocery store I was just sixteen years old. If it had not been for a ten-cent cigar I might still be selling dried apples over a counter. One day Bill Jones came in to get a smoke. Jones was the head of the Edgar Thompson Steel Works. I asked him for a job there. I did not know a thing about the steel business. Not for a moment did I at that time sense that the era of steel was just beginning. Had I done so I should not marvel the way I do at the result. But as it was, I was not interested in the grocery business, I knew that things were going on in the steel mills, and I thought I would take a chance. I think it must have been my nerve that made a hit with Jones. He gave me a position and by the time I was twenty-one I was chief engineer of the company.

"Things happened just as in a fairy tale. At thirty-five I was president of the Carnegie Steel Corporation. In the course of events a dinner was given me by the Chamber of Commerce in New York. Mr. Morgan sat at my right hand; Harriman, Frick, and Carnegie were all there. I was called upon for a speech, and partly as the result of what I said the Steel Corporation was formed and I became its president. But I was not happy there. With Mr. Carnegie I was a czar. In the Steel Corporation I had too many bosses, and one of them was Wall Street. So I got out and formed the Bethlehem Company. That was twenty-five years ago, and in all that time we have never needed business."

"Do you believe in luck?" I asked.

"Luck, opportunity, chance—call it what you will—there is something that certainly gives some men more than an even break," said Mr. Schwab. "In my lifetime I have known thousands of men with more ability than I have—some I am certain were better executives, others were much abler engineers—but things somehow or other just did not go with them.

"The smallest and most inconsequential thing may have the most vital effect on a man's life. I often wonder what I would have done if Bill Jones had not bought that ten-cent cigar. For, surveying myself impartially, and appraising myself fairly, I can find no special ability, no one trait in which I excel. I love life and people. I am what you would call a good mixer. After a short acquaintance people like me, and I in turn have an abiding trust in them."

"And you managed to make money in spite of that?" I asked.

"Yes," he replied with a laugh, "but think of how much I might have made if I had not been so trusting. Speaking seriously, I have never gone after money as such; I have never started or done anything just for the sake of money. I would be a very much wealthier man than I am had I done so. Just to give you an example of what I mean, take the companies that Bethlehem has bought up, such as, for instance, Cambria. I could have purchased it personally and sold it at a profit to Bethlehem; instead of which I let Bethlehem buy it itself. Never in all the years that I have been connected with a corporation have I sold anything to it. During the war, before we entered it, Germany offered me $100,000,000 not to sell ordnance to Great Britain, but I refused the money.

"What I have tried to do has been to build. It has been a joy to see businesses grow under my guidance. To plan, to adjust, to arrange and manipulate, to find the proper men for the proper places, to start new companies and reorganize old ones, in these things I have found my pleasure."

I asked Mr. Schwab about the changes that had occurred in the fifty years he had been doing this.

"In that time there have been vast changes not only in the methods of production but also in the methods of business and the attitude between employer and employee," he replied.

"As for the production end, the inventions and discoveries in that time have been epoch-making; but I do not propose to go into the technical changes. That would be too scientific and naturally vary according to the product manufactured.

"But just to give you some idea of the other changes: fifty years ago concerns in the same line of business were rivals, now they are competitors. There were many more trade secrets; the other fellow's product was usually not good; you sold yours by running his down. Then the lesson had not been learned that what would benefit one member in a certain line of production would benefit all; that conferences between them would result in a common advantage; that creating a market for a product would mean more business for every one.

"It is in the last half-century, too, that the world has seen the mobilization of capital and engineering that has resulted in the wonderful era of progress in which we live. Industry has brought together and welded into single organizations thousands of human beings with different habits of life and thought. For the success and happiness of these human beings and of society in general, mutual relationships had to be adjusted on the basis of fair dealing and coöperation.

"The result has been that there is a new concept of management of business—industry was humanized and men became self-respecting workmen and citizens and factors coöperating in the success of business.

"I have always used my best efforts to further the interests and better the conditions of the men who worked for me. The first thing that I have always bornet in mind has been that they were human beings with the same desires and motives as my own. When their ideas did not coincide with mine, I realized that they were as certain that they were right as I was sure that I was. I do not know whether you know it or not, but I was put in charge of the plant at Homestead while the great strike was on there. Thirty-five years later, when I was no longer connected with the company, the men there gave me a dinner. I had to speak, I knew that I could not ignore that strike. So I got up with Carnegie's book in my hand and said that in speaking of the trouble I would read from that book and what I read was this: 'As for the strike, if Charley had been here there would not have been any.'

"Management has come to realize that conflict between labor and capital is destructive of the interests of each; it is unnecessary and mutually expensive. The result is a new code of economics, a code that aims not only to provide food, clothing, and shelter, but also to place a true dignity on labor, a dignity that yields a fuller and happier life.

"But this happiness does not mean the abolishing of work, for work is the cornerstone of real happiness. It lies in the payment of fair wages for efficient services; steady, uninterrupted employment; safeguarding lives and health; good physical working conditions; provision to lay up savings and to become partners in the business through stock ownership; and, finally, some guarantee of financial independence in old age."

I asked whether standardization of labor conditions now was as favorable for the success of the individual as formerly.

"The conditions are more favorable, because there are so many more opportunities," said Mr. Schwab. "Take the question of wages, for instance. There was an adherence to a policy of uniform wages regardless of individual effort. Such a policy sought to discourage effort and to reduce the individual output to a standard set by the least efficient worker. But we have traveled far in our ideas on the question of reward for service. We now realize the essential benefits derived from relating compensation to the contribution made by the individual.

"As a matter of fact, there are more good positions than there are men to fill them, or, at least, men who have had the opportunity, if you choose to call it that, to show the required ability. The Steel Corporation had difficulty in filling Gary's place, and the Westinghouse Company did not find a successor to Tripp in a whole year.

"Yes, in those fifty years I have seen a vast improvement in the whole line of business. I am an optimist and look to seeing even greater strides forward. I have never been a calamity howler, even at times when I have been in pretty tight places. I have always been a hard worker, and I have always managed to look at the bright side of things.

"When I first went to work for the Thompson Steel Company I was a stake driver and my salary was so small that I taught the piano in the evenings for one dollar a lesson."

"Tell me something about your interest in music."

"Now, listen," said Mr. Schwab, "I am a business man pure and simple, so please don't stress this music. Some one once wrote that it was through my singing that I met Mr. Carnegie. Now, as a matter of fact I met him in the regular channels of business, but people like to invent romances.

"I first studied music under a priest at Loretto, Father Bowen, and then under a Sister of Charity. We always had music in our house. My father was very musical and my sister, who is a Mother Superior at present in Loretto, is an accomplished musician. As for myself, I originally studied the piano; then I learned to scrape a tune on the violin, and later I took up the organ. Music has given me a tremendous amount of enjoyment in life, and for twenty-five years Archie Gibson, whom I consider to be one of the finest organists in the country, has come here to the house whenever I want him to play for us.

"I am essentially a home man. Outside of public dinners, I have not dined away from my home in fifteen years. This is a pretty large house, but there is not a room in it that was designed for anything but living purposes. I have no large assembly rooms here, nothing for big functions. I love my friends; I love to entertain them. But all the entertaining I do is more or less informal. Every Sunday afternoon I am at home to them all; as many as want can stay for supper. Among those friends are many musicians. When they play here it is with a different spirit from that of a public appearance. Here Kreisler is Fritz, and never at a concert have I heard him play the way he does right here in this house. I can say the same of Sembrich, Schumann-Heink and a host of others.

"That is the kind of music I love. I am not partial to opera. It is too conglomerate an art. I prefer a more intimate and less formal style. The costumes and scenery add nothing to my pleasure, and the librettos for the most part are banal. I suppose I am too much of a realist to appreciate seeing a man or woman take fifteen or twenty minutes to die, warbling all the time."

I got up to go, and Mr. Schwab arose also. Coming over to me and putting his hand on my shoulder, he said:

"The other day you drew me as I appear. You did not soften my wrinkles nor make my hair one bit darker than it is. Go ahead and write about me, but tell the truth. I am not giving any advice on how to succeed. I hate that kind of article. I have no use for the successful business man who lolls back in his chair with his thumbs in his pockets and says do this and don't do that and you are bound to get on. For nobody can tell any one else what to do. Things just happen, that's all. I am not a Pollyanna, but I am not ashamed of being an optimist. The world is a pretty good place in which to live, and money isn't the only thing that counts in it. I have never been so interested in business as not to be able to enjoy a good book, a good picture, or good music. I have had a lot of joy in this life which money has not brought me. But above all I am thankful for one thing, and that is the God-given gift of being able to see the good in other people and of making them see whatever good there is in me."

XXVII

THE belief in luck which is so characteristic of Mr. Schwab is also held by Julius Rosenwald.

"Entirely too much stress," he said to me one day, "is put on the making of money. That does not require brains. Some of the biggest fools I know are the wealthiest. As a matter of fact, I believe that success is ninety-five per cent luck and five per cent ability.

"Take my own case. I know that there are any number of men in my employ who could run my business just as well as I can. They did not have the luck—that's the only difference between them and me."

When I asked him to tell me something about his life, he replied:

"That's an old story; in fact it is sixty-seven years old. I can tell you something that is much more interesting. I suppose that it was because I was born in Springfield, within a stone's throw of Abraham Lincoln's house, that I am particularly interested in his life. I am reading Beveridge's book now, and I read Sandburg's work when it came out. I want to tell this story because it shows that often authors are wrongly discredited.

"Sandburg gives a very good picture of the times, and among other things, he tells of the difficulties that Harriet Beecher Stowe was laboring under when she wrote 'Uncle Tom's Cabin.' Now, it happened that when I was traveling in New Mexico, I heard that one of her sons was living there, so I went to see him to find out all about it. He had not read Sandburg's book, so I sent him a copy, and he wrote to me and told me that it was all wrong—that they always kept a maid and that his mother had plenty of leisure in which to write.

"The next time I saw Sandburg I repeated to him what I had learned, and he explained the whole thing to me. It seems that the man whom I had met was the youngest son; by the time he was old enough to remember, Mrs. Stowe had not only written her famous book but had made enough money from it to afford the comparative luxuries which he mentioned. So you see both of them told the truth."

This story and its investigation are characteristic of Rosenwald. It shows his interest in small matters and at the same time it gives a good idea of his thoroughness—a thoroughness which enabled a country boy who came to New York to work in his uncle's clothing store, in a short time to open his own establishment on Fourth Avenue, near where it runs into the Bowery. It was the same spirit of investigation and infinite attention to details that enabled him to see the possibilities in Chicago, to realize that there was a market there for summer clothes for men, for that was the period when white waistcoats and alpaca and seersucker suits were the vogue. Successful in this, he soon saw that in Chicago there was a big field for low-priced clothing, and accordingly he made new connections and enlarged his business.

One of his principal customers was Sears-Roebuck, a firm which had started selling watches by mail and had developed into a mail order house. The senior partner wanted to increase the business and saw Rosenwald's ability. That was in 1895.

Julius Rosenwald

Rosenwald bought an interest in the business. At that time the capital stock was valued at $125,000; to-day its market value is many times that and Mr. Rosenwald owns more than half of it. And as he puts it, "that business has grown to its present proportions without the introduction of one cent of outside capital. It has made the money by means of which it has been enlarged."

Though Mr. Rosenwald is known primarily as a business man, and although he has held several important public offices, it is in his philanthropies that one sees the real man. There is more of the true Rosenwald, more of the essential quality of his personality in one of his philanthropic schemes than there is in any of his business plans.

"I am absolutely opposed," he told me, "to any system of philanthropy that stores up huge sums of wealth and permits trustees to spend only the interest on the principal. To begin with, this is economically all wrong; but, what is more important, it shows an absolute lack of confidence in the future.

"Do you remember the manna of the Bible which melted at the end of each day?" he asked. "I believe that gifts for the good of mankind should be spent within one generation of the donor's life. I can give you any number of examples where comparatively large sums of money are tied up for some particular purpose, the usefulness of which has entirely disappeared. To give you but one instance, when Benjamin Franklin died he set aside a certain sum of money, ten thousand dollars if I remember correctly, to be lent, as he put it, to married artificers under twenty-five. He computed that at the end of one hundred years the sum would be equal to one million dollars and this was to be expended for the construction of sidewalks in Boston and to pump the water of Wissahickon Creek into Philadelphia.

"Unfortunately there was a dearth of such artificers—or perhaps I should say fortunately. At all events, a large part of the principal has remained idle and there is not enough capital for the projects mentioned; nor is it needed for the purposes for which he intended it. I have tried to circumvent this fault in the provisions which I have stipulated shall govern the so-called Rosenwald Fund, for its final disposition has been set for twenty-five years after my death."

I interrupted to ask, "What are the purposes of the fund?"

"It is a development of many years of personal gifts," Mr. Rosenwald explained. "In the words of the charter, it is incorporated for the 'well-being of mankind.' For ten years it limited its activities almost exclusively to the negro rural schools; then it began to broaden its scope.

"There are many fields for this endeavor. The simple question of material necessities is one; the wise assistance, not by donations but by investments of capital, in housing or projects for coöperative farming which might serve as experiments in fresh methods and new types of organization. Then there are the problems of public health, of education, experiments in schools, coöperation with the government on various schemes, support of research, the development of promising individuals, and any number of similar subjects.

"Only recently the thought came to me that the government has made every provision for the separation of married people, and to-day our divorce courts are working overtime handing out decrees. I have an idea that if certain boards were established to hear the troubles of unhappily married couples, not necessarily with the idea of separating them, but rather with the purpose of disentangling their difficulties, much good would come of it and many homes would be saved."

I reverted to the subject of the negro schools and asked what was the reason for his interest in them.

"I am interested in the negro because I am also interested in the white," Mr. Rosenwald replied. "Do you know that one-tenth of our population is black? If we promote better citizenship among that proportion of our people, it goes without saying that our entire citizenship will be the better for it.

"Of course all of the states themselves helped with this project and appropriated money, and the colored people also secured donations; but it made me very happy when I knew that in fourteen southern states, March 1, 1929 was set aside as Rosenwald Day in all schools which are attended by colored children."

Now Mr. Rosenwald is absorbed in the building of a museum in Chicago, modeled after the Deutsches Museum in Munich, in which the history, in tangible form, of most of our modern inventions will be housed.

But of all the gifts that he has made in his lifetime, the one that has given him the greatest pleasure is one that probably cost him least in actual money.

"With Ingersoll," he told me, "I hate a stingy man. If you have only a dollar in the world, and have to spend it, spend it like a king. I'd rather be a beggar and spend like a king than a king and spend like a beggar.

"The reason I am quoting this is the fact that one of the smallest gifts I ever made is the one which meant more to me that any other, and at the same time was a case where a beggar spent like a king.

"I was fourteen and I had worked all summer for a few dollars a week. In the fall my parents celebrated their china wedding. I took all that I had and went out and bought a set of dishes. Proportionately, no king could have spent more lavishly. But looking back over the fifty-three years that have elapsed, no gift that I have made since then has left a more cherished memory."

XXVIII

As he leaned back in a big Italian chair in the vast living room of his Fifth Avenue apartment, leisurely talking, two hundred newspapers were awaiting words from him that were still unwritten. Great presses would not start their daily grind until this work was done, but into his huge beamed room that might have been in a Venetian palace Arthur Brisbane had brought none of the nervous tension of a newspaper office.

Sitting there as if he had not anything else in the world to do, his heavy-lidded blue eyes sparkling behind amber-rimmed spectacles, he might have been a retired business man, except for an alertness and an all-absorbing interest and curiosity— qualities not associated with ideas of retirement. For thirty years he has turned out his trenchant but simple phrases for millions of newspaper readers, and his literary output would fill many library shelves.

But this has been only a part of his activities. He has bought and sold newspapers; his real estate transactions are tremendous; yet he still has time for other business interests—and for leisure. He lives in New Jersey, maintaining his New York apartment for entertaining and luncheons and dinners. In the midst of a busy day he will find two or three hours for a more or less formal meal away from his office. At sixty-six, with many occupations, he still searches for more ways to employ his spare time.

There is a quickness about him, both in speech and in manner, that denies his age. No one thirty years his junior could be more active in thought or word. In physical vigor, too, he seems young, though perhaps he has not the strength he had when with one blow he knocked down Charley Mitchell, who was then the champion prize fighter of England.

He talks incisively and employs short sentences. His conversation sounds the way his editorials read. He translates abstruse thought into words of one syllable and he does this in no pedagogical manner. He thinks that way. He can apply the Darwinian theory to April Fool's Day or the philosophy of Jeans to the price of beef, and he can do it in such a manner that they become clearer by comparison.

There is a typical so-called Yankee shrewdness about him despite the fact that he was born in Buffalo. His sister told me she cannot recall the time when he did not have money; even when he was as young as ten he knew how to drive a good bargain.

But there was a peculiar softness in the voice of the alert but venerable editor as he took me into a small room and showed me a portrait that his father had painted of himself when he was a boy. It was with pride as well as sentiment that he pointed out other ancestral portraits, for he believes strongly in the influences of heredity.

"The best cart horse in the world," he said, "can't beat the worst race horse. Breed makes the difference. We talk of boys starting out with financial advantages. They are usually handicapped. A poor boy succeeds because he is poor, a rich one despite the fact that he has money. In nine cases out of ten wealth is the greatest obstacle a boy must overcome."

Arthur Brisbane

Turning to the portrait, he continued: "I suppose it was on account of my father that I went into journalism. He had very radical ideas and in order to give them publicity he bought a weekly column on the front page of the *New York Tribune* and there expounded his views. I am paid for doing badly what he did well and paid for, besides.

"When I started in to work Horace Greeley had hardly ceased telling young men to go West. I could not see the need for this. New York looked perfectly good to me. Though I went to the little red schoolhouse, I had five years' study in Europe, and when I came back I started to work for *The Sun*. I was nineteen years old at the time and I was much upset that the Constitution prevented any one under thirty-five becoming President. I couldn't wait that long. That's the reason I became a newspaper man."

I asked him what was the difference between the newspapers of those days and the newspapers of to-day.

"To compare the newspapers of to-day with the newspapers when I started would scarcely be possible. How can you compare a child three years old with one fourteen or older?

"When I began to work on *The New York Sun*, it consisted of four pages, two sheets, which carried everything—news, editorials, advertising, foreign dispatches. Not much advertising. Charles A. Dana refused one advertisement because the advertiser insisted on spelling cigar with an 's'—segar. A modern newspaper man would let the advertiser spell it, if he wanted to, with a 'z.'

"I was correspondent of *The Sun* in London at twenty-one. I had left the local staff and gone to Europe thinking that I was leaving journalism for good."

After several years as London correspondent Mr. Brisbane returned to New York to become editor of *The Evening Sun.* In speaking of those days he said:

"We ran the paper for some time on what might be called a literary basis. Such writers as Charles W. Tyler, Richard Harding Davis, Frank Wilson, afterward editor of *The Police Gazette*, wrote brilliant 'stories.' Davis began his Van Bibber stories then, based on a story by Manchecourt, which I translated for him from *La Vie Parisienne. The Sun* then had the biggest evening circulation in New York, which shows—as W. R. Hearst said when I went to work for him—that 'there are a dozen ways of making a paper successful. The important thing is to adopt some one way, and stick to it.'"

From *The Sun* Brisbane went to *The World.* In those days *The World* meant Pulitzer, and in speaking of him Mr. Brisbane said: "Joseph Pulitzer was an inspiration to hard work for every man who knew him well. Few knew him well. He worked at his newspapers literally from the moment he awoke until he went to sleep at night.

"Only success appealed to him, and his idea of success was results, circulation. You could not tell Joseph Pulitzer: 'We are holier and purer than our competitors. That's why they have more circulation than we have.'

"One day Joseph Pulitzer woke up to discover that W. R. Hearst had hired the entire staff of *The New York Sunday World*, with the exception of one capable lady. Mr. Pulitzer asked me to take charge of *The Sunday World*, and 'hire anybody in New York you want to.' In ten weeks our readers were increasing at an average rate of eleven thousand a Sunday. Pulitzer's delight was intense. When circulation came so easily, he, as sometimes happens with owners, had an attack of 'respectability.' Both *The Sunday World* and *The Sunday American* were excluded from certain clubs. I had no objection to this since it compelled club members to buy the paper.

"Mr. Pulitzer did not like it, and decided to overcome the objections of clubhouse committees by displaying such intense 'respectability' as would impress them. He sent me this message: 'Please have on the front page of the magazine in next Sunday's *World* a fine portrait of General O. O. Howard, head of the army, done by Mortimer, and an interview with Howard.' Mortimer made fine portraits in pen and ink. General O. O. Howard would have talked fine platitudes. The following Monday I sent Mr. Pulitzer this telegram: 'Sorry we did not have that O. O. Howard picture and interview. Instead, on the front page, I had a wonderful picture of Kate Swan in the electric chair and circulation is now up fifteen thousand.' Mr. Pulitzer telegraphed back: 'You know perfectly well I am blind, and must rely on you. Congratulations.'

"Above all, he was a man of quick action. He had been fighting a proposal to sell United States bonds at 104, saying that they were worth 110. One day his wife, a very brilliant woman, responsible for much of his success, asked him: 'Joseph, why don't you buy some of those bonds at 110, instead of talking so much about them?'

"Instantly, Mr. Pulitzer called up Dumont Clark, then president of the American Exchange Bank, telling him to bid $1,100,000 for $1,000,000 par value of the proposed bonds. He bought them at 110, sold them later at a much higher price, and broke the effort to sell the bonds privately at 104, forcing a sale to the public.

"A powerful man was Pulitzer. His one eye, with defective sight, seemed strong enough to look through a stone wall.

It was said that he would 'use a man, and throw him away like a squeezed orange.' But he never did it unless the man was that kind of man. Above all else he knew how to translate thought into action; that is what any successful man must do to keep on going.

"I may have an idea, but unless I do something with it it is worth nothing. Let me tell you a story. When the new tunnels to Jersey were first talked about I thought the property over there would be bound to increase in value. My idea in itself was not worth a hang, but I put the idea into action. I went over there and bought property. There is one piece that I have in mind that I paid fifteen thousand dollars for. A few months later the man from whom I bought laughingly said he would have accepted five thousand dollars for it. To-day that particular piece of land is renting for sixty thousand dollars."

He continued: "I had an idea that a tower would be a fine sort of structure for apartments. I erected the Ritz Tower, the first apartment house of that type in the city. It was a good idea, so good in fact that all you have to do is to look across the park to see how many have followed it."

But I wanted to hear more about newspapers. I referred to the growth of tabloids.

"I can only speak about tabloids as a spectator," said Mr. Brisbane, "but their growth and circulation do not surprise me. Size, in my opinion, has little to do with their success. They ask themselves, 'What interests nine million out of ten million people near here?' and they concentrate on that. They realize the force of pictures and recognize the fact that a strong picture can portray in a second what would require half a page of words. A full-size paper run on the same lines, in my opinion, would get more circulation than any tabloid, because people like a big picture better than they like a little one.

"Of course, the taste of the public continually changes. A strong man starts a paper, his personality goes into it and the paper is a success. Were he to live forever and his personality remain uniformly strong and progressive the paper would be eternal. For a paper to live it must continually absorb new ideas, which are its food, and keep up with the procession."

"Where will that procession lead to?" I asked.

"You mean the newspaper of the future? Who can tell what will be produced for the kind of men who will cultivate one eye for use in the telescope, the other for use in the microscope, and both for ordinary things on earth? That future man may have a skull that will be an absolute sphere, except for small openings for the eyes, nose, and mouth. He may weigh only twenty pounds or less, since his hardest work may be pressing a button. His wife, maintaining her size, and increasing her beauty, as mother of the race, may carry the husband suspended at her girdle, as the female parasite crab carries her little husband under one flipper.

"But one thing is as certain now as when it was said long ago by an old Greek teacher of oratory: 'To convince others, be yourself convinced.' The newspaper man who believes something and knows how to convince others of it will sell his newspaper. No matter what kind of newspaper you are printing, large size, tabloid, conservative, radical, you will succeed if you are saying what you really mean and are saying something worth while. If not, you won't succeed.

"Of course, I believe that moving pictures will largely take the place of books in education and condense by at least fifty per cent all educational processes. The radio, too, will become more and more important in conveying instantaneous news, and will, perhaps, educate the newspapers along the line of brevity."

I asked him whether he had spoken on the radio, "No," he replied, "I am a dictator, not an announcer. Don't misunderstand me. I do not mean I am another Mussolini. I mean I dictate too much into a machine, with the result that I have lost the sense of accent and emphasis and I cannot make much of a speech. Why, I once was addressing a group of professors in Chicago and I noticed them looking very queerly at me and I suddenly realized that I was dictating, even to punctuation."

He got up to look at the drawing.

"You have given me the brow of Sir Walter Scott," he remarked with a laugh, "and the chin of Charles Dana Gibson. I might have amounted to something if I had had a chin like that."

"Do you believe that facial characteristics reveal a man's ability?" I inquired.

"Practically always. Look here," he said, going to the large refectory table that stood in the middle of his room. On it were two inscribed photographs. One was of Gibson, the other of John D. Rockefeller, Sr.

"Couldn't you tell both of those men would make their mark in the world?" he asked. "I will acknowledge, however, that Gibson looks more like the trust magnate and Rockefeller like the artist. Perhaps, after all, each would have done better in the other's calling."

It was after three o'clock and my drawing was finished, so I suggested that I should go along.

"I guess I had better be going, too," he said, "as I have to write my editorial, and my train leaves for Allaire at five o'clock."

"Isn't it written yet?" I asked in surprise.

"Oh, no, but I have plenty of time. I usually dictate it in twenty minutes to half an hour. Let me drop you off at your place and on the way I'll show you how I work."

He put on a soft gray hat which only partly hid his high forehead. The collar of his overcoat was turned up, and, with a huge bundle of newspapers and magazines in hand, he took me down to the ground floor in his private elevator.

"Here's my machine," he said. "It's a second-hand one. I think I have bought more second-hand automobiles than any one else in the country."

The chauffeur opened the door. The interior resembled a baggage car. On one of the folding seats was a dictating machine, and suitcases, rugs, and papers were strewn about the floor. Though the car was large there was just about room for the two of us to squeeze in.

This is the way he makes use of his time. On his way through the city he sees things that strike him and he immediately dictates his impressions. The rest of it he does in the office. By the time he is ready to catch his train his stenographer has transcribed what he has dictated. A secretary accompanies him on the way to the ferry and across it and he corrects what he has dictated, so that when he gets aboard the train the day's work is finished. On the train he has a compartment and here is another machine with which he can start the next day's work.

As I got out of the car at my destination he leaned over and took up the mouthpiece of the recording device. Turning, he said, "Perhaps I write too easily, or rather take too little trouble. 'If I had had more time I should have written you a shorter letter.' Madame de Sévigné wrote that to her daughter.

I aim at brevity, but I miss it. I think, however, that I occasionally print useful quotations from others that stimulate thought."

As the door closed and his car started off through the crowded street I could see him sitting there dictating into the machine.

XXIX

I MUST confess I had been rather surprised to see a portrait of the older Rockefeller on Mr. Brisbane's table. There was something incongruous about this man who had written vitriolic editorials against trusts having the portrait of the head of the one-time largest trust in the country in his living room.

I have never met the father but I have drawn a portrait of John D. Rockefeller, Jr. His office is on the twentieth floor of 26 Broadway. Stand in front of the building some morning between nine-thirty and ten o'clock, and from one of the many motors that stop there you will see a young-looking man of fifty-odd years alight. Perhaps he himself has been driving the car. As he hands the machine over to the chauffeur and gets out he might pass for a successful lawyer, or, more likely, for an up-to-date college professor whose researches have been found to be of practical use to some tremendous business concern.

Of medium height and almost athletic build, he conveys the impression of strength and reserve force, of a man capable of handling a situation judicially and effectively. He dresses well, but not conspicuously. In fact, after meeting him one is likely to forget what his clothes are, for one remembers rather his keen gray eyes, his peculiar arched eyebrows, almost meeting above his well-modeled nose, and his broad, generous mouth. His head, though in reality long, seems broad on account of the squareness of his jaws, which swell just below his ears and sweep along, merging into a firm, bold chin. His color is almost ruddy. His hair, coarse and wiry and streaked with gray, is cut quite short. His walk gives an impression of physical fitness, of being in training yet not overtrained, which bears out the stories of his frequent visits to the handball courts.

As he enters the building and passes through the white marble corridor the chances are that he will glance up at a heroic bust that dominates the entrance hall. It is the likeness of a man past eighty, on whose face are shown without compromise the marks of time. There is a strong resemblance between the bust and the younger man—the same penetrating eyes, the same sharp nose with its characteristic curve. The principal difference in the two heads is that the older man's is slightly more oval and the curve of the face less broken by the squareness of the jaw.

Here are the founder and the dispenser of one of the greatest fortunes that has been accumulated on this earth. The father's life is still to be written. It is the romance of the country boy who rose to world supremacy in business and, having become the world's richest man, in turn became one of its leading benefactors through wise philanthropy and systematized scientific humanitarianism. To his son this modern Crœsus handed over the disposition of his colossal fortune.

Rockefeller endowments amounting to almost half a billion dollars are administered by carefully chosen boards of trustees. Throughout the entire world trained minds in all branches of science and art are devoting their lives to the benefit of humanity, with the knowledge that they have the freedom

John D. Rockefeller, Jr.

of unlimited resources at their command. It is through John D. Rockefeller that Carrel and Flexner can bend over their microscopes with free minds unburdened by material worries. Explorers are digging in the tropics and braving the polar seas, architects are designing new and better houses for the poor, college professors are provided with opportunities to make original researches, and social and religious movements are aided. John D. Rockefeller, Jr., is working in behalf of his father in these and countless more such activities.

The younger Rockefeller spends part of each day conducting his affairs in a large room wainscoted in dark oak, with windows that overlook the harbor. There is a large flat-topped desk carved to match the woodwork at one end, and around it stand a number of chairs upholstered in a bright vermilion leather. Behind the desk Mr. Rockefeller was seated one afternoon. It was a dull day and the gray light from the windows was augmented by an electric globe above; its rays, falling on his head and the red chairs, brought them into strong relief against the dark background.

It is not difficult to interview Mr. Rockefeller. He speaks freely on almost any subject and seems to feel that by reason of the position he holds in administering his father's fortune he owes a certain obligation to the public and should be more than willing to discharge it.

I mentioned the bust of his father and asked him whether he liked it.

"Yes," he said, "I like it; it is all good, except the two wrinkles above the nose. These convey to me a certain expression of fear, and that is one emotion that I am certain my father has never experienced. Perhaps I am wrong when I say fear. Probably it is apprehension, but that, too, is entirely foreign to his nature. If at any time he has had that feeling it was so fleeting that it is not a characteristic trait.

"In all my life, however, I have seen only two representations of any one whom I have intimately known that I consider faultless, and those are the two portraits of my father by Sargent. I was looking at one of them the other day. Examining it I could see in it the man I know. There was he to whom I had instinctively turned as a child for food and clothing and shelter and then for companionship. He responded and became my pal and from the outset had my confidence and friendship.

"I could see in that picture the friend who was never so occupied with his own business or pleasure that he had no time for my interests. On the canvas is my father as I know him, who, in all the years of my close association with him from earliest childhood, never told me what to do or what not to do. Sargent has shown in that painting why no influence in my life has been as powerful as his silent influence."

As Mr. Rockefeller sat there in his chair his hand toyed with a Phi Beta Kappa key that hung from his watch chain. I mentioned it and asked him whether he felt that a college education was needed nowadays for success in business.

"That depends largely on the individual," he answered. "I do not believe in forcing any boy or girl to go to college. As it is, our colleges are overcrowded by too many young people who are there only for a good time, and that is not why colleges are established.

"The Standard Oil Company has a special department for the training of foreign representatives and one of the requisites for admission into that training school is a college education. With such an education must go something more than ability, persistence, industry, and thrift; for, while all these are necessary for success in business, the real foundation is character. That is essential and indispensable.

"But do not confuse reputation with character. Reputation is what people think we are; character is what we really are. Now, by character I mean several things; the first is integrity; the second is obedience to the law, even when we do not feel the entire justice of that law; a third requisite is clean living, and by clean living I mean irrespective of the changing point of view in modern times. Way down within us we know what are the things that make us physically fit, mentally vigorous, and spiritually sensitive. Last, a vital component of character, I should say, is singleness of purpose. 'No man can serve two masters.' Upon singleness of purpose one's value to an employer largely depends.

"Those are the fundamental qualities underlying character, and to my mind none of them can be ignored if any continued success in business is looked for. Money is sometimes made by trickery and sharp practice, but successful business must be established on something more firm.

"As I have said in a speech: 'Corporations and individuals who set themselves up as superior to law are bound to be condemned eventually in the court of public opinion, so that even the most worldly-minded is bound to ask himself whether it pays, and to admit that no business, any more than any individual, can be successful and at the same time not be law-abiding.'

"While it is natural that every ambitious and self-respecting citizen should want to make a living, on the other hand it is well to remember, in this money-mad age, that the real purpose of our existence, after all, is not to make a living, but to make a life—a worthy, well-rounded, and useful life."

Mr. Rockefeller had mentioned "this money-mad age." I asked him whether the present social conditions did not make it difficult for a man to live a worthy, well-rounded, and useful life and at the same time make a living.

"Men do not live merely to work; they live also to play, to mix with their fellow-men; to love, and to worship," he replied. "To the extent that a man is free to realize the highest and best self, just to that extent is our social organization a success.

"It is only natural that evils have developed as a result of the increasing complexities in industrial conditions, but with these complexities have come new devices of progress. We cannot give up the corporation and industry on a large scale, nor can we give up the organization of labor; human progress depends too much upon them.

"Present conditions are not by any means perfect, but we shall get nowhere by going around and saying that the world is ever to be doomed to a warfare between labor and capital.

"Human nature is the same as it was years ago; there are the same cravings, the same tendencies toward sympathy when it has knowledge, and toward prejudices when it does not understand. In large part the difficulties that exist in our social state are due to nothing but misunderstanding.

"There is much talk of the opposing forces of labor and capital. To my mind they are essentially the same—human beings imbued with the same weaknesses, the same cravings, and the same aspirations.

"I do not feel that I am foolishly optimistic when I say that an age which can send moving pictures across the Atlantic through the ether will devise some means of permitting men really to see their fellow-men, to penetrate, as it were, the barriers that have grown up in our machine-burdened civilization.

"Of course I do not feel that scientific methods alone can solve our problems. There is need for spiritual assistance from a church that will promote applied, not theoretical, religion, a church with a sympathetic interest in all of the great problems of human life, in the social and moral problems, those of industry and business, the civic and educational problems; in all such as touch the life of man.

"For such a church to have real influence, denominational emphasis must be set aside. In large cities there must be conveniently located religious centers, strongly supported, and inspiring their members to participation in all community affairs. In smaller places, instead of half a dozen dying churches, competing with each other, there should be one or two churches uniting in the spiritual life of the town; this would mean economy in plant, in money, in service, and in leadership."

Several people were waiting to see Mr. Rockefeller; it was time for me to go, but before I left him there was one more question to be asked.

"Which is more difficult, making money, or spending it?"

He rose and smiled.

"Spending it," he answered. "Of course, I have never made any, but I find it very difficult to spend properly. I have no end of advice given me by people who are not directly concerned; but the very people who think it is so easy before they have the spending of it in charge are the ones most puzzled if they have an opportunity to show their ability to distribute it wisely.

"As for charity," Mr. Rockefeller concluded, "it is injurious unless it helps the recipient to become independent of it."

XXX

ONE of the greatest of the philanthropic enterprises he and his father have sponsored is the Rockefeller Institute for Medical Research which in the thirty years that it has existed has spent over forty million dollars in the service of health.

The head of that Institute is Dr. William Henry Welch. Recognized though he is by his fellow-workers, Dr. Welch is not so well known to the general public as are many other physicians. The reason for this is not hard to understand when one meets this short, square-set, energetic man who is now past eighty years old. Intensely interested in the welfare of humanity, he has been content to help without seeking applause. In the laboratory and in the classroom he has scored his triumphs and he has sought neither publicity nor gratitude. Public recognition or notice has not meant as much to him as has personal satisfaction in a job well done. He is thorough rather than spectacular, and the painstaking searching for some hidden element of truth never wins the acclaim that is accorded a lesser but more sensational endeavor.

Americans may be looked down upon by Europeans as a money-getting people with no respect for intellectual greatness, yet when I asked the taxi driver at the station in Baltimore to take me to the Welch Library, it was with an awed voice that he asked me whether I was going to call upon "the doctor himself." It was the same tone that another driver

William H. Welch

had used in Berlin when I told him to go to 6 (I think it was) Haberlandstrasse. This man had inquired, with the same mixture of awe and respect and local pride, whether I was calling on Professor Einstein.

Baltimore still retains much of its ante-bellum atmosphere; about it still cling the memories of the days when "patriotic gore" flecked its streets. Its old red brick houses with their white marble window trimmings and doorsteps look wonderfully like the backgrounds of some of Howard Pyle's Civil War drawings. It would be no surprise to see some crinoline-skirted belle with a little parasol on her arm emerge from one of them. There is a quietness about the city that is reminiscent of old world towns, and an air that is more conducive to study than one finds in most of our other cities.

Into these surroundings Dr. Welch fits remarkably well, for, in spite of years of study in the principal universities of Europe, he has managed to retain that old-fashioned attribute of neighborliness. In manner he belongs to the period when the people had family doctors who kept their instruments in back parlor closets, and who were friends as well as physicians; who, before they had prescribed anything, had instilled such a feeling of confidence that the patient began to notice an improvement; who did not hesitate to stop at the drug store to make sure the medicine would be sent in a hurry.

I caught my first glimpse of him as I got out of the taxi in front of the huge white building that bears his name and which is a fitting tribute to the man who since 1884 has been one of the leading figures in the medical school of Johns Hopkins University. Up the hill was trudging a small figure, hands clasped behind his back, with vigor and determination in his step that belied his fourscore years.

Dr. Welch carries his head to one side, giving him an inquiring look which is heightened by the keenness and alertness of his light blue eyes. His forehead is high, his jaws full and square, and he wears a sparse mustache and beard. Recognizing me by the portfolio that I carried, he led me up the broad flight of marble steps in the hall, past a bronze bust of himself, into his private office. He seated himself at his desk and took out of the drawer a huge cigar, though an intimate friend had told me that he had been ordered by a physician to stop smoking forty years ago. Into that room he seemed to have brought back with him from his numberless trips to Germany, where he studied, an air of "gemütlichkeit" that is so characteristic of the German professor. Born in Connecticut, there is no trace of the New Englander about him, and although he went to Yale and to the College of Physicians and Surgeons in New York, Strassburg and Leipzig and Breslau have apparently left more impress upon him than New Haven.

This does not imply that he seems at all foreign. He is distinctly American, but with his native Americanism is a cosmopolitanism that does not recognize boundaries. Moreover, in talking with him one immediately sees a broadness of vision and a breadth of interests that are sadly lacking in many younger men who have attained prominence in his or in other professions. This age of highly developed specialization does not make for general culture; time is too precious for young physicians to give thought to other subjects. With Dr. Welch it has been different. With a career which began as an instructor in Bellevue Medical College fifty-two years ago and which has embraced not only the founding but also the deanship of the Johns Hopkins Medical School, as well as a professorship of pathology and a directorship of its School of Hygiene and Public Health, he has managed to combine other interests.

His college work did not interfere with his being president of the Maryland State Board of Health for a quarter of a century, nor has it prevented him from giving his advice to any number of public committees. Nor has his own profession so dulled his artistic sensibilities as to close his eyes to either the beauties of nature or the appeal of art; they have not been so glued to a microscope as to make him blind to the charms of a tree or a landscape. In fact it was with difficulty that I succeeded in getting him to talk about medicine at all, so interested was he in Sargent's method of painting a portrait, for with Drs. Osler, Kelly, and Halstead he is one of the subjects in that masterpiece by Sargent, "The Four Doctors."

At last, however, he began. He leaned back in his swivel chair, his head cocked to one side; mentally and physically as alert as a man forty years his junior, he recounted the changes that had taken place since that autumn of 1871 when, after a year of teaching Latin and Greek in a school in Norwich, New York, he matriculated in a medical school.

"I was graduated in 1874," he said, "and after a year and a half at Bellevue Hospital as an interne I went abroad to complete my studies.

"At that time, you must remember, the germ theory as the cause of disease was hardly known. The entire history of medicine changed when that theory was established.

"Leaving out of account superstitious views, rational medicine during antiquity placed small importance upon contagion as compared with miasm, conveyed through the atmosphere, to account for the origin and spread of endemic and epidemic diseases. True, the Mosaic sanitary code and certain lay writers stressed contagions, but with Hippocrates and Galen and the other great doctors of those early times emphasis was laid on miasm.

"In all the years that elapsed up to the time that I was a student, it would be difficult to exaggerate the importance of this doctrine in the history of preventive and curative medicine. Indeed, it has survived up to our own time and has been displaced from its dominant position only by knowledge of the living agents of infection.

"For while contagion at last was recognized, its recognition occurred before the reason was known. As long ago as the sixteenth century an Italian physician did everything but discover that diseases were caused by living organisms. Two centuries later Jenner practiced vaccination and then came Pasteur, who was delving into the mysteries of bacteria and the processes of fermentation and putrefaction when I went to Europe. Lister immortalized his own name by applying the Frenchman's discoveries to the prevention of accidental, surgical infections even before the actual agents of these infections had been recognized."

Dr. Welch relighted his heavy black cigar and continued:

"You see I go back pretty far. Of course, I am not a contemporary of Hippocrates, nor did I have a speaking acquaintance with Galen or Francastorius, but as we look back at it now it is surprising to think of the advances in medicine since I was a student.

"The truth is that medical and sanitary science was groping in the dark before the discovery that microörganisms were the cause of infection. At last, however, the light came from the torch kindled by Pasteur. For a quarter of a century he had been laying the foundations of modern bacteriology, but he did not actually attack the problems of human infection until about the time when Koch, under whom I was studying, entered the field and introduced those technical methods which led, in that golden decade in the eighties, to that marvelous series of discoveries of the parasitic microörganisms causing cholera, tuberculosis, puerperal fever, typhoid, diphtheria, pneumonia, and other infectious diseases.

"The mauve decade, in medicine, was marked by the introduction of vaccine, serum therapy, and prophylaxis, and the exploration of the highly important domain of insect-borne diseases. The end of the last century was crowned by the discoveries of Walter Reed and the conquest of yellow fever.

"So you can see what has happened since I first took the Hippocratic vow. Bacteriology, by revealing the microörganisms concerned in those diseases which are of the greatest racial and social importance to mankind, and by providing methods for the study of their characters and behavior, transformed public health from a blundering empirical set of doctrines and practice to a science, and laid secure foundations for its further development.

"Now," he said, "that I have bored you with a history of the development of medicine and hygiene, come downstairs and I'll let you feast on one of Sargent's great masterpieces."

Downstairs trotted this little man eighty years young and, opening the door of a great room, with pride he pointed to the painting. He told me that Sargent had painted his head in one sitting, but that he had any number for one of the hands. He described how one day Sargent had walked up and down the room waving his arm and saying to himself, "This is no picture. How can I make it a picture?" And then came the idea of introducing a globe, and he asked the four doctors whether there would be an objection to that.

For a long time he told me anecdotes, and I felt that in a way he was prouder of having posed for Sargent than of being the eminent physician that he is. Then we returned to his study. On the way upstairs he stopped to show me a new statue, an antique figure of Esculapius that had just been presented to the library, and he spoke of its position in relation to the light, and the color of the marble slab that formed a background. He was interested in it, not only because it was a representation of the god of medicine, but because it was a work of art.

When we returned I suggested that he was a living proof of the falsity of the statement of his great colleague, Dr. Osler, that a man did nothing after forty.

"He did not mean that," he replied. "He was misquoted. What he meant was that every man had in him all that he would do by the time he was forty, though he might develop after that time. In other words, success might come to a man later, but that that success would be founded upon ideas which he had before he reached that age.

"However, a man cannot keep on forever. I resigned four years ago from the directorship of the School of Hygiene and Public Health. Then they made me professor of History of Medicine and I had to start this museum, so, in 1927, I went abroad again to study a similar institute in Leipzig and to buy books for the library.

"But no general rules can be laid down about individuals. I caught myself once addressing a group of young doctors and telling them that they should maintain a spirit of coöperation, and should allow nothing to divert them from their professional and scientific work. I found myself saying 'Resist the call to give general addresses, especially at a distance from home, to serve on committees, to assume time-consuming administrative duties, and to show visitors around laboratories, clinics, and buildings.' And these are the things I have done all my life."

Reverting to the subject of the change in medicine since he entered the profession, I asked him whether he thought the day of the general practitioner was over.

"Many changes have taken place," he replied. "Medicine is now as much preventive as curative. The hospital, a place that was once dreaded as a last refuge for the sick, is now looked upon as almost a necessity by those only slightly ill.

"But there is one thought that makes me look back with gratitude and love to the old-fashioned doctor. He treated people; the doctor of to-day treats a disease. The old family doctor, though he had a long beard where germs abounded, and even a spotty vest, knew his patient and in many cases the patient's family and his physical peculiarities. He did not have to jot down the antecedents or the history of a case on a card; he had it in his head and in his heart.

"If medicine were an exact science I would say: 'Yes, the family doctor has outlived his generation.' But it is not. There is something to mental healing, and the ounce of confidence which he instills often proves to be a pound of cure."

When I went downstairs he again came with me, and though the day was icy, without hat or overcoat he stood outside the door. I asked him to go in, for fear he might catch cold.

"Bother," he said, "I never catch cold."

Then he showed me where to get a taxi. As I entered it, I looked back. There he stood in the sunlight, a very small figure in front of the great monument which a grateful college has erected in his honor for the furtherance of his ideas.

XXXI

I HAD gone to Baltimore to see Dr. Welch, and from Baltimore I took the train for Washington. My work brings strange contrasts. Leaving Dr. Welch, whose life has been spent in saving lives and preserving health, I was going to the Capitol to see the Commander-in-Chief of the American Expeditionary Force.

I first met General Pershing in Paris, a Paris that was being shelled in the daytime by Big Bertha, thirty miles away, and bombed during the night by German planes. It was a sad and despondent Paris to which he had come, a confused and frightened city, where not only terrified and pale-faced children, but grown men and women rushed to safety when the sirens with melancholy wails warned of another attack from the skies.

His house was on the Left Bank, on the Rue des Varennes. It was large and furnished in rococo style, and I shall never forget my first glimpse of him as he came down the carved marble steps. The fat modeled cherubs, and the gilded wreaths with flamboyant bows of carved ribbons, the tapestry hangings and the flowered rugs, all seemed trivial and almost ludicrous in comparison with the rugged figure in khaki, which breathed business-like efficiency. There was a certain grimness about him, a determination of purpose, but withal a feeling of optimism and sincerity that made an impression which the years since have not dimmed.

Time has not changed him much. There is the same fire in his eyes, the same wrinkles of concentration above the nose. The mouth perhaps is a little more set, and the clefts on each side perhaps a little deeper.

His manner is always cordial but reserved. He is a quiet man, not given to the flare of war. Above all else he is an executive, the army is his working force, and like all working forces it must of necessity be kept fit.

No man ever headed our troops who looked more the part than he. Tall, erect, square-chinned and shouldered, he is the personification of all that a commanding officer should be. But there is a tenderness about his manner, almost a shyness, that, despite his impressive appearance, does not detract from the feeling of authority which he inspires.

There is nothing military in his present office except a bronze bust of himself in uniform and a portrait of a Revolutionary general, and as he sat before his desk in a striped suit he might have been the head of some great business.

The General is interested in art, he realizes its difficulties, and he knew that the light was so bad that it would be next to impossible to draw him where he sat, so he moved to a large chair beside the window. It was a big, heavy chair intended for lounging, but that meant nothing to him. He is one of those people who never lolls. Sitting absolutely erect, the sharp light from the high window throwing dark shadows under his brows, he recalled the first time that I had done his portrait. It was in March, 1918.

"At that time," he said, "we had but three hundred thousand men in France. My early cables had asked for one million men by that spring, to be further increased to three million. At my first conference with the Allied commanders it was

John J. Pershing

decided that a purely defensive attitude should be assumed on all secondary fronts, and that all surplus troops should be sent to the Western Front, which it was believed could be held until our forces should arrive in sufficient numbers.

"The prospects were not encouraging. All the expected shipments of men, animals, and supplies had fallen short and all construction of storehouses and railways was behind what we had hoped for.

"Secretary Baker arrived in France during that month and he and I went to the headquarters of the French army.

"On the twenty-first the great German drive began against the British right, penetrating thirty-five miles to the vicinity of Amiens. Plans for an Allied reserve had failed, and the French could ill afford to send many men from their own feeble front to check the enemy's advance.

"That was when decisive action was taken by the Allies. A commander-in-chief of all the Allied forces was appointed, the British came forward with tonnage that carried across over a million men in addition to the million sent by our own shipping, and all entered the race to reinforce the Allies before the Central Powers could force a decision.

"You remember what followed, the German attack in May which carried their line forward thirty miles, its progress suddenly stopped by two fresh American Divisions thrown in at Château Thierry and in that vicinity.

"The Prime Ministers cabled President Wilson that there was grave danger of losing the war unless the Allied inferiority in numbers could at once be remedied."

He was living those days over again. Slowly and as if he were weighing his words he recounted how by July we had one million men in France, and how he had urged that our best troops be permitted to attack the Château Thierry salient.

"On the fifteenth of July the Germans attempted to advance further at this point, and three days later the Americans and French launched a counter attack which drove the enemy behind the Aisne.

"This was the turning point of the war; from then on the initiative was with the Allies. But ultimate success required a new striking force and the moment was opportune for the formation of an independent American Army.

"After a year of the utmost insistence by the Allies that our soldiers should fill up their depleted ranks, at last in August we were able to organize an American Army, and our units were assembled to fight under our own flag."

He continued and told how in September our Army overcame the astonished Germans on the St. Mihiel salient. The American Army had become an accomplished fact and the enemy had felt its power.

Then came the Argonne offensive and at last the cutting of the German line of communications at Sedan and the Armistice.

"Yes," he said, "twelve years have passed, but I can still see our men in memory as they move forward in battle, eager, resolute, courageous. They did not count the cost, but each one thought only of his task."

He looked at me, and perhaps I imagined that there was a watery film over his eyes.

"If ever men were unselfish, if ever any died that others might honorably live, if ever war was pursued that peace might reign, it was during that time of untold sorrow when France was a modern Calvary.

"Coming from patriotic homes, those men were filled with a deep sense of responsibility, and they proved that a pacific spirit and a sense of justice had not weakened their virility or their courage.

"They showed that initiative and energy are as essential in the test of war as in the pursuit of peace. They vied with their Allied comrades in tenacity and valor.

"No army ever entered a war at a more critical period and none ever acquitted itself more nobly."

The talk then turned to the present revival of interest in the war and the publication of a number of war novels.

"Many of them that I have read," he said, "give a true picture of the horrors and sufferings that take place in the trenches. But with all its futile desolation the rack and ravage of war fall most heavily upon women and children. No one, especially one who has been in close contact with war, ever wants to see another. It is, however, not the man in the trenches alone who is the sufferer in the army. There is something worse than physical pain. There is the dread and awful responsibility that rests on those in command, and when I say this I am not minimizing in any way the horrors endured by the enlisted men. There were times when it was necessary to send half-trained boys into action, and it is a question as to who suffered more, the men who led or the boys who followed.

"Think of the feelings of a man who gives a command which he knows will make hundreds of widows and orphans. It must be done and in him is vested the terrible authority which when exercised, he knows, will not only cut off in the flower of their manhood untold numbers of his boys, but leave in its wake, weary, helpless and lonely women and children."

The General got up. For a few minutes he walked up and down his office. The silence could almost be heard. What thoughts were running through his head were his own. He sighed and again sat down for me to continue my drawing. I hesitated to talk.

At last I ventured, "Was it all worth while?"

"It is up to the world to-day to make that peace for which they fought as secure as anything human can be made. The outcome rests in the hands of those who are now charged with directing the affairs of nations.

"The broadening facilities of intercommunication, the exchange of friendly visits, the increasing coöperation among nations in finance and government, the favorable growth of public opinion among friends and former foes are all working together to create an international relationship of common understanding and good will."

"What about the League of Nations?" I asked.

"That is all right for European nations," he replied, "but we were very wise to keep out of it. There are many questions involved in European politics which do not affect us and it would be foolish for us to become mixed up in petty quarrels in which we have no concern.

"The United States showed during the last war that it did not need either treaties or signed agreements to make it do what is its moral duty. We recognize our obligations and we are in a better position to carry them out when we have nothing to limit our actions. With no secret understandings with any nation we entered a war to help those countries which we felt were fighting for the right. Removed from Europe, so that we can see things in their proper perspective, we shall always be in a position to act in a way that will be of most assistance to the progress of the world at large.

"I cannot state too strongly how I feel in this matter, and how much better it is for this country, not for itself alone, but also for the future of peace throughout the world, to have refused to become a member of the League."

I suggested that European ideas had changed since the war.

"All ideas have changed," he replied, "ideas of war and ideas of peace. The fallacious notion that war is an essential element of the national policy of government, and the erroneous belief that nations become great through aggressive undertakings carried on regardless of right and justice have always existed. Against such views the reasonings of cabinets and the creations of ententes have shown themselves powerless. The war showed that the expansion of any modern civilized nation at the expense of another cannot be permanent.

"In the future, nations that attempt to achieve greatness through unjust aggression are certainly going to incur the active hostility of all others. It would incur our hostility just as much though we do not belong to the League of Nations, as if we did."

"And what is the prospect of a lasting peace?" I asked.

"In order to make a lasting peace still more probable the leading civilized powers have agreed among themselves to the general principle of the elimination of war as an avowed instrument of national policy. This agreement need not interfere with the necessities for reasonable armament. For there may occur here and there armed rebellion against constituted authority, or crimes against international obligations.

"With the cultivation of friendly relations and good will toward one another, any differences between nations that may arise which cannot be readily adjusted will naturally be settled by arbitration.

"On the other hand, if, despite this agreement, some nations continue to accept war as essential to national policy, we must be prepared to see the most advanced peoples engaging in periodic wars of destruction in which future generations will suffer the same hideous loss of human life that we have suffered."

On the wall of General Pershing's present office hangs a portrait of Lincoln. He turned to it.

"Do you remember his words?" he asked. "'The better angels of our natures might be touched by the mystic chord of memory extending from every battlefield and every grave to every living heart and every hearth stone.'

"This prayer we have lived to see fulfilled here in our country. The bitterness and hatred that incited brothers to take up arms against each other has vanished.

"What we have accomplished in America between the different sections of the country is possible to exist between nations.

"If the people of the countries in the late war sincerely wish for peace, and to my mind there is not the slightest doubt of that, then there is hope that with old enmities already almost forgotten our former enemies will live in peaceful and profitable relationship."

XXXII

Very different in make-up and temperament from the head of the American Army in France is another general who also played an important part in the World War. There is nothing conventional about Charles G. Dawes. From the time he first took office as vice president and startled the country, and incidentally the Senate, by attempting to dust the cobwebs of senatorial procedure, down to the present day, no one has known what he would do next. Unawed by ceremony, he has seen fit to speak when he has felt the occasion demanded plain words. That is his nature. The result is that the country did not forget that it had a vice president nor what his name was. Dawes's personality rose above the office.

The sandy-haired, rosy-cheeked, kindly, fighting man could not help doing things. His vitality and nervous energy are all-pervasive. A student of history, he laughs at tradition; a philosopher by nature, he turns to material things; a musician by inclination, he becomes a leading financier; a conservative in business, he does not hesitate to propose radical changes.

He posed for me while he was vice president. His room adjoined the Senate Chamber. Its walls and ceilings were decorated with scrolls and shields. In the center was a large mahogany desk above which hung a huge crystal chandelier. Facing the entrance was a gilt-framed mirror above a white marble fireplace, while to the right hung a portrait of Washington painted by Rembrandt Peale, and to the left a huge closet from which, so the story goes, Andrew Johnson took his spiritual support before he was sworn in as president. It was in this room that Henry Wilson, Vice President under Grant, died. Here General Dawes, seated behind his desk, his underslung pipe in his mouth, posed and talked as I drew his portrait.

General Dawes likes to philosophize on life in general. To him people and their actions form a panorama from which he formulates theories. Intensely human and practical, he studies the lights and shades of human history. Archæology interests him and he reads much ancient history, but his researches into the past are translated into the present. Extremely characteristic of him is the fact that during the war, while he was in charge of purchasing the army's supplies, he spent much of his little spare time in the Louvre among Greek and Roman sculpture. Here was a Chicago banker, who had introduced business methods into an army, devoting his leisure to the study of ancient art.

It is difficult to get him to speak about himself. When I asked him to, he laughed and said he would not. "It reminds me too much of when I was young," he said, "and some little one-horse journal would come around and ask for your life's history and incidentally tell you that it was going to cost you thirty-five dollars to have it published."

It is useless to try to direct General Dawes's talk into preconceived channels. He speaks so quickly that at times it is hard to catch all he says, and he thinks so quickly that the association of ideas is not always evident, with the result that he appears to jump from one subject to another with no apparent connection.

Charles G. Dawes

In the same way that I found no opportunity to ask him certain questions I had in mind, his drawing turned out as he wanted, not as I had planned. He has been photographed so often with his pipe that I had determined not to introduce it in my drawing. But that pipe never left his mouth for more than a minute or two the entire time I was with him.

The subject of the World War was brought up. I asked him to tell me something of his work in it.

"What do I know about the war?" he said. "Ask the boys who were in the trenches. My job over there was a prosaic piece of business. General Pershing made me the head of a board of ten officers representing all the purchasing departments of our army and also the General Purchasing Agent in Europe for the A. E. F. That, of course, gave me unlimited discretion and authority to devise a system of coördination of purchases and while much depended upon this work it was, after all, a business proposition pure and simple. This purchasing of supplies in Europe worked out to be a much bigger thing than we expected, for two-thirds of the entire tonnage consumed by our army was obtained in Europe.

"But the things that I did in the war are not the things I remember best. In all the reviews, celebrations, and gatherings that I have attended since the war the picture in my mind has been what went on to make them possible, and I have wondered whether the millions buried in the wheat fields of northern France knew of them.

"Have you ever thought what is behind those boys who stand lonely in those front-line trenches, waiting for they don't know what? There they stand, the new frontiers of a country. Behind them, pushing irresistibly forward, are all the forces that a civilized country can muster—its ingenuity, its wealth, its resources, its man power. Think of those boys out in the observation posts, miles from home, of those that fall so that the overpowering force behind can advance."

"And was it all worth it?" I asked.

"Now this is getting too much like an interview," he replied. "I have been reading Hadley's 'History of the Roman Empire.' After Cæsar's death, and with it the end of the great wars, there were wrangling and uncertainty for six years. Finally Octavius became Augustus and the reaction of humanity after one hundred years of terrible warfare throughout the civilized world brought a peace unbroken for two hundred years. That gives us hopes, to say the least.

"But, irrespective of all other results, those boys who were in the army did learn one thing at least, and that is respect for authority. Now I for one believe that authority can best be maintained when fortified by reason. The officer must command the respect of his men, he must be obeyed by them; but in my opinion the officer who at times explains what seems to be an unreasonable order is more apt to be obeyed blindly when the occasion demands than he who treats his men like unreasoning automatons. And in this way authority commands respect.

"Of course it is essential that the authority of officers be preserved. That's the reason they have set rules for the method of communication between privates and the higher officers. For, believe me, if there were too much rubbing of elbows between officers and men it would soon be discovered that there were many captains who should be in shirt sleeves and many men in shirt sleeves who should be captains.

"When Napoleon sent his brother Joseph to Italy in command of an army, he said, 'Hold no council of war.' He knew his brother's shortcomings. Mediocrity requires aloofness to preserve its dignity. Genius alone can afford to mingle. In fact, it loves to mix in order to demonstrate its superiority. In spite of all that has been said to the contrary, it doesn't like to hide its light under a bushel. The man who paints or writes superlatively does not destroy his efforts after he has accomplished them. Say what you want, he loves public appreciation.

"This does not mean that geniuses alone want approbation, or that they are unique in desiring to show their abilities. The superbly ignorant resemble them in this.

"And," he continued, with a twinkle in his eyes and a look, as I thought, in the direction of the Senate Chamber, "if combined with ignorance there is sufficient impudence, success sometimes results. In fact, a book on the success of ignorance could be filled with notable examples. Remember that if the empty vessel makes the greatest sound, then the empty vessel is bound to be heard.

"Together with ignorance goes desire for ceremony which, while more or less necessary in army life, is not so requisite in times of peace. Of course the value of ceremony as a social power is unquestioned. It cannot be dispensed with without destroying one of the useful agencies of governmental and social discipline. At times the individual must use ceremony as the best means to noble ends. But to my way of thinking it is well to beware of too much ceremony, whether it is directed toward the submerging or toward the exploitation of the individual.

"Here I sit in an office that has the halo of tradition. Outside are officers and what not. A certain amount of scenery and stage setting are essential to give the office—not me, mind you—its proper importance. My title is Mr. Vice President, but do you suppose it makes any difference to me personally how I am addressed? To my friends I am Charlie, but to others, whether I am General or Mr. Vice President is unimportant. After all, a title is a handle. If I don't count without that title, I am not a bit better with it."

While he was talking, softly from another part of the Capitol came the strains of a military band; through the open door were heard Civil War melodies. Later I discovered it was the ceremony attendant on the return to some of the southern states of flags captured by State of Maine troops during the Civil War. General Dawes heard the music.

"Have you noticed," he asked, "the effect of music upon soldiers? I remember when we first landed in England. We reached Borden at eleven o'clock at night. The men had had only a sandwich each at noon. It was cold, dark, and rainy. And then occurred a demonstration of the reviving effect of music, for there appeared to lead us to camp a British band. It played American marches and airs as we marched in the dark and it meant much to all of us—that we were welcome, that we amounted to something.

"The following day London greeted us. We were the first American troops to pass through the British capital, but I think that our men were not so uplifted as when we marched along that lonely road, hungry, at the end of a weary day, to the tunes of our homeland.

"Aside from the rhythm, the association of ideas with music plays an important part in its effect. I was at a review of a Scottish brigade by Marshal Haig. And when the bagpipes struck up 'The Campbells Are Coming' it was not those magnificent and battle-worn troops that I saw. It was the Sixth Wisconsin Volunteer Infantry marching down the

Emmitsburg Road on that second of July in 1863 with my father at their head, his fife and drum corps playing the same air; for all my life I had heard that this was the tune they had played as they advanced at Gettysburg."

Realizing that music had meant much in his life, I asked General Dawes where and when he had studied it.

"I never studied at all," he replied. "You see, my parents were afraid I might become a musician, with the result that they would never allow me to take lessons. And when I say that I never studied I mean that I never received any instruction in any instrument. I always loved music and what little I know I taught myself. The flute is the smallest of all instruments, so it was the easiest to smuggle into my room, and then, too, it is not as noisy as most others, so it was the one I learned to play.

"When I grew up I made a lot of friends among musicians and for years a number of them came to my house in Chicago and we had trios, quartets and quintets, in which I often played a part."

"What about your 'Melody in A Major'?" I asked.

"When I wrote that, I created for myself no end of trouble, and it is always bobbing up to confront me. One of the musicians who used to come to my house very frequently was Francis Macmillen, the violinist. I got this tune in my head and I set it down and he used to play it. I never gave the thing a name. Some publishers heard him and wrote to me asking if they might publish it. Like a fool, I said 'yes.'

"Shortly after this I was walking down State Street and happened to look into a music shop. Imagine my feelings when I discovered not only the window filled with copies of it, but my name plastered on the glass in large letters.

"Here was I, presumably a perfectly sane and respectable banker, turning out tunes. I feared that my friends would say that if all my notes were as bad as my musical ones, they were not worth the paper they were written on.

"Later on I went to hear a concert by Kreisler and on looking through the program what should I discover but that he had selected it as one of his numbers. Now I am not going to deny that I was pleased, particularly when afterward I made inquiries and learned he had picked it out without knowing who was the author."

XXXIII

IN THAT distant day before General Dawes was consorting with royalty, one Herbert Hoover was Secretary of Commerce in President Coolidge's Cabinet. That was when I first met him. His house was on S. Street, a few doors from where President Wilson lived and died, and he had asked me to breakfast with him so we could get to work early on the drawing which I wanted to do.

I remember distinctly my first glimpse of him. He was standing with a long stick in his hands beside a pool of goldfish in the grounds behind his house. Some dead leaves had dropped into the water and he was trying to get them out. A cool wind was blowing as he turned to greet me and I particularly noticed that one lock of smoothed hair had broken loose from the rest and drooped low over his forehead.

He looked up from underneath his brows, a fairly heavy man with an almost awkward smile. His handshake is soft, repressed, and his voice gives evidence of the same restraint. Punctiliously polite, he is cordial without being effusive. There is a reticence about him that it is difficult to overcome, a reserve that appears impossible to penetrate.

His niece was stopping with him at the time and we three ate together. His manner with her was as detached as with me. Over the strawberries and the bacon and scrambled eggs the conversation was impersonal, almost forced. A great police dog which sat beside him alone broke the formality. Unawed by conventions, he rested his fore legs on the Secretary's chair and begged for bacon. The young woman left—she was going to school—and on her departure we talked of the younger generation. It was then that his eyes, ordinarily cold, assumed a kindlier look. And yet, despite a certain sympathetic interest, one instinctively felt it was the problem that was absorbing, rather than people. Rationally he could understand, emotionally they were as far away as the dinosaurs.

"The great difficulty in education," he explained, "is how much to leave to choice and how much to prescribe. As a member of the Board of Trustees at Leland Stanford I have often run up against that question. Are our young people securing at the colleges as well-rounded an education as in the days when specialization was not the order?

"Some of our students make a point of picking out easy courses; others, thinking that their lives will run along certain lines, specialize in such studies as they believe will aid them. After they have graduated they change their minds and are left without the benefits of a general education. More and more I have noticed that our colleges are turning out specialists rather than scholars.

"Of course I realize that the old system whereby a student, no matter what his bent, was compelled to take certain studies in which he had no interest, and for which he would have no further use, also had its faults. It is only by a compromise that the advantages of both systems can be retained."

We had gone into the living room and there by a window the future president sat smoking a large black cigar while I made my drawing. He had shown me a portrait of himself which his wife liked and which had been painted some years before,

Herbert Hoover

and he had cautioned me not to make him look like a Mellin's Food baby in my drawing.

It was in my meeting with him before he became president that I feel that I got to know Mr. Hoover best, if indeed one may say that he got to know him at all. For about him is a curtain of secretiveness that in more or less casual meetings precludes any deep insight into the man.

Mr. Coolidge has the reputation of being more or less of an enigma; his silence has been stressed ever since he first entered public life. Yet that silence is eloquent compared to Mr. Hoover's speech. There is a ruggedness and spiciness about the New Englander that lend color to his actions as well as his personality; there is a positiveness even in his most ambiguous statements that convinces one that he knows his own mind. Mr. Hoover has none of these assertive traits. He appears to lack color, and it is this fact which makes it difficult for the White House correspondents, some of whom have filled the same post during three or four administrations, to send interesting stories concerning him to their papers.

Several drives through the city of Washington with the then Secretary of Commerce come to mind. On one of them he was much pleased because Congress had voted him a new car without question while there had been opposition to other members of the Cabinet having theirs replaced. At another time we were speaking of the Mississippi flood which had just about that time subsided. From the topic of floods the conversation turned to that of earthquakes and hurricanes. It was then that he made a remark which has always stuck in my memory, and which to me revealed the man. I shall not attempt to give his exact words but the gist of them was that up to the present, the power of our tall skyscrapers to withstand either a convulsion of the earth or a terrific windstorm was unknown. And he expressed a keen interest in what would happen should either of these cataclysms overwhelm a city. What particularly struck me at the time was the cold engineering question which he puzzled over; the other results of such a catastrophe apparently did not concern him at all.

And yet it was as a humanitarian that Mr. Hoover first made his reputation. But as one sees him and speaks with him, as one begins to realize his approach to any question it becomes more and more evident that he is above all else an engineer, and that even when he sat distributing food to the people of Belgium, he would not permit his feelings to be touched. He acted as if it were a question involving fuel for furnaces rather than sustenance for the starving.

This does not mean that he does not feel keenly; it implies rather that he keeps his feelings in the background, almost as if he were ashamed of being human. But when it is remembered that as a ragged boy he worked his way through school and college, that his student romance with Lou Henry culminated in his marriage, it seems certain that but few people know the real Herbert Hoover.

Before he became president he told me that the only exercise which he took was standing before the window and inhaling deeply a number of times. Since he has been in the White House his daily bouts with the medicine ball have been added. But the life of a president is confining, and before Mr. Hoover entered public office his profession had kept him much in the open.

Seven o'clock has long been his rising hour. It is interesting to learn that he shaves himself with a safety razor, and a little before eight he comes downstairs, but prefers to walk rather than use the elevator.

The presidential menu does not vary. It consists of fruit, bacon and scrambled eggs, and one cup of coffee. Unlike his predecessor his first meal of the day has not assumed great importance. In fact, he seems in a hurry to have done with it in order to have his first cigar, which incidentally is large and heavy.

Mentioning this cigar again brings Mr. Coolidge to mind. He invariably clipped the end of his cigar with a knife or a cutter and carefully adjusted it in a pasteboard and quill holder. Mr. Hoover squeezes off the end of his with his nails and puts the cigar itself in his mouth.

By nine o'clock each morning he is seated in front of his mahogany desk in the executive office going over the mail which requires immediate attention. When he has read this he begins to dictate his replies. He does this slowly and evenly. Trained in method, he usually knows exactly what he is going to say before he says it, and it is not often that he asks his stenographer to repeat what has been said.

If he is redrafting a paper which has already been typed he hardly ever looks up from it, but with a pencil in hand, he will note the changes on the first draft as he makes them to his stenographer. Should a question of fact in the matter arise, instead of noting it for future corroboration, or disproof, he sends immediately for the person who can supply the correct information.

At one o'clock he goes to luncheon. While he was Secretary of Commerce he often ate at his desk where sandwiches and milk and peanuts, of which he is extremely fond, were the menu. Since he became president this meal is taken at the

White House and is of a more substantial character and often guests are present.

He is back again in his office at two and from then until four he sees people with whom he has appointments. After that he is again with his secretaries and continues dictation.

He likes to leave his office by six, but this is not always possible. However, at seven-thirty he dines and when there are no visitors this meal is served in the small colonial dining room. He is neither a fussy nor a large eater, and when he is particularly rushed he eats most sparingly.

Ten-thirty is his usual retiring time, and only important matters will keep him up past that hour. It is then that he goes to his own room to read for a time in bed the latest detective story upon which he can lay his hands.

Despite the tax that has been put upon him Mr. Hoover looks better now than when he was running for the presidency. I remember going to see him while he was campaigning and he was thin and appeared very worried. He posed for me the first day he was in office and the appreciation of the heavy responsibilities that he knew were in store for him showed itself on his face.

At most times he is very serious looking and it would be difficult to imagine him ever laughing uproariously; that is not his nature. His humor is distinctly a mental process; the slightest distortion of a fact would spoil any joke for him. On the other hand he is shrewd in his observations. On one occasion he was speaking about the changes that had come over Washington.

"The so-called Cliff Dwellers," he said, "the old families who have been here for years, are rapidly dying out. A new society is taking their place. Now when any man makes a lot of money in a small town, let us say Podunk, he immediately buys a house in Washington. Through his business interests he gets a letter of introduction to his Senator and to the representative of his district. He is invited to semi-public functions and his wife joins some literary clubs and in a comparatively short time they are members of the new social class which is in evidence here."

He did not say this in any spirit of criticism. It was a simple statement of facts, and yet though he did not mention it, it was evident that he was amused by the entry of small town manners in the capital of the country. In a way the subject seemed one that Sinclair Lewis would delight to write about. For undoubtedly Babbitt in Washington would give him another opportunity for a display of fireworks and would cause as much discussion as when he hurled a bombshell into that long thoroughfare which wends its way from New York to San Francisco and passes through Gopher Prairie, Zenith and hundreds of other towns of similar character—a bombshell which rattled the cans on the grocery store shelves of Ole Jensen and the windows in the emporium known as the Bon Ton Store.

XXXIV

IT WAS years and years ago that I first met Sinclair Lewis. At a typical Greenwich Village party his brilliant conversation made such a deep impression that although there were a number of other guests I remember none of them except him.

Sophisticate and satirist though he is, Sauk Center, Minnesota, where he was born, has left an indelible mark upon him. Tall, red-faced, red-haired, with very blue eyes, in all his awkward movements and almost jackknife-like poses, he reminds one of a freckle-faced boy with a broad grin in a Briggs cartoon.

It was the day after he was notified of the award of the Nobel Prize that I made my sketch of him.

As he leaned back on a sofa, or nervously jumped up and walked around the room, shortly after he had heard of the award, protesting that prizes meant nothing, that he was just a writing man, that he wrote as well last year as he did now, I could not help feeling that all this was an innate modesty and shyness—a self-depreciation of the country boy—and that away down in the bottom of his heart Babbitt himself could not have been more pleased had he been voted the best citizen of Zenith.

But the personalities of authors are often the antithesis of their writings. Mark Twain seemed to be rather acrid and sour; the sardonic Shaw is sweet and kindly and, indeed,

Sinclair Lewis

somewhat like a lovable old Santa Claus; and here was Lewis, who laughs loudly at mankind, decrying the value of prizes, and at the same time trying to learn Swedish so that he would be able to make a reply in that language when he received the award in Stockholm.

Indeed, his entire personality is apparently a mass of contradictions. He scorns patriotism and declares that America is the only country in the world in which he cares to live; and, while he said this, he showed me his old passport and expressed his anxiety to get abroad again as soon as possible. He laughs at sentiment but a great part of his conversation was about his wife and his son, Mickey. He has made fun of the Babbitts and, at the same time, he has no use for the ill-kempt superior souls who sit around bare tables in Greenwich Village discussing art—an aversion for which one might find an explanation in his own Greenwich Village days and his heritage of Sauk Center morality.

His father was the doctor of the town, which may account both for Kennicott in "Main Street" and for Arrowsmith. When he was seven years old he determined to be a writer, for he had been impressed by the respect and awe with which the village editor was regarded. When he was fourteen he wrote his first story, but it was four years later before he succeeded in selling any of his work. That was when he was attending Yale, where he wrote poetry and short stories for the college magazine, and gained a reputation for being a good—and tireless—talker.

After three years at New Haven, Lewis left to join that strange colony which Upton Sinclair founded in New Jersey; he became the furnaceman of Helicon Hall—for every member of the colony was assigned to some form of menial labor—and this job gave him plenty of leisure for writing. It is not hard to imagine the effect this communistic experiment had upon a youth from Minnesota whose outstanding experience with a radical up to that time had been an association with his Sauk Center tutor, who, though an Episcopalian clergyman, had had the temerity to preach evolution to a body of Fundamentalists. When he tired of Helicon Hall Lewis came to New York and lived in a tenement in the gas house district.

A trip to Panama, and a final year at Yale followed, and then he became a reporter for an Iowa paper. This job did not last long, and for a number of years he drifted about, selling a story here and there, and working as a reporter, reader, or publicity man in various parts of the country. Then he became advertising manager of a publishing house. By this time, he had written three novels, which, although they had fair success, gave no hint of his later point of view. Then came "Main Street."

"So you see," he said, as he leaned back in his chair, his lean legs crossed and his hands clasped behind the back of his head, "I have had a varied life and the twenty-seven years that have passed since I sold my first story have been filled with pretty hard work at a tough game. And a lot of the time I had to do stuff that I hated."

There is nothing dignified about Lewis. The humor of most dignity appeals to him too much to permit him to assume it. Indeed, about him is something of the actor, and when I asked him what had happened to Main Street in the last ten years, he immediately became the inhabitant of a small town boasting of its progress.

"Gosh," he said, "you wouldn't know the place, its so changed. Remember the mud? Well it's all paved now, right out past the city limits. And the trolley cars have gone. Yes, sir! We had them all ripped up and the most comfortable buses you ever rode in pass through our city every half hour.

"When you first knew the street half of it was filled with story-and-a-half wooden buildings. You won't find one of them left.

"Remember the Minniemashie House? Tall, lean structure, three stories of yellow wood. They covered it with stucco and made a regular hotel out of it. Tiled linoleum on the floor and not a brass cuspidor in sight. And that dirty old dining room with the soiled tablecloths and the catsup bottles? It has been turned into part cafeteria and part dining room with glass-covered tables.

"Dave Dyer sold his drug store to a chain outfit, and I'll bet you neither St. Paul nor Minneapolis can boast of a better place.

"Of course, the saloons are gone. They were a disgrace to any self-respecting village. Oh, yes, we have got a couple of speakeasies in their place, but they are so dirty that no decent citizen likes to be seen in them. We have our stuff in our homes or else in the lockers at the golf club.

"I don't think we had a golf course when you were there. We laid that out shortly after prohibition came in. But there wasn't anything else for us to do when they closed the bar at the Minniemashie House. By the way, the name of it was changed to the Harding, but that only lasted for a year or two; now it's called Gopher Mansion. They decided it was a little risky naming it again after a president.

"And then, there's the Bon Ton Store. Haydock and Simons owned it ten years ago. Well, do you remember the little errand boy, Ikey? He bought them out and enlarged it so that you wouldn't know it."

And he continued, jokingly describing the architectural changes that had occurred in the decade that had passed since he immortalized the principal highway of any small town.

"But speaking seriously," he continued, "even if these changes have taken place, Main Street is still Main Street and will always be so. For essentially and basically Main Street is also Broadway. Indeed, I am beginning to wonder if it is not also Unter den Linden and the Avenue de l'Opéra and Regent Street.

"Of course, Main Street is progressing, but so are Broadway and all of the other streets in the world, and there have been on it just as many changes, comparatively speaking, as there have been on Regent Street.

"Though the people of the world vary in certain characteristics, essentially they are the same. The only difference between the Babbitts in this country and those in France is that over there they wear gray silk gloves. I have seen them and heard them in England too. Shell spectacles are not a part of their make-up, but in many an English town I have met good, hearty British Babbitts whose conversation, apart from its pronunciation, might be duplicated in any Kiwanis luncheon in Iowa or gathering of Lions in Kansas."

"Has Babbitt changed much also?"

"Of course, he has. Do you think that he has any sympathy with Vergil Gunch who wastes his time reading detective stories? No, sir, not he. Of course, business had been going along well until the slump—and he has some definite ideas on how that could have been avoided—but the trouble has been right along that he has only been able to give about two or three hours of his time to mental diversion. But there's nothing he likes better than to get into an easy chair, with his slippers on, and after he has lighted his cigar with his patent lighter—which he now fills with jelly instead of fluid—to get deep into a good biography. And of course he keeps the radio going all the time. But he keeps it down low unless there's something good on.

"But you know," he continued, "despite all the changes. there was something present ten or fifteen years ago that is lacking to-day. There was a certain pioneer spirit in those days. Of course, as far as churchgoing was concerned they had narrow ideas. If you did not attend an evangelical church every Sunday, the opinion was that you ought to be lynched. On the other hand, there were a certain juice and zest that are lacking to-day. There's more talk about automobiles and the radio and what proportion of water to use, but there's less conversation. People are not interested as much in scandals or politics or abstractions as they were.

"The old pioneers have gone. They have been replaced by people who own bathtubs and sedans and limousines, strange glass-topped porch furniture, even speed boats and country homes—people who are determined that these things shall not be endangered by the success of radical theories and who are more interested in them than in mere speculation on the soul of man.

"This is an age of radio, of the talkies, where religion is road paving, patriotism the relation of weather to Sunday morning, when 'contract' is discussed with a sanctified fervor, and when even the sky is becoming cluttered with airplanes.

"This is an age of industrialism. But one must recognize its supremacy to-day or else be submerged. Main Street recognizes it and so does Babbitt. They have to."

He got up, and strode across the room with his hands in his pockets.

"But this age will pass just as the others have. People will come to resent having an entire evening spoiled by the boom of a dynamic speaker and hearing morons bawl out idiotic banalities. I have faith that the very passion in the worship of the Great God Industrialism, together with his attendant deities, will bring its own reaction. Even Babbitt progresses, and his grandsons will laugh at his gods much as he does at the chin whiskers of the Smith Brothers."

"Then you have hope for the country?" I asked.

"Hope? I should say I have. It's the greatest country in the world, and its people have the greatest potentialities."

So, fearing that Mr. Lewis would sing "The Star-Spangled Banner," I left.

XXXV

IT WAS some time after I had seen Lewis that in a conversation with Gilbert K. Chesterton the subject of Main Street came up. The ponderous Englishman at once took issue with the picture as drawn by the vitriolic American.

"When the pioneers of this country started westward," he said, "they traveled in covered wagons with closed minds.

"The Puritan is likely to be a fanatic. He believes in the simplicity of human nature. If there is any defect he thinks he can find one thing to cure it. He does not realize either the complexity of the world or the complexity of human nature.

"He suddenly decides that drink is the cause of much misery and he promptly adopts prohibition as a panacea for all ills. When by chance, prosperity, as a result of a thousand and one causes, strikes your land after the adoption of this evil, he promptly attributes the prosperity to the measure which he has adopted for the spiritual welfare of mankind. But when prosperity departs he does not blame it on what he considered its cause. He promptly goes looking around for another remedy.

"In other words, he is by nature a professional reformer, and is constantly looking for ways to improve the world. When he walks along Main Street he is not willing to accept what he can see. Behind the attractive grocery stores he goes rummaging among the packing boxes and crates, finding a spiritual pleasure in discovering rotten fruit and spoiled olives. He is more gratified by finding one potato with an ulcer than a bushel of them without any. For that is something for him to reform.

"Indeed," he went on with a chuckle, "I feel that it is that Puritanic idea of reformation that has played a large part in Mr. Lewis's writings. He has tried to delve behind the scenes on Main Street, but all that he has found were ulcers on potatoes. The real motives, the simple but full lives of these people have escaped him, at any event he has endeavored to improve and reform them.

"The antimacassar on the back of a fine old chair has blinded him to the beauty of the lines of the furniture. In his way I find him much like the lady who was trying to bring Ibsen to Main Street, except he is trying to bring Mencken there. And I am not sure were he to succeed whether the people would laugh more at Mencken or Mencken at the people."

The first time I met Chesterton was in London. I had an appointment to draw him, and instead of going out to his country home he had suggested that I make the sketch in the office of G. K.'s *Weekly*. In spite of his detective stories, he had always seemed to me a survival of the literary man of the eighteenth century. Reynolds's portrait of Johnson always substituted itself in my mind's eye for his photograph; and in his work, in spite of a certain modernity, I could always detect the guiding hands of Addison and Steele.

I had walked down the Strand from Trafalgar Square. It is one of the ugliest streets in the world, a battlefield on which the ghostly forces of Victoria are just beginning to give way before an army of modernists. In the chemist shops, in the tobacconists, and behind the red velvet sofas in dingy hotels,

Gilbert K. Chesterton

the specters of Victorianism still cluster, but the hands of the wreckers are fast dislodging them.

Down past Aldwych I strolled, longing for a little bit of the London of Johnson, or even Dickens, and turned sharp right into Essex Street. I was looking for No. 20, and came to a stop before a structure some six stories high, such as any Main Street over forty years of age might contain.

To find the successor of Dr. Johnson in an office building was, to say the least, disconcerting, for associations do count, and to transplant an eighteenth century character into a mid-Victorian surrounding was difficult. When I did find his office, I felt as if I had been transported back about a hundred years.

It is a dirty office and very small. An appalling amount of material is crowded into one small room. Against two walls are high book shelves filled with papers, while two large walnut tables covered with what at one time was green oilcloth, are burdened with files of memoranda. An old letterpress, a pitcher and basin in the corner, wastebaskets full of pamphlets, all add their touches of character, and had Ebenezer Scrooge walked out from one of the two doors that led to other rooms he would have been as much a part of the picture as was the fat boy in a much worn coat who sat at the table opposite the door.

As I entered, he was leaning far over the table, licking postage stamps. In front of him were thousands of large envelopes, at his elbow were sheets of stamps. He stopped his performance to say that Mr. Chesterton had not arrived, handed me a current number of the publication, and went back to his task. First he licked a stamp, then he placed it on an envelope, then he pounded it with his other hand to make it stick, then another lick, another envelope, and so on, quite mechanically.

How long I sat fascinated I do not know, but I was awakened from reverie by heavy footsteps outside, the quick opening of the entrance door, and the appearance of a large, heavy-breathing man, who made everything in the room, including the fat boy, dwindle into insignificance.

He muttered something about being sorry that he was late and walked rapidly into his own room, followed by the fat boy, who quickly returned and ushered me into G. K's sanctuary.

The first thing that strikes one about Chesterton is his abounding good nature. The complexion of a baby, wavy blond hair, a drooping reddish brown mustache, kindly blue eyes, all contribute to this impression. He was sitting, as I entered the room, at the head of another long office table. Behind him was a tall bookcase filled with many books, principally paper covered ones, and this room, like the outer office, presented the same picture of absolute disorder. Papers were strewn everywhere, the furniture was old and worn, and Chesterton, sitting there in the midst of this chaos, immediately brought to mind Johnson sitting in much the same kind of room writing furiously in order to finish "Rasselas" and thereby be enabled to pay his mother's funeral expenses. The atmosphere was intensified when, looking through the window, I caught a glimpse of the old Temple, very little changed in all these years, and realized that within a stone's throw was Goldsmith's grave.

"I want to apologize for this office," said Mr. Chesterton, "it is not much of a place compared to what American publications have in the way of editorial rooms. It must seem very small and stuffy to you."

But I assured him that it was exactly the kind of place I had hoped to find in London, but up to then had not found.

"In fact," I said, "it is precisely the setting in which I could picture Dr. Johnson."

"Yes," he began, "it is an old-fashioned place, and it is in the very neighborhood in which Johnson lived. He worshiped at St. Clement's and that is the reason they put up that statue to him over there behind the church; and a strange statue it is to put up to Johnson. If he was one thing, he was a big man, and in the shadow of that church he is absolutely dwarfed, and that Johnson never was."

Chesterton's voice is pitched high, and as he talks he draws in his breath with almost a whistling noise conveying a certain self-appreciation of his own remarks. He smiles often, disclosing a missing front tooth in his lower jaw, which intensifies the impression of absolute disregard of personal appearance.

Leaving Johnson, he talked about himself and his journalistic experiences.

"A week after I had left Warsaw that great political crime, the murder of the Bolshevists, occurred," he said. "I have had this strange experience a number of times. Invariably I leave a place of interest just before it becomes really interesting. In the first days of the Zionist quarrel in Jerusalem, I saw the mobs gathering and heard the cries against the Jews; but the first real riots broke out a few days after my departure. Just after I left Madrid things began to happen there; and while I was away from London and trying in vain to get back, even more interesting things happened here. This may sometimes be a relief to a humanitarian, but it is something of a tragedy to a journalist."

I began talking about the interest in spiritualism as one of the results of the war and asked Chesterton how he accounted for Conan Doyle having embraced it.

"To my mind Doyle hit the bull's-eye when he wrote the Sherlock Holmes stories," he said. "He was very successful with them and as people liked them he kept turning them out. He turned out many, and as Holmes always discovered the criminal, Doyle in time began in his own mind to associate himself with Holmes. This often happens. People say that an author puts a lot of himself in one of his characters, when as a matter of fact he puts a lot of his favorite characters in himself. It is a case where Nature begins, as Whistler said, to catch up to Art."

From Doyle and his detective stories it was an easy step to lead Chesterton to talk of his own efforts in that field.

"Yes," he said, "I have done a number of them; it has been great fun doing them. They are a sort of game to me and I have often started out with one idea and before I have finished I have made an entirely innocent bystander the guilty party. The real way to do them, however, is to forget that you are writing a detective story at all. Just start out with certain facts; a murder or other crime has been committed; a number of people are involved; you, no more than your reader, have any idea as to the guilty party. Then go ahead and unravel the crime as if the problem were actually put up to you."

While at work on Chesterton's portrait I remarked that in arranging to make sketches of various British officials one encountered little red tape and that there seemed to be more democracy in England than in America.

"Yes," Chesterton answered, "in some ways there is. I imagine that here a Prime Minister is much more democratic with his secretary, than in your country, but on the other hand, in America I think that the secretary is much more democratic to his Minister. When I was traveling in America

I had occasion to spend several days on a railroad train. Our porter was a nice-looking colored fellow, and one day I engaged him in conversation. I found him intelligent and fairly well read, in fact learned much about the section through which we were passing from him. I had been speaking to him some time when the call bell rang and he had to leave me, which he did with these words, 'So long, see you again soon.'

"Now that to me was true democracy. He was not in the least impudent—he had said to me exactly what he would have said to any friend of his; but can you imagine what would happen to an English porter who said the same thing? In other words, we have the forms of democracy and not the spirit, and I fear the forms without that essential idea that goes with them are dangerous."

There was a commotion without and I looked around as the fat boy entered, bringing two cups of tea. My drawing was finished, so I left after the first cup and accordingly do not know whether Chesterton, like his prototype, Dr. Johnson, drinks seven at one sitting.

XXXVI

THE mere mention of tea at once brings to mind that active old yachtsman, Sir Thomas Lipton. It was on the occasion of his last attempt to lift the *America's* cup that I first met him.

Keen, active, and alert, he belied his fourscore years. Perhaps his hair was a little whiter and thinner and his shoulders not quite so square as they were when he made his first attempt to win the cup, but there was still the same bubbling humor in his sharp blue eyes and there was the same engaging smile. His complexion was as ruddy and vigorous as it was when he trod the deck of the first *Shamrock*.

The greatest change in his appearance was the way he trimmed his mustache, a mustache that was characteristic of the Lipton of old. The ends retained the same whimsical turn, but the white hair on the upper lip was clipped short, so that the two curls, together with the goatee, would have given him a Mephistophelian expression, were it not for the benign humor that radiated from his countenance.

Though he was bronzed, as all men are who sail the seas, he looked more like a physician or a college professor than a man who had spent part of his life aboard ship. His humor, though, was his dominating trait. The minute he began to speak, whatever academic air he had, vanished. His was a distinctly Celtic humor, heightened, when he spoke, by a mixture of brogue and burr. It was that strange mingling of Gael and Scot that gave

Sir Thomas Lipton

to Sir Thomas those divergent attributes that were so marked in him. When I asked him about his nationality he said:

"I am Scotch-Irish or Irish-Scotch, depending upon what company I am in."

It was his Irish ancestry which prompted the humor of the remark, it was his early Scottish environment which was behind its shrewdness.

Indeed, kindliness and canniness were the keys to the success of this son of two poor Irish emigrants who went to Glasgow, where young Thomas was born. It was canniness that enabled him to become one of the leading merchants in the world, it was kindliness that made him probably the best-loved Briton who has come to these shores.

But it was not as a cup contender that he first came. Indeed, his first trip occurred long before any international yacht race to which he was a party. Sixty-odd years ago the boy who had helped in a little provision shop, and who later had run errands for a stationer for half a crown a week, heard the call of the sea. Mooning along the docks on the River Clyde he built strange dramas about the lands to which the old square-riggers sailed—countries where fortunes were easily won.

One day the call was too strong to be resisted. Quietly packing his few belongings, he left the gray stone town and started on his first great adventure. Through the old, round, brick building which had once reechoed to the notes of Jenny Lind, the penniless immigrant entered the largest city of the New World. Upon his last visit he passed by the same building in a flag-bedecked ship, the guest of that same city, cheered by thousands, as he once more put foot on this soil. The intervening years held an almost incredible story of success.

It was not long after the Civil War when he first came here. Times were hard, particularly so for a friendless boy with no money. He tried his hand at many jobs, even that of hoeing cotton in South Carolina. It was not long before he decided that he might just as well work at home as in this strange land where he knew no one. When he had saved up enough to pay his passage, back he set sail for his native land.

"But," he said, "even if my pocketbook was not bulging with American dollars, my head was filled with new ideas that I had gathered in this country. My father and mother were keeping a little shop in Glasgow. The principal things that they sold were butter, eggs, and ham, and their customers were the people whom they had known for years and who lived in the immediate neighborhood.

"What I had learned over here was that shops did not depend entirely upon the people who lived near them. Already in those days the great American idea of advertising had taken hold. I don't know whether I should call it altogether an American idea, for one of the men who developed it to a great extent happened to be a Scotsman. However it was in America that I first saw the great benefits to be derived from it, and when I got back to my parents' little shop that would barely hold six people, I was filled with enthusiasm for a new plan. I so impressed them with it that my father decided to risk his little savings in trying it out."

The shop grew slowly at first, but eventually another one was opened and then others. This was in Glasgow, but young Lipton soon saw that there were the same possibilities in many towns, and before long he was opening similar stores in the larger cities of both England and Scotland. In order to supply them with teas, he bought plantations in Ceylon, and eventually, when he owned some six hundred stores, he went into coffee and cocoa growing, and even acquired a packing house in Omaha, Nebraska.

I asked him when he built his first *Shamrock*.

"Some sixty-nine years ago," he said with a half-roguish smile in his eyes.

"You see," he said, "no one can live in Glasgow and not love the water. The great Clyde River, filled with shipping from all parts of the world, is bound to affect a youngster who sees it almost from the moment of his birth. As a boy I used to frequent the docks and talk to those strange, gruff men who had sailed all over the world and who came on land with stories stranger and more fascinating than fairy tales.

"It was only natural that as soon as I was old enough to own a knife I should cut boats out of blocks of wood.

"On puddles near our house I sailed my first yacht, a boat crudely made and having paper sails, but a boat that was in my eyes the trimmest ship that ever glided through the water. It bore the same name as the yacht now at Newport.

"That was a long time ago, but in all the years that have since gone by I have never lost my interest in ships. Of course, I have often said that business is my vocation, yachting my hobby, and that is true; but it has been a hobby that has yielded me many happy hours, and also a few disappointments."

He smiled as he said this, and I asked him what he would do if he did not win the cup this time.

"Try again as soon as I can build another boat, but I do not think that will be necessary, for the present *Shamrock* has so far beaten everything in sight.

"You know, when Mr. Adams's boat, the *Resolute*, beat mine last time, you made him Secretary of the Navy in

〖 335 〗

gratitude, so when I come back with the cup this time I have no doubt my government will do as much for me. But I will not play quite as fairly as you people, for, once I have that cup over there, and I am in command of the naval forces, every time you send over a challenger I'll order out a couple of gunboats to fire shots along your boat's course, so that it will be impossible for it to win.

"But, seriously, seventy-nine years is too long for any nation to hold the trophy. After I shall have held it fifty, I shall be perfectly content for America to regain it."

As he sat in a large armchair, his hands clasped in his lap, and spoke of plans and purposes, interspersing his remarks with his sly humor, he breathed a spirit of optimism. It was clearly evident to him that this world is a pretty good place in which to live, that life had been a marvelous game, in which the bitter never outweighed the sweet. It was difficult for him to be serious long, and whenever he could turn his answer into a joke he did so.

Although his humor was ever to the forefront, behind it, deeper but perhaps even a little more powerful, was a certain Scotch dourness, a seriousness of purpose, unswerving and irresistible, begotten in the gray mists in the land in which he was born and in which he toiled. It did not come to the surface often—he hid it, almost as if he were ashamed of it—but it showed itself when he replied to the question as to whether a poor boy of to-day had as much chance to succeed as one in former times.

"Of course he has. Times have naturally changed," he said. "Modern inventions have made the world an entirely different place. But take the *Leviathan*, on which I crossed the ocean on this trip, and the little packet on which I made my first crossing. Do you think that the oil-burning engines, the radio, or anything else aboard the new ship has affected the feelings of the people? There are the same joys and griefs and hopes in the breasts of the passengers to-day as there always were. External conditions cannot change them, nor can they change opportunities. In fact, if anything, they only make opportunities greater.

"Success in life depends upon the individual, and no one who goes around with a long face, who keeps saying the world is not as good as it was, that he has no chance to-day, can ever hope to succeed. Indeed, that person is beaten before he crosses the starting line. To begin with, he is headed in the wrong direction; he is going backward instead of forward, and he is looking for squally clouds and rough water, even if the sun is shining and the sea is calm.

"But very often this wrong way of looking at things is the result of wrong upbringing. It is home surroundings that, to my mind, set a boy or a girl on the road to success. As you know, my early days were not the easiest, but our home, though perhaps it was not beautiful, was clean and inviting and comfortable, and presiding over it was the bravest and noblest woman in the world, my mother.

"When things were not going as well as they should, there was nevertheless a smile on her face. She has always been my guiding star. It was from her that I learned to look toward the future and not to the past. It is expecting better things that brings them; it is the conviction that they will come to pass that provides the incentive to work to bring them about.

"The boy who starts out in life with honesty and courage, convinced that he will get along, is provided with proper weapons to succeed, and modern conditions will prove no more formidable to him than the old ones did to the boys with the same ideas."

He was intensely serious as he spoke, and then suddenly came the look of humor in his eyes.

"Indeed," he went on, "modern conditions are going to help me lift that cup."

"What are you going to do with it after you have won it?" I inquired.

"That's a fine question for a person in a dry country to ask," he shot back. "Don't you know cups were made for one purpose only? That's for tea."

XXXVII

THIRTY-FIVE years ago Walter P. Chrysler was an oil wiper working for five cents an hour. To-day he is the head of one of the largest automobile companies in the world and is regarded as one of the outstanding figures in the motor-car industry.

"The man who makes good is the man who starts his job with enthusiasm," said Mr. Chrysler in his office, "and who does a little more than is expected of him. Give the boss a little more than he expects and he will see that you are rewarded. And if he doesn't—the best thing to do is to find another boss."

Seated behind a large flat-topped desk, which was placed diagonally in one corner of the room, this tall, powerfully built, sun-tanned man issued crisp orders.

It is not the peculiar shape of his head, which narrows above the temples, that one notices on first meeting Mr. Chrysler, nor is it the strong aquiline nose and the square jaws; it is the piercing black eyes, which seem to bore through any object upon which they are focused.

"It is not strange that I am in the automobile business," he said. "My grandfather drove a covered wagon across the plains, my father was an engineer on one of those old wood-burning engines of the Union Pacific Railroad, so you see transportation is in my blood."

Mr. Chrysler's voice is deep, and he speaks quickly, so quickly that he runs one word into another. One feels that he realizes the shortness of life; that as much as possible must be crowded into its span.

He leaned back in his chair and passed the palms of his hands over his sleek hair, and went on:

"I was born in a little Kansas hamlet—it wasn't even a town—called Wamego, near Ellis, and it was there that the shops of the Union Pacific were located.

"I went to school until I was seventeen. Of course, like all country boys I had had summer jobs in the grocery store, but it was at seventeen that I really went to work, and I have been working steadily ever since."

Shrewd business man that he is, there is nevertheless in Chrysler a touch of the philosopher. He leaned forward and clasped his hands on the glass-topped desk.

"You know," he said, "the poor boy has a great advantage over the kid whose father is wealthy—a great advantage, I mean, in shaping his future life. He can only get pleasure in constructive things. The wealthy boy gets pleasure in spending money, and in most cases he does that in a purely destructive fashion. I still have a real working model of a locomotive that I built, and I not only made that, but I even had to make the tools with which I worked."

For four years he worked in the Union Pacific shops, then something happened that had a distinct effect on his career.

"One day traffic had been very heavy," he said, "and a locomotive pulled in with a broken cylinder head. In two hours a mail train had to leave, and there wasn't another locomotive to be had. A chap by the name of Hickey was the Superintendent of Motive Power, and he called me into his office. 'That locomotive has to be fixed in two hours,' he said. 'Can you do it?'

Walter P. Chrysler

"Believe me, that was some whale of a job. But I said I would tackle it and I put in as hard a spell of work there as I ever did in all my life, but the engine was finished on time.

" 'Walt,' Hickey said to me, 'I didn't think it could be done. I can't pay you anything extra. But I won't forget.'

"And he didn't. Three months later, on his recommendation, I became general foreman of the Colorado and Southern shops at Trinidad. I had given the boss a little more than he expected and I had received my reward."

Chrysler made good here as he had done in the first job. In nine years he had become superintendent of motive power of the Chicago and Great Western system.

"I was getting a pretty good salary," he said, "but I was thirty-three and I realized that I had gone as far as I could in the line I was in. Mechanical men never got further than being the heads of their own departments. Executive positions were not given to them. Tradition prevented my promotion, but it did not prevent my taking another job.

"And that is something which I have never hesitated to do all my life. When I have seen that I have gone as far as possible in one direction, I have been willing to take a chance in an entirely new field, even when doing so meant an actual pecuniary loss for the time being.

"So at a salary of about half of what I had been getting I went to work for the American Locomotive Company in the position of works manager. I saw possibilities there for future advancement. My job meant more than the actual construction of locomotives—the element of competitive sales entered. In two years I was general manager and the company was operating at a profit.

"From what I am telling you I don't want you to get the idea that I object to punching a time card. As a matter of fact, at the office entrance of the Chrysler Company in Detroit, card number one has my name on it and every morning I am in that city that card is punched at eight o'clock. But what I am trying to drive at is that I was interested not only in the construction details of engineering, but also in the purely business side of it.

"As a matter of fact," he went on, "engineering is the foundation on which all sound manufacturing is developed. Engineering, finance, design, production and sales are the tools with which the management works. Efficiency is achieved only when each of these functions is scientifically managed. And to my way of thinking, the running of large corporations is just as purely mechanical as the building of a locomotive —or an automobile.

"I suppose you are wondering how I happened to switch from locomotives to motor cars. Well, you see in the early part of the century horseless wagons began to chug over our roads. It did not take a prophet to see possibilities in these primitive cars. The day of individual transportation was dawning.

"Way back in 1905 I went to the Chicago Automobile Show. There I saw what struck me as a marvelous car. Its price was five thousand dollars and I had seven hundred. But I wanted that car. Not to drive, but to see how it was made. I managed to borrow the rest of the money and I had the car shipped home. By the time I had taken it apart and put it together again I knew a lot about the inner workings of motor cars.

"That was just nineteen years before I brought out the first Chrysler, but I had done some tall thinking in the meantime, and I had been in a number of jobs. In order to get into the automobile business, I had to do exactly the same thing that I had done in order to get out of the mechanical end of the locomotive business.

"I gave up a twelve-thousand-dollar job to take one at six thousand dollars with General Motors. I finally became vice president there, but then I left. After the war I reorganized several other automobile companies, but all the time I was dreaming of that car of my own. In 1924 my dream came true. I started to build it.

"To-day all our ideas of motors have changed from what they were. A quarter of a century ago, the automobile was an inventive hope. In the early days of the twentieth century the budding automobile industry was experimenting with an almost endless variety of self-propelled vehicles and there was no agreement among engineers.

"It was the phase when the industry hoped that the cars built would run. It was easy to see the place that the motor car was destined to occupy in modern life, but not so easy to see the form of the final product which is to-day a vital factor in our existence, which is changing our cities and remaking the habitable parts of the globe.

"We were on our way, however. Naturally the first experimental cars were costly. If the automobile was to grow in public use and become a factor in modern life, stability had to come.

"The second phase was the production of more nearly standardized types in such volume that they should come economically within the reach of the mass of the people. To Henry Ford must go the credit for having the vision of quantity production at low prices. He set the pace through the years of the second phase—the period of low-cost cars.

"A step behind came the great quantity production era. We thought then that the ultimate status of the industry was

[[345]]

attained. With all the essential variants—size, number of cylinders, variety of models, and luxury of finish—other companies followed the Ford lead; great plants sprang up. Quantity became the keynote of automobile development.

"And logically following quantity was an era of lowering prices. In spite of the interruption of the war period the downward trend of prices continued steadily, with quantity output ever growing.

"An inevitable reaction from quantity production and low prices is a demand for quality. The universality of that trend affecting all products suggests that it is perhaps sociological rather than economic. When an article universally needed becomes cheap enough for practically every one to possess it, the demand for higher quality, better style, and greater luxury naturally follows quickly.

"And so," he went on, "we now have arrived at the third stage; the problem is now quality production on the most economical basis. Miracles of manufacturing have been accomplished in the last five years, and those miracles have all demonstrated the practicability of building the finest quality cars in large quantities.

"Quality from the lowest to the highest priced car is here to stay. It is an essential of the modern utility of automobiles. We must have power and the capacity for speed, which is inherent in power, to cope with modern traffic conditions.

"And speaking of traffic conditions leads me to speak of traffic congestion. That is an economic ill of the first magnitude. Regulation and distribution of traffic by the construction of highways and byways, instead of by-laws and ordinances, is the need of this country to-day."

XXXVIII

ASK any ten people to name the three largest corporations in this country and nine of them will include Standard Oil in their answers, yet it is doubtful whether one out of those nine could tell who is its president.

This is in a way characteristic of the man who heads the Standard Oil Company of New Jersey, for while the name of Rockefeller still blazes forth on the front pages of the newspapers, and although in their time Rogers, Archbold, Flagler, and Bedford were often in the public prints, Walter C. Teagle has remained comparatively unknown.

From the day in June, 1899, when at the age of twenty-one he returned to Cleveland from Cornell University, having completed its four-year course in three years, and his father handed him a pair of overalls and told him to go to work, up to the present, he has been too busy working to bother about publicity.

It is but natural that he should have taken to oil, for his maternal grandfather was one of John D. Rockefeller's original partners, while his father owned an oil refinery that had been bought out by the Standard Oil and of which young Teagle eventually became the vice president. His rise from that position has been a steady one; besides having been an officer in many other companies, he has directed the export policy of the Standard Oil of New Jersey, has been largely responsible for opening new fields and devising new methods of sales, and for the last thirteen years he has been its president.

Mr. Teagle's work for the company has carried him to the four corners of the globe, and for years necessitated his living out of the country. He combined in his work the duties of publicity man with those of executive, for he not only succeeded in creating a demand for the company's products but also laid plans for their distribution and delivery. In Asia he was up against the already matured plans of rival companies, but this did not deter him. Through his efforts Standard Oil tankers became a common sight in Chinese and Japanese harbors.

Coupled with this business ability goes an aptitude for making friends, and also of not antagonizing competitors, so that to-day one of his closest cronies is Sir Henri Deterding, the head of a rival concern, whom he originally met in the Far East.

More than six feet tall, weighing well over two hundred pounds, with a weatherbeaten complexion and an almost lumbering walk, he looks more like the captain of a vessel—a man who has braved the rigors of storms at sea and poured oil on troubled waters—than like the head of a vast corporation who has directed the production of the oil.

In fact his entire manner, his booming voice, his hearty laugh, the way he snaps his square jaws, all smack of the sea and bring up pictures of the old Yankee skippers. And after all, perhaps this is not strange, for upon those sturdy men who sailed out of New Bedford and neighboring ports, much of the country depended for the oil supply of those days; the whale oil that fed the flickering lamps in American homes. Man had not then learned to drill into the earth for his lighting fuel, nor had engines been constructed that would get motive force from the same fluid. And so, in a way, this bluff, genial

Walter C. Teagle

man, in his oak-paneled office, with windows overlooking the harbor, is a direct descendant of those old-time mariners, who, on shipboard, directed the earlier industry.

On his desk, as on theirs, was a pipe, a straight one, with a mouthpiece almost bitten through, and maps, not of a small part of the ocean but of the entire world.

I mentioned these thoughts on oil.

"The world does move," Mr. Teagle replied. "Only twenty-five years ago the principal reason for refining crude oil was to produce kerosene. It was practically the only commodity that could be sold. Gasoline was an unwelcome by-product that was difficult to dispose of.

"In a quarter of a century electricity has practically displaced kerosene as an illuminant, while the development of the gas engine has not only transformed our entire business but also changed our entire mode of life. Though our great cities are important factors in our civilization, after all our real prosperity and our greatness rest with the people in small communities and in agricultural areas. It is for them that the automobile has effected a great change, for it has removed the loneliness and handicaps of rural life, and has brought them within visiting distance of larger communities, and in so doing has necessitated the reconstruction of the primitive roads that existed at the beginning of the century

"But one thing you must remember," he continued. "This country has been favored as no other with natural attributes to foster this desire for change and travel, which is a distinguishing characteristic of our people. There are more reasons than one why we have gone chasing around our land in automobiles while the citizens of other countries have had to walk. The motor fuel supply has been at our call. Not by accident, but by fortunate circumstances, an abundance has been available to our people. The entry of crude petroleum into the field of commerce was coincident with an era of commercial expansion. Oil fields were discovered at a time when our people were a pioneering folk and the uncertainty of oil drilling captivated their adventurous spirit.

"Our country is not the only one that produces oil, but a production great enough to fill our needs was possible at home; there was no necessity on our part to go to other lands. Great Britain and the other European nations that are commercially comparable to the United States have not the raw materials, while most of those countries that have oil are hampered by climatic conditions less favorable than ours.

"The development of an oil field to-day is an expensive proposition, and before returns begin to be commensurate with the investment a minimum of at least twenty-five million dollars must be expended. Thus the physical obstacles and the large amount of capital required in foreign fields have convinced American business men that dollar for dollar an investment here would yield greater returns than elsewhere. Foreign companies have realized the same thing, with the result that there has always been a foreign exploitation of our petroleum and even companies primarily formed for the marketing in this country of petroleum from other lands have eventually found it more profitable to produce a large proportion of their crude oil here."

As he was speaking, through one of the doors of the room a secretary entered. In this hand was a stack of letters. In whispers he consulted Mr. Teagle. The amber cigar holder, with its long black cigar, was gripped further in his teeth.

"Look through our files," he said, "and about February, 1927, you will find a letter from these people giving us the figures that they now ask for."

It is this remarkable memory that is one of the secrets of the man's success. Almost instantly he can quote figures years old. And coupled with this memory is a most methodical manner of doing things. In his upper vest pocket he carries a little black book, in which he jots down ideas as they come to him. Then, too, he appears to give off dynamic energy and one immediately feels his entire absorption in his business. As a matter of fact most of his evenings are spent at his home, near Greenwich, going over papers which he carries from the office in an old brief case with a trick lock that nobody but himself can open. He does not care much for the theater or for the opera.

"But," he said, "don't think that I work all the time. I do not play golf, but I get off in the wilds every now and then and hunt and fish, and then too I like a good game of 'contract.' In fact, on my last vacation somebody at the club said that I hunted and fished all day and played bridge all night, but I did come back wonderfully rested.

"I guess I have one hobby, and that is dogs, and by the way, this is not a very good day for you to make a sketch of me, because I just heard that my best prize winner has been defeated for a cup.

"But these are hobbies; my real interest," he went on, "is in the oil business, and, believe me, in these days of big business no one can hope to succeed who is not tied up heart and soul in what he is doing.

"I remember a little fellow, bald and unobtrusive, who started in on the Stock Exchange about twenty-five years ago.

He specialized in a food product that was not very well known at the time, but that fellow got to work; he learned that business from beginning to end and he talked the future of this food product from alarm clocks to pajamas. To-day that man and the stuff he boosted are sensational successes of the time. His enthusiasm, based on faith that in turn was based on knowledge that was based on hard work, won.

"I have in mind another chap who was fifty years old and flatter than Kansas when for the first time he took his little red book out of his pocket and started in to sell life insurance. Now that's no easy job in New York, but he himself told me that he became enthusiastic over the idea of service; he forgot what he was going to make out of it, but the idea in the back of his mind was that he was saving families from destitution on the death of the bread-winner. He communicated that earnestness to the people with whom he was doing business and in ten years he had earned enough out of his commissions to retire on a comfortable competence.

"These are not exceptional cases. Right here in this company I could show you any number of examples of men who have succeeded by their enthusiasm. Every large company in the world is constantly on the lookout for new men to fill satisfactorily new positions that are bound to be created as new business is undertaken. And let me tell you right here that there are always more big positions to be filled than there are men to fill them."

He had spoken of new business and I asked him about the future of oil.

"No one can answer that," he replied. "At the present time it is used either in its semi-crude or finished state as fuel for automotive engines; as kerosene for illumination and heat;

as light distillate oils for the Diesel engine, and as fuel oil for steam generation. What its future will bring forth no man can tell.

"But this much I can say. The American oil industry has always displayed conspicuous foresight, initiative, and resource in the past, and in the face of an ever increasing demand it has made petroleum products more easily available at a cheaper price than in any other country in the world. In fact, the reason for the widespread consumption has been the low cost. The price has produced alike the demand and the product to meet the demand. Price which is fixed by competition finds the oil and produces it. Price controls and limits its use. As the American public signals its needs to the industry, the response will be as it has been in the past, a supply of those products ample for all the requirements which the future may require."

XXXIX

IN THESE days when changes occur so rapidly that it is hard to follow them, publicity brings renown that would have startled our fathers. When the chimney of Walter Damrosch's house caught fire some passers-by, seeing the smoke, turned in an alarm. After the fire was put out, Mr. Damrosch asked the firemen down into his dining room to have a cup of "tea." As he did so, one of them turned to him with, "Say, don't I know your voice? Aren't you the feller that tells us all about the pieces you play every Saturday night?"

Then and there a discussion of music ensued. It is immaterial whether the "Eroica" was preferred to the "Fire Music" of the Valkyrie. The point is that the firemen were interested in good music.

As Mr. Damrosch told the story, he was tremendously pleased, because it was another bit of evidence that the missionary work which he set out to do is bearing fruit. The music of the great masters is being brought right into the homes of the people—music that has heretofore been unknown to them.

That this will ultimately mean much to the hearers, that it will work not only for their spiritual welfare but will serve also as a counteracting influence to the various factors tending to the breaking up of home life, Mr. Damrosch firmly believes. It is but natural that he should, for his own life has been spent in musical surroundings.

Walter Damrosch

Contrary to general belief, Mr. Damrosch was born not in this country but in Breslau. His father, a physician, had given up the stethoscope for the violin, and played at Weimar when Liszt conducted there. His mother was an opera singer who was one of the first Ortruds in Wagner's "Lohengrin."

It was a toss-up as to whether Walter Damrosch would be a painter or a musician, but a house that was frequented by Wagner, von Bülow and Rubinstein was bound to exert an influence upon a child who was gifted in two arts, and eventually he decided to follow in his father's footsteps.

In his own home to-day he has many mementos and portraits of those times. On his desk is a large picture of his father, long-haired and bearded, who was largely responsible for the introduction of Wagner's music into this country. There is a little study of Liszt, done from life, and paintings of Mrs. Damrosch and her father, James G. Blaine.

Above the piano in the music room hangs a large portrait of a blond-haired, dreamy-eyed young man, with a strong aquiline nose and a determined mouth. Mr. Damrosch showed it to me. He was standing directly under it, and the light from the window fell on him in much the same way as it had fallen on the subject of the painting.

The daylight that came into the room did not reach into the farther corners. Within the pine-paneled walls, among early Dutch pictures, there was an atmosphere of mystery. The painting, behind the tall, erect figure with its strong face and white hair, looked a little like a ghost. The past and the present were both there. The Damrosch of the late eighties, who was the contemporary of Lehman and Eames and the De Reszkes, and the conductor of the thirties—of Debussy and of Honegger's "Pacific 299"—were both looking at me.

The time that has elapsed since the portrait was painted has seen a great development in the musical taste of this country and a large part of that development has been due to Walter Damrosch. He began to conduct when music was a luxury indulged in by the fashionable few who lived about Gramercy Park and lower Madison and Fifth Avenues. He helped to make good music popular and he is still wielding a baton for the benefit of the people of the entire nation.

During the intervening years he has not only led the opera but also several symphony orchestras. He has composed chamber music and operatic works. When the war broke out he volunteered his services and went overseas to organize a school for the instruction of bandmasters in our army.

"I have seen the musical taste of this country develop from what was almost a primitive instinct into a discrimination that demands the very best in music in all its forms," he told me. "And what I see now, which assuredly was not in evidence when I first began my career, is a love of music among the so-called plain people. It is this love which makes for the creation of a national school of music.

"The Italian workman knows his Verdi and the German peasant his Schubert and Schumann. For years Italy and Germany have been leaders in music. To-day the farmer out west, miles from a large city, who heretofore has been denied the opportunity of listening to what is best in music, properly rendered, can sit down after his day's work and hear the masterpieces of all times played, very often, as they should be."

Mr. Damrosch talks very precisely, as millions of listeners over the radio know. His voice seems to me to be characteristic of a man who, having an almost didactic approach to an art, has also a keen business-like capacity for the financial details that are necessary to the fostering of any art project.

"While any art," he went on, "can be created in poverty, its popularization requires financial assistance. No college can exist only on the money received as tuition fees from its students. There must be an endowment fund which will go toward its upkeep. In the same way, there is not an art museum in the world that can continue from the sale of its tickets and catalogues. The same is true of any orchestra. It is absolutely essential that it be supported by the people who can afford that form of public service, and the larger the sum that is subscribed, the smaller can be the price of the tickets to the public at large, and the better the artists it can employ.

"Radio has worked a miracle. It has, in effect, erected a concert hall in every hamlet throughout the country. In fact, it has gone even further. It has turned every home into a potential palace of music, where the finest can be heard. Now, too, the children in our public schools, instead of singing 'Jingle Bells' and other similar compositions to the beat of a lead pencil held in the hand of some teacher, are being introduced to the great classical compositions of all times. For many of the children that means the opening of a door to untold treasures."

I asked how he felt about the broadcasting of modern music.

"So long as it is music," he said, "I believe in it. But unfortunately, I think much that is broadcast under the name of music does not fall in that category. By that I do not mean to say that there is not good and interesting music being written to-day. But there is also a lot of trash. Luckily it will soon die a natural death. It has always been so. While every great musician is an innovator, his art, nevertheless, is built upon what has gone before, no matter how much it may differ from it.

"Catholicity in music was a distinguishing characteristic of my father. He made a great fight for Wagner, Berlioz, and Liszt, who in those days were moderns. However much he admired them, and often though he conducted their works, he kept me pretty close to Bach, Beethoven, and Handel when I started to study music. 'The moderns,' he used to say to me, 'will take care of themselves.'

"I believe that is true. The great trouble has heretofore been that classical music has been regarded as non-understandable—by people who had never had the opportunity of hearing it. They looked on it in much the same way that they looked on heavy books in the library which could be appreciated only by specialists.

"What is happening now is that these very people turn on their radios and cut in on some delightfully charming composition. They do not know what it is, and when it is finished they are surprised to learn from the announcer that it is by Beethoven or Mozart."

Mr. Damrosch went on to speak about the little talks he gives before playing his pieces.

"While the essential attribute of music," he said, "is to produce esthetic emotion through the medium of sounds, very often the so-called literary side of music will create an added interest in the composition. I do not try to instruct my listeners, but I know that many of them are not acquainted with musical forms, and often I try to give a concise outline of the particular type of composition that I play as well as the idea that is expressed.

"All of these things contribute to a greater appreciation of music, but this does not imply that they are necessary for the enjoyment of any piece of good music. Nothing is essential for that but its performance in a proper way. And that is the reason I am so much interested in the work I am doing. It has been pioneer work. But I have been no keener in my interest than the people who are connected with the radio industry. From the highest official down to the man who arranges the orchestra seats, each one of them has done his best to help. As you sit in your living room and turn the switch that fills it with music little do you realize the technical difficulties that have been overcome, or some that still vex us.

"The placing of the various instruments has been a problem in itself, and as it has been worked out it differs essentially from the way in which the musicians are placed when playing in public. That is the reason concerts in the studio sound better than concerts broadcast from large halls.

"That is but one of the problems that we have encountered. There have been countless others of a technical nature, and besides these there is always the question of programs. However, I know we are progressing and creating a larger interest in musical art."

XL

AFTER the tumult and the shouting had died at the Democratic Convention in Dallas in 1928 there was one dramatic note which stood out above all others. It was that moment when a man in the prime of life, but walking with canes to the rostrum, began to speak in a mellow voice, calmly and deliberately.

"I come for the third time," said he, "to urge upon a convention of my party the nomination of the Governor of the State of New York. The faith which I held I still hold. It has been justified in the achievement. The whole country has now learned the measure of his greatness."

It was not only the sweltering audience in Houston which became interested; the people with radios throughout the country at once sensed that this was no ordinary nominating speech. Without any futile attempt at suspense, simply, directly, and sincerely, Franklin D. Roosevelt stated at the outset his purpose—The nomination of Alfred E. Smith for the presidency. Compared to the bombastic effusions that had gone before, his earnestness and simplicity seemed all the more striking. With no striving for theatrical effect, honest and straightforward, he represents the best influence of the college man in American politics to-day.

Mr. Roosevelt was born in Hyde Park, Dutchess County, New York, the son of James Roosevelt, who was president of the Delaware & Hudson Company. Like Theodore Roose-

Franklin D. Roosevelt

velt, his famous distant cousin, and, in fact, like most of the Roosevelts, he went to Harvard from which he was graduated in 1904. While there he was managing editor of *The Crimson*, the college daily, and also a librarian of the old Hasty Pudding Club. After his graduation he attended Columbia Law School, and, having been admitted to the bar at the end of three years, he went to work for the legal firm of Carter, Ledyard & Milburn.

He had been practicing law but a short time when he was offered the nomination for State Senator. This, however, did not mean much. For years Dutchess, Columbia, and Putnam counties had been represented by a Republican in the Senate. In fact, the Republican nomination was regarded as the equivalent of election. But young Roosevelt did not see it that way. He accepted the nomination in no spirit of party sacrifice; he was determined to win and made a whirlwind campaign. Employing an automobile, then a novelty in campaigning, he thought no village too small to be visited. For weeks he made six speeches or more a day, and by the time election day came around most of the voters had seen the candidate and obtained a fair statement of his opinions regarding the issues they were called upon to settle at the polls.

The tall young man, with clear blue eyes, sharp aquiline nose, strong mouth and chin, made a favorable impression upon the people, and when the votes were counted the candidate of the Republican bosses was defeated by the young man who had fired verbal fusillades at the men who for years had run things in those counties.

But he had not been in the Senate a week when he showed that he was as much opposed to Democratic bosses as he was to those of the Republican Party. Charles F. Murphy of

Tammany Hall had given orders to the Democratic Legislature to elect John C. Sheehan to the United States Senate. That was before senators were elected by popular vote. But Roosevelt was not taking orders from Murphy. His mind did not work that way. He was regarded as the leader of the insurgents in the Senate, though he disclaimed it.

"Leader?" said he. "I should not claim that title; there really was no leader, there was no need for any. We just determined to stay out. Our districts wanted us to. We laid no dark and deep plots to confound the enemy. We waited for public sentiment to perform that function."

It did. Sheehan was defeated. Roosevelt was reëlected to the State Senate in 1912. Then, in 1913, President Wilson appointed him Assistant Secretary of the Navy, a post he held for seven years and from which he resigned when the Democratic Party made him its candidate for the vice presidency in 1920.

It was in his New York house that I made a drawing of Mr. Roosevelt and had a talk with him. The house is filled with ship models and naval pictures. And as he seated himself in his library, its walls lined with books, the man who had just returned from a meeting of the Democratic National Committee seemed much more the scholar than the politician. On the table beside him, surrounded by hundreds of papers and magazines, was a glass-inclosed model of the *Constitution*. Above the fireplace hangs a marine by Claude Lorraine, while resting on the tops of the bookcases are prints and engravings of war vessels and a portrait of John Paul Jones.

In that room there is no likeness of his illustrious cousin. That hangs in the bedroom, on the wall facing the bed. In that room is also the original of one of the first cartoons in which the late President figured. It is by Nast and shows him, still a very young man, standing before President Cleveland—a sort of prophetic picture.

"It's going to be much easier for you to make a drawing of me," he said, "than to get that article. The trouble with me is that I have never specialized in any one thing; I am interested in too many things. and the result is that there is nothing to say about me.

"Take my library, for instance. It is almost accidental that I have so many naval books. It did not begin that way. When I was at college I was librarian of one of the societies, and I started collecting. But a general library, such as I wanted, was out of the question, and I just happened to gather one on our naval history. To-day I have practically every book and pamphlet that has been published on the subject.

"I have a small collection of ship models also, not as many as I would like, but they take up too much room. I have also built a number of them.

"However, the thing in which I am most interested at the present time is the sanitarium down at Warm Springs, Georgia. In 1921, I contracted infantile paralysis. It left me with very little power in my legs. I determined that I was going to be cured. I heard about the curative powers of these springs which, in addition to containing mineral properties that are beneficial, have a temperature of eighty-nine degrees. I went down there and started a course of treatment, exercising as much as possible in these warm waters. In a short time an improvement was apparent, and this improvement has been steady and progressive. I felt that here was something of inestimable value to the world, here was a means of benefiting thousands of crippled children. The place, however, needed development, and I accordingly interested some philanthropic friends in starting a foundation, and we are now getting excellent results.

"Another hobby of mine is forestry. Up at Hyde Park we have a large acreage in woods. You see T. R. was the Roosevelt who chopped down trees; I like to plant them."

Endeavoring to turn the conversation to politics, I asked him how it came about that a Roosevelt should be a Democrat.

"Nearly all of them used to be Democrats," he answered, "all except T. R.'s father; he was the only Republican of his generation.

"After all, one has but to compare the two parties to see why most of the Roosevelts have been Democrats. Place two facts of history side by side by way of example. Eight years of Democratic administration in Washington produced a slate free from election scandals, free from a single act of public dishonesty on the part of any responsible official. These years included the responsibilities for the conduct of the vast operations of the World War. On the other hand, the succeeding years have given to the nation examples of public turpitude which we would like to forget.

"If we select the proper leader the United States can regain the world's trust and friendship. And in foreign affairs we can point the way to the reduction of armaments; we can coöperate officially and wholeheartedly with every agency that studies and works to relieve the ills of mankind; and what, to my mind, is very important, we can for all time renounce the practice of arbitrary intervention in the home affairs of our neighbors.

"Needless to say these are my own individual ideas, but, thank goodness, with the spread of education throughout the land, the younger generation is learning to think for itself."

XLI

THE younger generation is a much discussed subject Youth has always proved of interest to age, and to each passing generation the succeeding one appears an enigma.

One day I happened to notice in the paper that Booth Tarkington was in New York on a visit and it occurred to me that it would be interesting to learn what the author of "Penrod" had to say about the boys and girls of to-day.

I called him up on the telephone, and while he declared that by this time the generation of which Penrod was a type had grown to manhood, and that he knew but little about the present youngsters, nevertheless he was most cordial about making an appointment.

But it is unsatisfactory to talk with a gentleman from Indiana in the living room of a Park Avenue hotel. The stock steel engravings of Benjamin Franklin and Lafayette express none of the personality of the temporary tenant, nor does the near Duncan Phyfe furniture give any hint as to his taste in interior decoration. There is a singular sameness of artificiality about all hotel rooms, from the monotone carpet to the French telephone. And then, too, it is hard to hear the murmur of the Wabash above the clank of the trolley cars a short half block away.

Mr. Tarkington did not leave me long alone in the cold formality of the hotel room. A man nearing sixty, he does not look much over fifty, and, though rather stoop shouldered, this seems a fault of posture, not a sign of age. A tall building opposite threw the room into shadow and it was necessary for him to sit very close to the window. Remarkably keen-looking, well-groomed, a cigarette in his long, thin fingers, he seemed in every way a man of to-day, capable of seeing things as they are, with a knowledge of the past, but with his mind open to the present; a man whose feet were firmly planted on the ground and who was in no danger of being swept away by sudden fads or fancies. There is nothing of the dreamer about Mr. Tarkington; nothing of the studied negligence of the professional writer.

Almost as soon as I had begun to draw he asked me whether I had read a book which tried to show that Sargent was not an artist. I told him I had not seen it, and he went on:

"But I am not surprised. They have denied God, why stop at Sargent?"

"To whom do you refer, the younger generation?"

"Not necessarily to them," said Mr. Tarkington, "but rather to a certain class of disgruntled individuals who hate the world and the people in it, and who believe, as a matter of course, that every thing that is established is wrong. It goes without saying that this class has an immense influence on young people, for the rising generation is always looking for the faults of the one immediately preceding it; but this is as it should be; otherwise we should not have progress in the world.

"It is not only our ideas that the youngsters criticize, but also our clothes and our household articles. Have you ever noticed that anything less than thirty years old is old-fashioned? As time goes on it becomes quaint, then interesting, later on

Booth Tarkington

rare, and finally it looms forth as an antique. And so, the furniture and bric-a-brac used by our parents to adorn their parlors and got rid of by us to make way for the uncomfortable mission atrocities, our children are beginning to drag down from attics and are using in their own homes. But, of course, we did the same things when we were young."

"In what way then," I asked, "does the present youngster differ from Penrod?"

"Essentially he is the same; superficially, he is entirely different," Mr. Tarkington replied. "Human nature does not change very much, but environment and the material things which surround us naturally influence our ideas of life. Remember the period in which the Penrod stories were laid. The garage had not replaced the stable, the man who owned a car still kept it in a building in which stray wisps of hay lurked in the cracks between the boards on the wooden floor; the odor of horses had not been driven out by the fumes of gasoline. It was not a cold-blooded mechanistic age, and efficiency had not swept over the country like a plague.

"Not that I object to efficiency, everything is all right in its proper place, but what I am trying to get at is the reason for the apparent change in the young. I believe the boy of fifteen years ago was very much the same as the boy thirty years ago. The big change has come in the last fifteen years, and to my mind one of the biggest factors in that change is the automobile. Of course, I am speaking particularly of the boys in middle western towns; they are the ones I know best.

"Before the automobile became so common, some families had horses, the majority did not. If a boy went to call on a girl, what did they do? They sat on the porch, the doors and the windows of the house were open, a gas lamp was usually within fifty feet of them, and if they wanted to go some place they walked a half a mile or so to the village drug store and had an ice cream soda. If by chance the boy's father did have a horse, it was hitched to the red-wheeled buggy, but they could not get very far with that, not far enough, anyway, not to be recognized. But to-day space has been eliminated by the motor car. When a boy takes a girl out in an automobile I have no more idea where they go or what they do than their parents have. You see I am too old to find out, but unless I do, I can't write about them.

"Girls, too, are much less chaperoned than they were. This is a logical outcome of the growing economic independence of woman and in many ways it is a fine thing. Mothers to-day look back at the time when they had to drag their own mothers along and many a harmless party was spoiled, and the result is that they give their daughters much more freedom than they had. Besides, girls are working and demand rights of which their mothers would never have dreamed.

"Why, when I was a boy, people threw up their hands in holy horror if a girl hinted that she would like to go on the stage; to-day a girl can become a scientist or a chorus girl and nobody will say a word."

The remark about girls becoming scientists led to a question as to what Mr. Tarkington thought of colleges at the present time.

"To my mind," he said, "the principal trouble with the colleges to-day is that there is too much education and not enough human nature. I know a boy who was graduated from Princeton last year and he was so educated that I was afraid to speak to him for fear that I should show my ignorance. The only person who appeared to be cultured enough to hold a conversation with him was a professor of Greek. The finest things that I found in college, and what I retained long after I forgot my Latin and Greek, were my friends, but judging from the amount of knowledge that boy had, I can't see how he found time to make any.

"Knowledge is a fine thing, but if it goes to the making of an intellectual snob it defeats its own purpose and breaks down the inherent and natural sense of democracy that exists in the young."

"Do you mean that the Penrod of to-day no longer plays with Herman and Verman?" I asked.

"Left to himself he invariably does. The boy whose father owns a Rolls Royce is tickled to death to go for a ride in the dilapidated flivver belonging to the father of a friend. Speaking of these very things brings up another reason for a great change in children, and that is the fact that the luxuries of fifteen or so years ago have become the necessities of to-day, with the result that what used to be a treat is now tiresome.

"I have a friend who has a daughter eight years old. At her last birthday her parents could not think of a thing to give her that she had not already had. At last a great inspiration came to them. They finally hit on something that would be a complete surprise. They gave her a live baby elephant. By the time that girl is sixteen they will have to blow up an entire navy to give her a thrill.

"Now, if that child is blasé at an age when we were getting the time of our lives out of circuses, it surely is not the child's fault. What our generation does not seem to realize is that it is responsible for what the younger generation is to-day. Take all this sex talk that is so prevalent. There is no doubt that we, revolting against the false modesty and prudery of our child-

[377]

hood, and inspired by such plays as Wedekind's 'Spring's Awakening,' may have gone a little too far in clearing up the sex mystery. In order to get away from the foolish reticence of our parents, we may have stressed sex too much, and the result is the younger generation is sex-conscious. In fact, it goes around with the idea that it has suddenly made a great discovery: there is such a thing in the world as sex. Strange as it may seem to them, sex existed long before they were born. Spring was spring ever since this world began, and youth has always been youth. The boys and girls who two-stepped to the 'Washington Post March' and those who waltzed to 'The Merry Widow' had the same feelings as those of to-day, and I don't honestly think there is much more side-stepping.

"There is no doubt that there are dances that would not have been tolerated years ago, dances indulged in solely to awaken emotions—I begin to feel old when I talk this way—but I wonder whether the proportion of young people who indulge in these is any larger than the proportion that found equally exciting pastimes in years gone by."

"Do you believe," I asked, "that there is a lowering of moral standards?"

"For the large part, I don't think there is," Mr. Tarkington said. "Of course, youth is impetuous. It always has been. It has seized on the idea that we have given it and perhaps it has gone a little bit further than we expected. But if the pendulum does not swing far to one side, it will never get to the other. The principal thing that I fear may result from our children going to this extreme is that our grandchildren may be brought up in the same way as our grandmothers. And that would be a calamity.

"As a matter of fact, I think that a large part of the so-called let-down in morality is rather a change in vocabulary and a freedom of speech. I wonder how much more there is in the 'petting parties' than there was in the old-fashioned 'spooning.' What is the difference between 'sex appeal' and 'coquetry,' 'charm,' and 'allure'? As far as I can see, they are all 'It.'

"But even this change in vocabulary is not so marked as some of the twenty-year-olds imagine. With a great air of superiority they go around and say, 'Why, you people used to call legs "limbs."' Now, as a matter of fact, who did that but maiden aunts who could boast only of a couple of toothpicks?

"The older folks are saying: 'The young girls wear nothing to-day.' I leave it to you, are their dresses cut a bit shorter than those of their mothers? But so far as this curtailment of clothes is concerned, I can see that it has done nothing but make it unnecessary for a bunch of men to congregate on corners on windy days. In other words, we have removed the veil—I don't say seven—from a lot of things that required no mystery. And the very fact that mystery no longer exists makes natural things as they should be, natural. But here again when our children take a natural view of things, some Aunt Maria—for they still exist—excitedly exclaims, 'What has become of the modesty of our ancestors?' Thank goodness it is buried with them.

"There is another thing very similar to this. When we were young and were told to do a certain thing, very often there were good reasons why we didn't want to, but we knew enough to keep our mouths shut. Realizing the injustice of this method, we have treated our children as reasoning human beings. When a child is told to do something to-day which does not seem right to him, he asks 'Why?' Now this is perfectly proper. Still, the minute he demands to be treated in the way that we have taught him he should be, some one is bound to say, 'What has become of parental authority? Where is the respect that we had for our parents?'

"Of course, in a civilization as complex as ours, there are countless contributing causes to these superficial changes. Much has been said about the sex trend in literature, but that is not as new as it seems. I remember a copy of 'Sapho' in my father's library, and the English translations of Zola have served as models for any number of our modern novels."

"But surely," I remarked, "books like these are more universally read than they used to be."

"Up to fifteen or sixteen, the average boy still reads Henty and his successors. So-called love stories are 'mush' to him. After that he reads what his elders do, and as sex talk is no longer taboo I don't feel that it has much effect, that is, on the average boy or girl. But there is one class on which this type of writing has had a direct influence. The sex novel, the sex play and the psycho-analytical books have all contributed to the creation of the young intelligentsia who, in striving for apparent sophistication, do very foolish things. There are undoubtedly more of these than there used to be. Before the last few years those that there were, were the near-Bohemians. They did as they pleased and blamed it on their souls and temperaments. Now they find justification for their actions in the dangers of repression and the resultant complexes.

"One cannot speak of this sex literature without also mentioning the movies as they are to-day. At one time, there was a prevalence of pictures in which there were gun fights and hold-ups. To my mind that kind of picture did have a bad effect on the youngsters—by youngsters I mean on the boys ten, twelve, or fourteen years of age. To-day I feel that the influence of the movie is nil. The younger ones have as much use for love on the screen as they have for it in books. The older ones have as much sense as we, and after they go to them they wonder why they did.

"I think I have told you what, to my mind, are the superficial differences between this generation and the preceding ones, but now I am going to tell you something else. When I started out I intended to be an artist. I studied in the art schools of Paris. Once I managed to sell a drawing to *Life*. That was way back in 1894. Though I have given up art as a profession, it was my first love and I am still true to it. It means much to me and always will. But in spite of a life-long interest, I'll confess that I cannot understand modern art. Do you think the younger generation can tell me what it means?"

XLII

To the younger generation must be left the answers to many of the questions that are puzzling the world to-day. Already they have begun to give them. A twenty-five year old boy spanned the ocean in a plane while older and perhaps more experienced heads hesitated and waited for more favorable conditions. Lindbergh's flight was an expression of youth. It was the younger generation's first answer to one of the world's old questions, old as Icarus himself.

One day off the Irish coast the steward brought word into the smoking room of an ocean liner that the "flying fool" had landed in Paris. Many of the passengers did not even know his name, but there was a scene there that I shall never forget. Yet few realized the true import of that flight; few realized that in those previous thirty-six hours a boy had opened the way to the junk heap for the speeding boat and had made the air as subservient as the sea to man's will. The world sped forward years in that day and a half, carried along by the will of youth.

I first saw Lindbergh in the American Embassy on the Avenue de Iéna. Two or three days had passed since he had landed at Le Bourget and my first glimpse of him was obtained as he stood on the stairs of Ambassador Herrick's house and answered questions that the press of the world hurled at him— a tall almost awkward figure who, hesitating, replied to inane inquiries. And yet there was the charm and bashfulness of

Charles A. Lindbergh

boyhood, the bewilderment of one who had done something of which he did not fully recognize the signifigance. It bore out the story that before setting flight he had gone to young Colonel Roosevelt and asked for a letter of introduction to the American Ambassador.

After the reporters had left I went up to his room with him. The haze of perplexity was still evident. In body he had come to earth, mentally he was still at sea. And yet there was a discernment of realities and a keenness sufficient to prompt him to put himself in the trusted hands of the Ambassador. True to youth, Lindbergh had shifted responsibilities. And tired Herrick, reclining in his bed and eating his *petit déjeuner* in true French fashion, as he picked up large strawberries by their stems and dipped them in sugar, expressed fear that Byrd might land before he had finished with Lindbergh.

It was a new experience for the American representative. Men did not drop from the skies every day and the rigid rules of etiquette were stretched. Diplomacy is not accustomed to dealing with the unexpected. Yet Herrick liked it though it tired him. He liked the boyishness of the adventurer and the almost childlike obedience which he gave.

Weeks afterwards, hunched, snarling Briand said in his office in the Ministry of Foreign Affairs: "The first reception which we gave to Lindbergh we would have given to any one who had made the trip; the following ovations were as much for the sweet, simple boy as for the daring aviator." From an appreciation of bravery it became a glorification of youth.

And it was youth that I saw in that upper room in the American Embassy on that May afternoon in 1927. It was youth, forgetful of the dangers, though still stunned. It was youth, anxious about a new suit of clothes which he had just ordered, for the very ones on his back were borrowed and fitted none too well.

He is not articulate. He seems unimaginative. And yet when I asked him when he first got the idea of crossing he said: "I was carrying the mail. In the daytime I could see what was below me. But in the nighttime it was different. Looking down, often there would be nothing but blackness, and I had to strain my eyes to catch some familiar light which would be my guide.

"One night I was traveling eastward. It was terribly dark and I had to keep my eyes wide open to catch the guiding light. As I flew through the blackness and saw nothing, suddenly the idea came to me. Suppose I should miss my bearings and keep on flying eastward. Eventually I would strike Europe."

He smiled. It was a sort of shamefaced smile, as if he were half-ashamed for having let himself go. And then the talk changed and he spoke of the crossing. The shield was once more in place and it was "We" not "He" that said words. It was not revealing, it served to carry him further away than did the silence.

Often I have thought of that time, of the crowds outside the embassy iron gates, of the only talk that one heard on the boulevards and avenues, of the conversation over the tables outside the cafés. Paris forgot she was French, the drone of a motor had drowned out even the "Marseillaise." I had seen Paris in war time. While bombs from German airplanes overhead were dropping, old men pruned rose bushes in the garden of the Tuileries. But even the shears, which would not stop for the enemy, halted as this messenger from over the seas sailed through the skies, and business which carried on as best it could under German guns, ceased in homage to youth and bravery.

It was the world's expression of praise of accomplishment. And yet even as I sat in that room drawing the first human being who had flown alone across the ocean, as the cheers of thousands were still literally sounding in his ears, memories arose of Langley and his dashed hopes as his airplane crashed into the Potomac, and Lillienthal and his death as he tried to soar in a motorless plane. And the thought came, too, that one sudden gust of treacherous wind, over which no one had control, might have put an end to this flight before its object was accomplished.

How close are failure and success.

*The type used for the text is Monotype No. 37 E. Set,
electrotyped and printed by The Maple Press Company,
York, Pa. Illustrations reproduced and printed by the
Fredrick Photogelatine Press, Inc., New York, N. Y.*